Are You

...A combination of earthy sensuality and fiery idealism? If you have *Venus in Virgo and Mars in Sagittarius*, you value a healthy, beautiful body. Your motto: Don't fence me in! Getting possessive is the fastest way for a lover to lose you.

...Someone who'd rather cuddle up by the fire than go out dancing? Intense, possessive, your motto is *All or nothing at all.* If you have *Venus in Cancer and Mars in Scorpio*, you want to invest your entire being in a relationship and need a lover who'll do the same.

...A creative dreamer with a new mate around every corner you turn? Sweet and cuddly, but able to let go and move on, you know one day you'll find true love, but for now you love the one you're with. If you have Venus in Pisces and Mars in Gemini, you snuggle everyone you meet.

SEXY, SIZZLING COMBINATIONS
THAT REVEAL YOUR SPECIAL LOVE STYLE

Don't be fooled by Sun sign astrology books that claim to give you detailed information about your love life. To do that, you need to know about the planets Venus and Mars, for they are the source of everything romantic and sexy about you. Internationally acclaimed astrologer Nancy Frederick shows you how to locate the exact position of Venus and Mars at your birth in the easy-to-navigate charts right here in this book. *If you know your birthday, you can instantly look up your Venus and Mars—right here.* Then she tells you what the planets reveal. To know the secrets of your love style, all you need to know is your birthday! And the same goes for that special someone who's caught your eye. Want to know what's boiling below that sexy surface? Read on!

Also by Nancy Frederick

The Astro Tutor

Dawn Any Minute
Hungry For Love
A Change of Heart
Touring the Afterlife
Starstruck
The Sportin' Life

The Lover's Dream
Love Games: Psychic Paths to Love
Palmistry: All Lines Lead to Love
Tarot: Love is in the Cards

Want to learn astrology in depth? Check out Nancy's popular astrology book, ***The Astro Tutor.*** Hope you enjoy!

Originally published in 1989 by Dell Publishing, a division of Bantam Doubleday Dell Publishing Group, Inc

Copyright 1989 by Nancy Frederick Sussan and 2014 by Nancy Frederick

ISBN-13: 978-0615985138
ISBN-10: 0615985130

(Heart and Soul Press)

Original ISBN:
ISBN 13: 9780440203575
ISBN 10: 0440203570
Dell Publishing

Heart and Soul Press

Love and Sex Under the Stars

Nancy Frederick

For my mother and father,
the two most loving, fun
and exciting people anywhere.

And for my Xandy,
who makes me prouder every day.

Table of Contents

Introduction

HOT AS A PISTOL?

POSSESSIVE AND SENSUAL?

DEMANDING AND MAGNETIC?

GENTLE AND TENDER?

What's your love style? We all expect different things from romance and we all require different things from love. Naturally everyone wants to meet that significant other and ride off into the territory marked "happily ever after." But what is the journey like along the way? It's a different trip for each of us. As a consulting astrologer, I counsel people on their love lives daily, and it's amazing how much a little self-awareness can improve a person's love life.

Venus and Mars are the planets of love and sex, and that is what this book explores. Through Venus we express affection, creativity, and the urge to merge. Through Mars we express energy, aggressiveness, and develop our individuality. Together the pair is responsible for how we love and make love.

Each Venus-Mars combination describes an archetypal love style. Naturally there are variations within the archetype, but inside each individual is this germ of truth which I have tried to uncover in my delineations of the 144 possible combinations. Remember, however, that Venus and Mars are only a part of the whole horoscope, and that there's no substitute for a complete reading. For example, you'll read that someone with a Venus in Gemini and Mars in Sagittarius is a freewheeling, independent individual who enjoys variety in love more than commitment. This is true. But obviously a tender, emotional Cancer with this placement will want more stability than a Mercurial Gemini with the same planets. Remember to consider that a horoscope is a vast and complicated map of a complete individual, and that here we are focusing on one small, but very valid sector that can provide insight about your romantic and sexual expectations and those of your lover. If you feel that the passage about you isn't right, there may be some modifying factors in other parts of your horoscope. It will contain some element of truth, however, and you can affirm this by randomly reading other passages. Chances are that your own is most strongly like you and will resonate the most profoundly with you.

Within each Venus-Mars combination is a lesson about the successful self-expression of the individual sexuality of that person. Through an in-depth, honest examination of your own placement, you can gain self-awareness and then can correct any behavior patterns or false expectations that promote unhappiness rather than the fulfillment you deserve. If your partners always disappoint you, then by getting in touch with your genuine needs, you'll learn to attract a more compatible mate. And, of course, the real fun is in looking up the Venus-Mars combinations of friends and lovers. If your motive is as innocent as choosing a suitable gift, knowing about your friend's Venus will help. If seduction is your goal, being forewarned is definitely being forearmed.

When love goes wrong, it usually isn't because of a lack of genuine feelings. We each communicate our love in different ways, likened to a code, and although we love each other dearly, if your code escapes your lover's detection, he or she will feel unloved, and ultimately you'll part. Venus and Mars together describe the code of every individual, and with a heart willing to open itself to another's style of loving, we each can nurture and preserve the relationships we begin.

It was with this goal in mind—to explore and create understanding for every different mode of loving—that I set out to write this book and, in so doing, to make loving as joyous as it should be for everyone.

Venus

Venus is the planet of love. Inside all of us is the desire to be seen, understood, appreciated, and ultimately loved because of who we are. It's not a winning smile, or beautiful breasts, or bulging muscles, or even a spectacular brain that seeks this confirmation from another. Rather, it's that indescribable spark of individuality that lights us from within that we wish to reveal without shame or embarrassment, for it's the promise of Venus that another human being will recognize that shining beacon of self—and with that recognition will come love.

The love of Venus is between individuals, each fully developed honestly, according to his or her own design. Venus seeks a soulmate, a partner in a one-to-one relationship that allows each participant to develop his or her uniqueness to the fullest, while creating a partnership that is greater than the sum of the two individuals alone.

Without rules, without conditions, without caveats, Venus says, "I see you as you're and I love you. I hope that you'll love me as well." For it's not in the nature of Venus to love without caring for love in return. Venus needs love as much as it desires to give love, for it feels incomplete and lonely without a partner. And so, feeling a longing for the company and wholeness it lacks, Venus desires to attract the one partner with whom it can bond, forming a strong and satisfying perfect whole.

The first step in understanding someone's Venus is to consider the placement by sign. Venus is one of the primary indicators of relationship needs, desires, and expectations in your horoscope. What's your particular love style? What can you expect in the way of romance from a potential partner? What's a good choice for a gift for a friend? Knowing something about the sign of Venus in a horoscope is a good way to begin to answer these questions.

Venus has much to do with the way we all relate. It describes our general romantic expectations, the way we seek pleasure, and the type of pleasure that is most enjoyable to us. Someone with Venus in Aries has a significantly different style of relating and set of values where love is concerned than the individual with Venus in Cancer. They both may believe wholeheartedly in love, but what that means to each of them is vastly different. The Venus in Aries person is aggressive, impatient, and direct. He or she wants to be swept away on a tide of passion that feels overwhelming and delicious. The Venus in Cancer person is more subtle, but just as determined to win the heart of a lover. Tender touches, shy, smiling glances, and the willingness to nurture characterize this sentimental approach. But both Venus in Cancer and Venus in Aries pursue the object of their affections assertively without waiting for that person to pursue them.

The sign placement of Venus describes the way we express our affections and the circumstances surrounding romance that feel most natural to each of us. Look at someone's Venus and you can learn the way in which he or she would like to be wooed, as well as what to expect in the way of courtship behavior. Do you desire hearts and flowers and midnight serenades? Or would you prefer a good, solid lover your parents would like? Venus gives you a very good idea about which you're likely to get.

Because Venus is about love, it's also about pleasure. How many times have you said, "Oh I love to do...." Both pleasure and love generate happiness, that warm spot inside that is stimulated and makes us all feel good. One test of compatibility is when you like the same things as your partner does. Otherwise you'll end up in different rooms, on different adventures, and very likely in different relationships. There are many shades of pleasure of course, and compromise is always an option, so as you learn more about what pleases your partner, you feel more confident about offering gifts, even small tokens of affection that mean little in the abstract, but when offered, mean so much.

In a woman's chart, Venus (as well as the Moon) describes the way she expresses her femininity, the essential nature of femaleness as she likes to share it. As what kind of woman does she see herself? Is she the motherly type? A sexy femme fatale? A clinging vine? A militant feminist? Her Venus will tell you, and it will help you determine if she's the sort of woman your heart yearns for as a mate. It will also tell you about her social ideals and expectations. How does she wish to be treated by a mate? Should you open the car door, make a proposition, dress up or dress down? Should you order tickets to the rodeo or the opera? Check her Venus.

In a man's chart, Venus describes the kind of woman he'd like to attract. Although his Moon is as important in his selection of a wife, his Venus is more romantic and sexual in its description of the way he sees women. Venus is his ideal of womanhood, the essential feminine principle that he seeks to express through the woman he loves. Does he want a soft woman to warm his hearth and cuddle in his lap, or an independent freethinker who can beat him at chess? Will he expect to lavish her with gifts, or does he want her to be content with quiet evenings in front of the television? Should she be gorgeous, or is her brain more important than her figure? Check his Venus. Is your new lover interested in a night of passion and a quick good-bye, or is this someone who is looking for a commitment? What are your own expectations along those lines? Often we attract people who refuse to give us the kind of love we need. Could it be that perhaps we are fooling ourselves about our own desires? Venus will give a pretty good clue. Each person has unique expectations where love is concerned, and we all have a right to fulfill our dreams and our individuality. The best matches are made between individuals who manage to be themselves in a way that satisfies their mates' needs for a partner. That is to say that when you naturally are what I need, then we will be well suited and happy together. By learning about another's romantic expectations, we're better able to compare them with our own. And without making judgments about which is "better," we can make more useful conclusions about whether we're on compatible paths.

Whether or not we find a mate in the eyes of a lover, the search for knowledge about that person brings with it a growing understanding and hence appreciation for the qualities he or she embodies. And knowledge and the resultant appreciation of another human being brings with it love for that person, which is the promise and the gift of Venus to every one of us.

Mars

Mars is the planet of ego expression—and action—and sex! The Venusian goal of the complete, individualized self is actualized through Mars. Not only does Mars say, "I get what I want," it also says, "I express what I am." It is not the job of Mars to consider other people, for it exists only for you—for your survival at its most primitive—and your self-actualization at its ultimate level. We all have the desire and the responsibility to become what we are, and we deserve to express that inner spark in order to grow and develop the promise of our completed individuality. It's through Mars that we do so.

Feeling free to assert yourself and the confidence in your own ability to carry any action through to a successful conclusion is the province of Mars. The strength of your constitution, your general vitality, your ability to be selfish, and your level of aggressiveness are all determined by the influence of Mars.

Mars is the planet of action, and everybody expresses this energy every day. The sign placement of Mars describes the way we express our aggressive urges. Someone with Mars in Aries reacts and acts in a manner significantly different from the individual with Mars in Scorpio. They both may be energetic, aggressive, and self-assertive, but they project themselves into the world in ways that are totally dissimilar. The Mars in Aries individual is independent, self-directed, and unapologetic. He or she easily puts personal needs above those of a partner, and while that can create some problems in practical areas of life, it can also mean many nights of passionate, overpowering seduction that can enthrall a willing mate. Mars in Scorpio is just as passionate, but it's a little craftier. This individual knows how to get under a partner's skin, in the manner of a Svengali who can use a mate's fantasies as fuel for the sexual fire. But both Mars in Aries and Mars in Scorpio are intense, sexually domineering, and unwaveringly strong.

Look at someone's Mars and you can learn about the type of activity he or she enjoys. Do you like to be outdoors doing something physical? Would you prefer to lie on a chaise and read a good book? Are you always leaping impulsively into new situations? Do you consider every potential action carefully before taking any action? Are you unabashedly selfish, or do you always consider the other guy? Mars will give you a good idea about the energy patterns of each individual.

In a man's chart, Mars (as well as the Sun) describes the way he expresses his masculinity, the essential nature of maleness as he likes to convey it. As what kind of man does he see himself? Is he a freewheeling cowboy? A shy sensitive type who loves to mother? A humanitarian? A sexy caveman? A sensualist? A show off? Will he be an authoritarian or can he compromise? Check his Mars.

In a woman's chart, Mars (and traditionally the Sun, although that is lessening as women now express the energies of their Suns directly) describes the kind of man she'd like to attract. What sort of guy turns her on? What's her sexual type? Check her Mars. Does she want an exciting, aggressive, athletic type? Does she want someone dependable who earns a good living and provides a stable home? Does she want an intellectual type? Does she want a sensitive, emotional artist, or would she rather have a rigorous military type? The sign placement of her Mars will describe very well the kind of guy who turns her on. And, of course, Mars will describe her own way of expressing her energies. For example, a woman with Mars in Capricorn is ambitious, organized, achievement-oriented, and she's attracted to men who embody these qualities as well. When faced with the placid, sensitive type who'd rather be at home reading a volume of poetry instead of outside, climbing up the ladder of success, she isn't very likely to disappear to slip into something "more comfortable"—she'll just disappear.

We all have Venus and Mars in our charts, and to a very great extent we all express both of these energies. Nowadays we all seek a better integration of our male-female energies. We each seek to express both sides of our natures, and we do it through Venus and Mars in our horoscopes, combined with the Sun and the Moon. Nevertheless, it still remains true that you can learn is much about the partner you seek through your Venus and Mars as you can learn about your own essential male and female energies from the same two planets.

Locating Your Venus and Your Mars

At the back of this book you'll find tables listing the positions of Venus and Mars between 1930 and 2025. If you find that either planet in your horoscope is listed at either the first or last day for any sign, you can use your birth time to find the precise location of your actual Venus and actual Mars. You may have to adjust that time based on Greenwich, England but I explain how to do that quite easily on the listings pages.

Without getting too astrologically complicated, we all are born in different time zones. That affects the placement of planets as well, for it's a different time in England than it is in Oklahoma City. The planetary charts were calculated for the zero hour, in Greenwich England. Thus—if you're born as a planet is moving into the next sign—you'll need to adjust your birth time to match the zero hour. This is so that the charts will work for people all over the world. If you look at the top of the charts, there is easy to follow information about how many hours to add or subtract. **This is only necessary if you were born as a planet was just entering or leaving the sign.**

If this still seems complicated, you can simply read the description of the sign next to yours (the sign preceding or following, as the case may be) in order to be sure that you're placing your planets correctly. You shouldn't have any trouble recognizing yourself. Most people will find that they were born in the middle of a Venus or Mars period, so no calculations will be necessary.

You'll find comprehensive descriptions of both Venus and Mars in every sign, as well as the description of every Venus-Mars combination. They go in order of the Zodiac, with Venus leading. So if you have Venus in Sagittarius and Mars in Taurus, go first to the Venus chapter and scroll down to where your Venus in Sagittarius is described. Then go to the Mars chapter and read the Mars in Taurus passage. Then go to the section with the delineations of all the Venus in Sagittarius combinations to find your own Venus in Sagittarius-Mars in Taurus combination.

The Four Elements

One way of grouping the twelve astrological signs is by element. There are three signs in each element, and they all share certain similarities with each other. Each element has several key words associated with it, and thus simply by knowing the sign (and thus the element) of someone's Venus or Mars, you already have some idea about the way that planet will function. The chart below helps.

Signs in the Elements and Their Qualities

FIRE	EARTH	AIR	WATER
Aries	Taurus	Gemini	Cancer
Leo	Virgo	Libra	Scorpio
Sagittarius	Capricorn	Aquarius	Pisces
Energetic	Practical	Intellectual	Emotional
Independent	Sensual	Outgoing	Shy
Friendly	Materialistic	Impractical	Secretive
Idealistic	Organized	Communicative	Sensitive

Thus individuals who have Venus in Taurus and Mars in Sagittarius, will express romance in a sensual way that is friendly, they will seek a practical, materially oriented partner, and they will express themselves in an energetic way, demanding independence and freedom of action.

In another example, a Cancer Venus, Gemini Mars individual will be emotional, shy and a bit secretive about expressing feelings, yet sensitive to a partner's emotions. This mate may be outgoing because of Mars, but the Cancer Venus will always hold back a little until there's a sense of intimacy and security with a partner.

For an easy first clue when analyzing the signs of Venus and Mars, consider their position by element.

The Astrological Modes

Another way we categorize the signs is via Modes—the way energy is expressed. The signs which share a common mode have patterns of energy in common.

CARDINAL	FIXED	MUTABLE
Aries	Taurus	Gemini
Cancer	Leo	Virgo
Libra	Scorpio	Sagittarius
Capricorn	Aquarius	Pisces
Pro-active	Steady	Flexible
Assertive	Stable	Changeable
Energetic	Completion-Oriented	Variety-seeking

A person with Venus in any of the Fixed signs seeks continuity. A break-up is a big deal, for this individual want to keep going, no matter what. This can be good in a marriage because it's easier to stay together than endure a divorce, but if the marriage is a bad one, it can be war for decades. But a person with a Cardinal Venus leaps into a relationship with passion, and may leap into a new one without looking back. Mutable people can shrug and move on or let go and forgive. They find different ways to approach any problem, which is good for compromise.

So if you meet a person with Venus in Pisces and Mars in Aries, you can expect to be wooed with assertiveness, but also this mate is flexible enough to allow you to express your own preferences.

If you're stuck on a mate with Venus in Libra and Mars in Sagittarius, you find yourself being charmed with energy, and taken on many adventures which are new and exciting.

The Modes show how much stability a person craves and how easily he or she is willing to compromise where your needs are concerned.

Planets and Rulerships

As you read through the various sections in the book about Venus and Mars in all the signs, you'll notice I mention rulers and use phrases like "well placed," "happy," "comfortable," when discussing how Venus or Mars work in certain signs. This is because of something called rulerships. Without getting too complicated, each sign is ruled by a certain planet, and planets found in the sign of their rulership function very well. They're compatible with that sign, like bread and butter, and express their inherent energies without complication or hesitation. Other signs and planets work less easily together, like liver and chocolate.

Planets are each meant to do a specific thing, and how they do it depends on the sign where they reside. That is the whole subject of this book—how the planets Venus (love) and Mars (action) express their energies while in each of the twelve possible signs. Their sign position describes each planet's basic thrust into life and they show how that energy is expressed in the world.

For example, Mars rules Aries, so in Aries Mars is totally comfortable. The sign and the planet have much in common. They're self-focused, assertive, and basically can go after what they want with no apologies. It works. On the other hand, Libra, Aries' opposite sign, is all about connecting with other people, so Mars here is a little out of sorts, feeling that it should concentrate on the other guy rather than you and your own needs. This can make it harder to get what you want. You still find a way to meet your needs, however. And the people around you who benefit from your consideration will thank you.

On the flip side, Venus rules Libra, so in Libra, the sweet, loving qualities of Venus are expressed with happy gentility. Venus and Libra understand each other. But when you put Venus in Aries, it gets a little selfish, for that is the nature of the sign. Venus behaves in ways that are not altogether natural for the planet to do. But it still seeks love.

I guess you could liken this idea to music and dance. In

fact, I'm always complaining about the weird music on the popular TV show, *Dancing with the Stars*. They play wacky songs that to me don't go with the dances. I think there should be Latin music for the tango, for example. When they play some pop song with a tango it looks odd, as though they don't fit, even if the basic syncopation is the same. It feels like the dance and the music are at odds. So if a planet is trying to function in a sign that feels less harmonious to its basic nature, its expression is different, and sometimes awkward, but it still expresses itself. Mars still tries to tango you into bed.

Does this mean that if you have a planet in your horoscope in a sign where it's not at its best that you're doomed? No, of course not. You're expressing the energy of Venus or Mars in a different manner. And of course you won't know it's different because you're the product of your horoscope. You don't say well gee, my Mars isn't in Aries, so I'm less assertive. You're as assertive as you are. It's you, and you express your energies naturally in your own manner, just as you were meant to do.

Venus in Aries

Aries is a fire sign, ruled by impetuous, headstrong Mars. And Venus is the planet of love, other-person-oriented, working by the principle of attraction. As you might imagine, the planet Venus and the sign Aries do not always function harmoniously.

Think of the Aries Sun sign people you know. They're exciting, charming, magnetic people who like to run around doing exactly as they please with no interference from anyone. They are frequently in the middle of some dilemma or other, caused by the way they go charging into new situations without taking the time to analyze the consequences of their actions. They are always starting new things, whether or not they finish up the old.

Aries people always demand the freedom of unobstructed self-expression. Whoever said, "Me first!" was undoubtedly Aries. And the individual who expressed the thought that you don't get what you want by sitting around waiting for it to come to you was also Aries, you can be sure.

If your Venus is in this headstrong sign, you don't mind going after what you want, whether it's a lover or something to own. You like meeting your own needs and fulfilling your own desires, and whatever it takes to make you happy, you're willing to pursue. You easily put your own needs first and rarely feel the need to be self-sacrificial, no matter what's at stake. You want love—on your own terms.

The man with Venus in Aries wants a woman who is independent and strong-willed enough to be a challenge for him. He wants to feel that he is conquering her in a fierce battle of the heart. He spots the woman of his fantasies (and he has plenty of fantasies, usually of the rough-and-tumble variety), and he's instantly by her side, ready to sweep her off her feet for an evening or a lifetime. The trouble is that there is no real way to tell which he has in mind.

He isn't shy and he isn't reserved. He doesn't hesitate for an instant to tell you how wonderful you are, to try to persuade you that he is wonderful as well, and that together you'll be a couple the likes of which the world hasn't experienced since Romeo and Juliet. At first you may be tempted to think that this fellow has an incredible line. But as you talk with him, it's easy to fall under his magnetic spell, and gradually you realize that he means every flamboyant word he says. Honesty is a strong element wherever Aries is represented.

Just as the man with Venus in Aries wants his woman to be strong and independent, he himself intends to be that way. Don't expect him to be amused by your jealousy, to be flattered by your possessiveness, or to tolerate any form of unreasonable behavior that attempts to curtail his freedom. He won't. Forget clinging, and forget wanting to know when to expect him. Expect him when he gets there, and be prepared to occupy yourself with your own pursuits the rest of the time. He may listen to your suggestions about reasonable behavior and he may be open to ideas of compromise, depending on his Sun sign, but it is more likely that he'll ignore you because compromise is not in his vocabulary, except as a term applying to other people. He will not allow you or anyone else to infringe on his rights or to do anything that he sees as a threat to his freedom. His past relationships may have been full of stormy scenes, and even as he ages, your Venus in Aries swain probably won't develop the ease with give-and-take that other people have.

What's the answer to this dilemma? To be in agreement, naturally, without having to discuss the issue. If you're the type of woman who needs a good deal of freedom yourself and desires to give your partner the same rights you demand, so much the better. If you don't mind being an adoring audience, being swept away into his passions and his fantasies, then you have a much better chance of achieving a satisfying relationship with this man.

Go out to noisy, exciting places with lots happening. If you like to stay at home in a cozy nest, you're probably making plans for the wrong lover. If you enjoy doing new things, and being the first one to try something, you're in good company. Plan on being active, on engaging in sports, not being a spectator, for Venus in Aries likes to do, not watch. And don't expect hearts and flowers, because this man is often too wrapped up in his own needs to think of the little niceties of courtship. But for a woman who would rather be swept up into an exciting whirl that is always unpredictable, the man with Venus in Aries is a terrific fantasy-fulfilling lover.

The woman with Venus in Aries has a much tougher time. It's hard for her to find a man who's strong enough for her, and she's often ambivalent about whether or not this is what she desires. She has the same fantasies of conquering and of being conquered as does her male counterpart, but often she is doing the conquering. The archetype of the female Amazon—strong, powerful, and supremely sexy—is the essence of the vision of self seen by the woman with Venus in Aries. She is aggressive. She's the type of woman who goes right up to the man she likes at a party, in a bar, or on the street. She likes the idea that she is unconventional, that her behavior is shocking and even a little bit titillating. The Venus in Aries woman likes the chase as much as her male counterpart does. But she isn't so sure she wants to be caught. It's hard for her to want to be committed to any one man, because that idea is so conventional as well as so inhibiting. And she refuses to be either. She must be free to express herself at all times. No one is allowed to dictate to her, and as soon as she feels that sense of confinement, she's on her way. It isn't that she's unromantic or that she has trouble falling in love; she just finds it difficult to remain in love or to want to stay put at all.

She's the kind of woman who makes her own fortune and runs her own conglomerate with hundreds of male subordinates. She's a goer, a doer, an exciting woman who approaches you, invites you on a date, then picks you up in her own plane that she pilots herself. She'd much rather be exciting than feminine, and while she may very well be the initiator in a love scene, she isn't very likely to curl up in your lap with a sweet sigh.

How do you deal with a woman like this? As an equal. Take her to exciting places after asking her first if she'd like to go. Drive a sexy sports car, and drive it fast. Appreciate her for the exciting, energetic woman she is, and never expect her to fulfill any traditional notions of womanhood. And don't expect her to compromise or to stay at home quietly knitting.

Whether you're a man or a woman, Venus in Aries is self-centered, freedom-loving, uncompromising, and quick to express affection in an exuberant, unhesitating way.

These celebs are among those with Venus in Aries: George Clooney, Jack Nicholson, Rihanna, Marilyn Monroe, Elizabeth Taylor, Mariah Carey, Bar Refaeli, Shakira, Eva Longoria, Rosa Parks, Lady Gaga, Audrey Hepburn, Sofia Coppola, Liza Minnelli, Janet Jackson, Bob Marley, Johnny Cash.

The impulsive, headstrong romantic nature described by Venus in Aries will be modified somewhat by the sign positive of Mars, the planet of action and sex.

Venus in Taurus

Taurus is an earth sign—ruled, traditionalists say, by Venus—although other astrologers feel that the Earth rules Taurus. In any case, the sign Taurus can be a very harmonious place for the planet Venus. Both enjoy luxury, pleasure, sensuality, and beauty.

Taurus Sun sign people tend to be down-to-earth types who like to look good, live well, and in general have a high capacity to appreciate and enjoy all the sensual pleasure that our planet has to offer. They seem to be calm, easygoing, reliable folk who would never start a riot, although they might start a luxury catering business.

If your Venus is in this sensual sign, you love beauty and pleasure, and you know how to enjoy yourself. You can soothe frayed edges with food and do sometimes self-medicate with sweet treats, but other times you just eat for the pleasure of it. You're not the sort to deny yourself anything, and you want to be sure that your life is filled with marvelous, sensual pleasures. In fact, you can happily spend all weekend in bed focusing on those sensual delights. Why not!

The man with Venus in Taurus wants a beautiful woman who is always elegantly groomed, perfumed, and ready to be adored. A broken, unmanicured fingernail can be as unattractive to him as a slow mental process might be to another fellow. He wants a woman he can show off to his friends as his beautiful and totally desirable female. He'll smother her in luxury, to whatever extent he can afford, and it's likely that he is no pauper, for he has the ability to attract material wealth to him. He'll buy her boxes and boxes of the finest chocolates, and he won't mind a bit if she's just a tiny bit plump, for he may be a little fleshy himself.

Nights at the theater, seeing frothy musicals, followed by visits to the finest restaurants are his idea of the perfect evening. Of course, his partner should wear her designer togs and jewels, even if everyone else is making an appearance in jeans. He may be a little too possessive of her because he thinks of her as belonging to him as surely as one of his many gold cufflinks, silver flasks, or diamond ear studs. It's not that he wants to control her behavior; he just feels that she is his, period.

In bed, he delights in long, lazy lovemaking sessions, with much touching, kissing, licking, and biting. His bed is the most comfortable nest in the town, with its down pillows and billowy comforter. And if she has suggestions for some innovation in the sex department, he's more than willing to go along, as long as acrobatics are not the order of the evening. How do you handle a man like this? Relax, curl up, and sigh with pleasure as he licks delicacies from your body and sensuously tickles your back for hours on end.

The woman with Venus in Taurus is every man's favorite mistress. She exudes sensuality and she's never ashamed of the fact that she loves sex, touching, and men in general. Her greatest pleasure is in creating a special atmosphere of luxury in which to indulge her man. She loves to be wooed with wine and gifts, and the one impression she wants to make is that of supreme artist at seduction.

She may be lazy, soft, and spoiled, and she won't care if you tell her so, for that's exactly what she wishes to be. Lazy is one of her favorite words. It means lying around alone or with a pal enjoying every potential pleasure available. Pliant is not a dirty word to her; her favorite perch may well be in your lap, where she will unashamedly accept all the petting you might want to lavish on her. Just make sure that she's the only lady in your life, for like her male counterpart, she can be possessive and jealous.

Venus in Taurus has the knack of turning a sex partner for the afternoon into one for the ages. Continuity is this lover's specialty, and it's fairly tempting to be lured into a lair where you know you can luxuriate for a lifetime.

What do you do with this sex kitten? Savor her magical sensuality. Indulge her with gifts and kisses. And wallow in every form of pleasure that she can devise for your enjoyment. After all, if you wanted a pal for the ball game or a camping partner, you wouldn't be interested in this food-loving, super-sexy femme fatale, would you?

Whether you're a man or a woman, Venus in Taurus is sensual, earthy, luxury-loving, indolent, and inclined to a manner of pleasant excess. It seeks a mate who sticks around and isn't afraid at all of commitment.

These celebs are among those with Venus in Taurus: Kanye West, James Franco, Jesssica Alba, Princess Diana, Amber Heard, Linda Evangelista, Ella Fitzgerald, Chaka Khan, Sarah Vaughn, Cyd Charisse, Liv Tyler, Debbie Harry, Traci Lords, Marlon Brando.

How well you go about expressing the uxorious urges of Venus in Taurus will be modified somewhat by the sign position of Mars, the planet of action and sex.

Venus in Gemini

Gemini is an air sign, ruled by the quick-thinking, always-moving Mercury. Venus is the planet of love, and it needs to be able to express affection without being bothered by intellectual considerations. It also seeks to develop a relationship with one significant other. In Gemini, both of these issues are complicated by the intrusion of the thought process, and in favor of the intellect and the need to be flexible enough to move along.

Sun sign Geminis have a lively kind of mental sparkle. They love to talk, to tell jokes, make puns, and to chatter. They are rarely overemotional, and they are always running from one appointment (date, meeting, party) to another, usually late. Their greatest fear is of being bored.

For that reason, they often refuse to get too close to anyone, because they can't bear the responsibilities having to deal with heavy emotions, or the feeling that they are being hemmed in or tied down. This isn't because they must express themselves at all costs, like Aries, but because the specter of boredom haunts them continually.

If you have Venus in this intellectual sign, you like the life of the mind. Talking about everything under the sun makes you very happy. You need friends and many social contacts, so you can feel fulfilled intellectually. You'd never choose a mate based only on physical chemistry because what turns you on is a sparkling mind. If someone can make you laugh, you love them forever. To you, love is going through life arm in arm, chatting, laughing, and sharing ideas.

The man with Venus in Gemini likes to play the field. He prefers an intellectually superior woman. He will never expect her to conform to any preset notions of behavior; she should be her own varied and interesting (the more interesting the better) self at all times. That way it's almost as good as having more than one woman.

He wants a lively little gal who can engage his mind, flirt like a champ, and make life exciting in a changeable way. She doesn't have to be what anyone thinks of as traditionally sexy. She might be skinny and flat-chested but have lots of spunk. The vamp is just too intense for his tastes. A woman like that could suck you in forever—before you ever found out if she had a brain or not. And then where would you be—stuck in a relationship with nothing more exciting to do than pointless, repetitive, silent sex.

The man with Venus in Gemini is a flirt. He loves to stand around at a party regaling any woman he encounters with his wit. You go ahead and do the same—he's not jealous or possessive at all. In fact, the more interesting to others you seem, the more interesting you are to him. Maybe there's a facet of you that he has yet to experience, and he loves the idea of discovering those hidden qualities.

Where might you encounter this mercurial man? In the library or the book store—in the light reading section. On a neighborhood walk. At the local radio station, where he may be the disc jockey. Anywhere things are happening and people are expressing ideas. Capturing him for your very own is another matter. You know to what lengths Scheherazade had go to in enchanting her man—no doubt a Venus in Gemini fellow. Night after night she regaled him, but not with her splendid body, her sexual expertise, or her home cooking. She wooed her man with words, and so should you, if you want this man to hang around and maintain his interest. After all, who else can whisper puns in your ear at the height of passion?

The woman with Venus in Gemini is no fragile emotional flower. She's outgoing, friendly, interested in everyone and everything, and she loves to stand around with a lively bunch of people and crack jokes. Chief among the gifts she brings to any man to whom she makes a commitment are her intellectual sparkle and her terrific way with words. She may send you a birthday card, but you can be sure that the verse inside was penned by her, not Hallmark, unless she is employed there, which is a distinct possibility. She can write light verse, create limericks, and is a swell punster.

This female is determined to be a sparkling and interesting companion. And she won't be content unless you appreciate her wit and can match it. In fact, she may want several guys in her life at one time, in order to keep the action lively and to keep from being swallowed up by boredom. She may have been the first to go to bed with two men at once, not because she's so sensual but because the idea was so interesting and the assignation provided a lot more in the way of variety than those she had previously experienced.

What happens if you're one guy and you want her all for yourself? Unless her Sun, Moon, and Ascendant are in more emotional, more relationship-oriented signs, it may be difficult. This is one woman who hates to be tied down romantically. *Forever* sounds like *boring* to this lady, although she does want to be your pal for a long time—as long as you stay interesting, that is.

Take her out to gatherings of your intellectual friends, where you both can roam, freely making contacts with other people. Then she might be willing to go home with you alone, to spend the balance of the night discussing interesting ideas. Buy her books, but keep them light. Don't be too emotional, too intense, too staid. Maintain your flexibility so that you can continue to grow and change, and she might want to stay around to discover the ever-new, ever changing you. Come to think of it, that's a pretty good incentive to become your most scintillating self.

Whether you're a man or a woman, Venus in Gemini is unemotional, intellectual, friendly, and reluctant to form lasting ties or commitments.

These celebs are among those with Venus in Gemini: Harrison Ford, Tom Hanks, Cher, Adele, Jennifer Lopez, Tina Fey, Sandra Bullock, Brooke Shields, Gisele Bündchen, Naomi Campbell, Heidi Klum, Courtney Love, Christina Hendricks, Helen Hunt, Frida Kahlo, Jackie O, JFK, Bob Dylan, Tupac Shakur, Jerry Seinfeld.

The mercurial, lighthearted nature described by Venus in

Gemini will be modified somewhat by the sign position of Mars, the planet of ego expression.

Venus in Cancer

Cancer is a water sign, ruled by the ever-changing, always emotional Moon. When Venus is free to express itself emotionally, a relationship that allows each person to communicate on the most intimate level possible can be created. Each partner can then go on to become more complete, a more naturally whole individual, without constraints, awkwardness, or confusion. Cancer is emotional, sensitive, nurturing, home and family oriented, and as such provides an excellent atmosphere for Venus, the planet of love and relationships.

Sun sign Cancers are sensitive. They are very concerned with emotions—particularly their own, and they never hesitate to let you know if you've trampled on those very important feelings. They love Mom a lot, and they adore all children. Growth and nurturing are the most important thing in the world to them.

Cancers are very concerned with security. Hard workers, they always try to accumulate enough money to feel that they and their family will be well taken care of. Food is always an important issue for anyone with planets in Cancer.

If you have Venus in this sensitive sign, you're sweet, nurturing, and tenderhearted, and you love your ice cream. Your inner child remains alive and vibrant all your life, and you easily recall all the childhood pleasures that made you feel safe and joyful. You like indulging in them all your life and with your own children. Your values are traditional and you know that a happy life means being surrounded by a warm family and security. You want to feel and give love that provides tenderness and nurturing.

The man with Venus in Cancer may be the best mother

you know. He loves to take care of people, is never embarrassed when confronted with a weeping female, squeezes orange juice for his mate when she's sick, helps diaper the baby, and is generally a thoughtful, New Age man. He likes a soft, sensitive woman who's cuddly, gentle, and a good cook. He respects all the traditional notions of femininity (and embodies quite a few of them himself), and thus likes a woman who wants to fulfill that role. After all, he's not asking her to do anything he's unwilling to do.

You'll find the Venus in Cancer man at the playground or building castles in the sandbox with some youngster, whether or not he's ever been a father. If you're standing around wiping runny noses and gazing about with the same dewy expression you see on his tender face, he'll find you. Or he may be in his mother's backyard, giving the lawn its weekly mowing. This man loves the sensation of home, the smell of warm muffins in the oven, the Parcheesi game on the floor. Invite him for dinner. The house doesn't have to be spotless, but it ought to be cozy. Cook dinner yourself, set a pretty table, and wear a frilly apron.

At dinner, enjoy the stories about his childhood (he has forgotten a total of barely ten minutes since the moment of his birth) and share your own favorites. Memories of your childhood and family don't seem at all long ago to this sentimental fellow. After dinner, take your time listening to music and each other's soft murmurs of relaxed happiness. What follows will be cozy, cuddly, and tender.

The woman with Venus in Cancer is sweet, tender, and loving. She may be as liberated a woman as you'll ever meet, yet she in no way sees the value of eschewing the gentler human emotions. Her idea of herself as a woman is someone tender enough to care for other people, whether her lover, her children, or her friends. She's a sensitive woman who likes to entertain at home in her warm and cozy nest.

Spending time with a group of happy, well-fed people makes her feel good. She's the lady who's always in the kitchen, with a roomful of people surrounding her. She wants to be married and to be a mother, and that's a number-one priority, even if she's also a full-time corporate executive, banker, or college professor. When her children are born, it isn't very likely that she'll entrust their full-time care to anyone else; caring for them herself is too important—and too satisfying.

If this is the lady you want to woo, you've chosen well. Just come down with a case of the flu and she'll mother you to health. Buy her a charm for her charm bracelet (she loves tender memories and their physical reminders). Invite her to your place and pamper her for a change. She loves being reminded of the days when she was mother's pet. It's perfectly all right to discuss your deepest feelings. She's glad to listen and willing to make you feel great about being the one thing you're supremely qualified to be—yourself. She has the ability to love you totally for no better reason than because you're you, and nobody has done that so well since your mother.

Whether you're a man or a woman, Venus in Cancer is sensitive, nurturing, emotional, and desirous of one reliable, long-term relationship that will be the backbone of a secure family and home.

These celebs are among those with Venus in Cancer: Angelina Jolie, Ben Affleck, Barack Obama, Keanu Reeves, Arnold Schwarzenegger, Natalie Portman, Cameron Diaz, Halle Berry, Camilla Parker Bowles, Mary Kate & Ashley Olson, Khloe Kardashian, Hilary Swank, Raquel Welch, Stevie Nicks, Judy Garland, Kim Cattrall, Grace Jones, Clint Eastwood, Donald Trump.

The caring, emotional nature described by Venus in Cancer will be modified somewhat by the sign position of Mars, the planet of ego expression.

Venus in Leo

Leo is a fire sign, ruled by the Sun. The Leo qualities of steadiness, generosity, pride, and egocentricity, as represented by the warm, radiant Sun, cause Venus to be steadfast and giving when placed in that sign. Leo tends to be a bit general and rather unemotional, whereas Venus likes to be specific and free to express emotions, but these minor points aside, Venus in Leo can work quite well, as long as the positive Leo qualities are being expressed.

Sun sign Leos are very people oriented. They like to be at the epicenter of whatever's happening. At their best, they are generous, supportive, stable, constant, and very loving. At their worst, they're selfish, self-centered, vain, arrogant, and domineering. Leos have a great deal of pride, wanting always to be respected and admired. They like important people and want to enjoy a certain level of prestige and status.

Because their ruler is the Sun, Leos are always warm, radiant people with sunny personalities. They're generally popular and work hard to maintain the goodwill of the people in their immediate circle. Leos care deeply about the impression they make, and they always want to live up to some code of worthiness that inspires the admiration of people they know.

If your Venus is in this sunny sign, you enjoy giving and receiving. Being immersed in a social whirl makes you feel happy, and you love to shop for clothes, shoes, and anything that makes you look good. All your life, your appearance is important to you, and it's unlikely you'll ever let yourself go. You want to be attractive to other people and to be appreciated for the treasure you know you are. You hold tightly in your heart the people you love and you want the same from them in return. Love to you is being able to share the good life with someone who makes it sparkle even more.

The man with Venus in Leo wants a woman he can point to with pride and admiration, and who inspires the appreciation of others who see her with him. She should be strikingly beautiful, radiant, interesting, warm, and loving. No matter that her heart may be in the right place, the woman who's a careless slob is not the sort he wants to share his name or even his limelight. This man sees his woman as an envoy, as his ambassador, and as such, she must live up to his standards and be able to reflect the appropriate light on him. She's an extension of him in the outside world, so she must be or do nothing to create a bad impression.

He's not strong on compromise, and he attracts a woman who likewise is used to being the unchallenged center of attention. Because he's so friendly and magnetically attractive, he can usually avoid the sort of strife engendered by his demands for attention. With such a sunny, outgoing personality, his idea of himself is not usually challenged, and he easily receives the notice and devotion he desires. The man with Venus in Leo likes to go out with lively people who're well off and well known. He likes to wear expensive clothes and could be accused of being a show-off if he weren't such an all-around nice guy.

The lady on his arm must wear elegant clothes, expensive jewels, and is escorted in the nicest car he can afford to the best places with the most substantive people. Together they make a splendid spectacle, and that's precisely how he wants it. If you're in love with a Venus in Leo man, go to the beauty salon after a shopping spree. A perfect hairdo and manicured nails may be just the props in the scene you're setting, but they're mandatory.

How many movie stars do you know? Politicians? Denizens of the social register? Invite them all to a formal bash, and invite him too. If it's an occasion to benefit a worthy cause, so much the better. Venus in Leo loves to shine in public alongside the glitterati, and to give with an open hand. After you've captured his attention, it won't be long before you've also captured his heart. And when that happens, it's a good bet that it will be forever, for Venus in Leo glows with a steadfast devotion that is unmatched by many of the other signs in the Zodiac.

The woman with Venus in Leo wants to be admired. She sees herself as a supremely attractive woman, the glittering diamond centerpiece in a jeweled tiara, worthy of notice, admiration, and adoration. Scarlett O'Hara, as she sat at the barbecue surrounded by dozens of admiring beaux whose only wish was to serve and dote on her, represents the epitome of Venus in Leo. Her presence, and indeed her affection, are gifts she warmly and regally bestows on the people she loves, and she may sometimes look down on them as her humble servants. Just as she sees herself as extraordinary, her friends are also special, the "in crowd," and she is loyal and devoted to them forever.

Your Venus in Leo lady can be very patient, but she is determined. If you're the one she loves, she'll overwhelm you with a persistent kind of ardor that's very hard to discourage. She expects to get her way and to have her desires fulfilled, whether or not you both agree on those desires. She's so warm, charming, and generally endearing, even when she's being exasperatingly regal, that it's hard to quibble. More than any other sign in the Zodiac, Venus in Leo likes to be wooed, and can likely be won with wooing of the right type. First of all, you must be attractive, well dressed, and the sort of companion that Mother, Father, and the president would approve of.

After you're sure that you can pass muster, start your campaign. Phone calls, lots of invitations to classy places, lavish gifts matched by even more lavish verbal expressions of admiration, and of course, candy and flowers, will get you started on the road to romance. The best way to win this lady's heart and her consent is by proving yourself to be the most fitting of all possible consorts. Once you've done that, you'll have caught a mate of whom you can always be proud and who always inspires the admiration of everyone you know.

Whether you're a man or a woman, Venus in Leo is friendly, outgoing, generous, and steady in its expression of affection in a warm, long-lasting, very loving way.

These celebs are among those with Venus in Leo: Tom Cruise, Nicole Kidman, Madonna, Pamela Anderson, Whitney Houston, Amy Winehouse, Gwyneth Paltrow, Coco Chanel, Salma Hayek, Selena Gomez, Dita Von Teese, Fiona Apple, Zoe Saldana, Alfred Hitchcock, Andy Warhol.

The sunny, romantic nature described by Venus in Leo will be modified somewhat by the sign position of Mars, the planet of ego expression.

Venus in Virgo

Virgo is an Earth sign, and although its ruler has traditionally been Mercury, many astrologers today believe that the true ruler of Virgo has yet to be discovered, and others feel that a group of asteroids rule this analytical, critical, service-oriented sign. Venus in Virgo is a difficult placement. At its best, Venus should be able to express affection toward a loved one without restraint, hesitation, or even good reason. Being loved just because you exist the gift of Venus to us all. But Virgo must always have reasons—therefore its critical faculties prevent action of any kind without discrimination, and a careful analysis of all pros and cons, a process which thwarts the irrationality and pleasure of romance.

Sun sign Virgos are critical, careful, and helpful. They like to work, and want to do a good job. If you have a problem, need to improve any system of organization, need insights from someone whose mind is discerning, precise, and always able to ferret out the best option, call your Virgo friends. They're naturally able to sift through mountains of details, producing a molehill of perfect organization from them. And they love to help.

If your Venus is in this cautious sign, you take your time making connections. You're careful, and you have very specific tastes. You know what your standards are, and it's important to you that your choices reflect those standards. As much as you like to help other people, your goal is not to be with a partner who needs to be rescued. You'd rather find someone who's as together as you are. Sometimes you have trouble finding love, and you don't know why, because you are very kind. It's just something inside you that pulls away, so if you work on this tendency, you can let it go. Then you can find the love you want in which each partner gives and receives equally.

The man with Venus in Virgo wants a lady, not just a woman, and this means perfect attire and grooming, and a sense of poise and tact that can't easily be faked. This fellow wants a cool, composed lady who's always controlled, serene, and capable, someone who's never tacky enough to wear her heart on her sleeve. And under her immaculate hair should lie a brain the equal of his. A dumb blonde on the order of those played by Marilyn Monroe wouldn't tempt this guy for half an instant. He's a Kate Hepburn/Julia Roberts fan.

This fellow loves to touch and be touched, and although he's quite comfortable with the physical aspects of love (only in private of course, and on fresh sheets), the idea of romance makes him nervous. Why, exactly, do people write love songs and stand outside in the freezing cold singing them to coeds with their hair in curlers? Wouldn't it make much more sense to treat the lady to a visit to Elizabeth Arden or hire a cleaning woman for her for a day? And doesn't all that mooning around people do waste an awful lot of time that could be spent doing something useful? This is the way his mind works. He's the sort of guy who approves of a woman who'd prefer a washing machine to a diamond.

If you're interested in a Venus in Virgo man, be practical. Go ahead and pamper him, but make sure you're buying useful things that you know he'll like. He probably doesn't need a tie pin or another tie, but he might love some special shaving cream, a new soap, a deluxe Scrabble game, or a cozy bathrobe. Breakfast in bed may seem a little decadent to this practical, hardworking sort, but go ahead, anyway; just be sure that the muffins are homemade and the eggs are perfectly scrambled. And your hair should be combed and your teeth freshly brushed.

If you're too busy to go out one night because of a deadline at work, go ahead and tell him. He respects you for your career ambitions and is delighted to stay in at night working by your side. He never expects you to wait on him as his masculine due, and in fact, he may be far more comfortable fetching and carrying for you. The man with Venus in Virgo helps out around the house, and he's probably as good at doing the chores as your mother is. He may be an artisan of some sort, and if he is, he makes crafts of excellent quality. He never leaves towels on the bathroom floor, hangs his underwear on a doorknob, or walks around in grubby socks. He's a tidy sort who likes to keep his surroundings as orderly as his emotions. As long as you're the woman he wants in his life, you have no fears of infidelity—cheating is just too messy for him.

In bed, he's earthy and comfortable, so despite all of this carefulness and precision, he's a pretty good lover. He wants to please you and works hard to do so. He may not be terribly emotional, but he loves to touch and is sensual.

The woman with Venus in Virgo thinks of herself as cool, calm, and collected, ever ready to intercede when there's a problem, and able to restore order to even the most difficult situation. She's a lady with taste, breeding, and good sense, and she has no tolerance for frivolity or nonsense of any type.

This intelligent woman may well be a fashion designer, a nurse, or a craftswoman, but whatever her profession, she is no clinging vine, and she doesn't need a man to support her or to advise her. She is self-sufficient and may well be the most organized, most competent woman you'll meet, despite the fact that she is a bit insecure about herself.

Venus in Virgo encourages her to express love via helping others. As soon as she sees a problem, or an area where her expertise would come in handy, she's there doing what she can to smooth ruffled feathers, restoring order without even a furrow to her brow.

If you've taken an interest in this pristine lady, go ahead and express your feelings, just do it tastefully. She wouldn't appreciate a John loves Mary billboard lit up in Times Square. A tiny silver locket with your picture in it is another matter. Or give her a class in something she's been wanting to learn: lace crocheting or pottery or translation of hieroglyphics—you get the idea. It doesn't have to be traditionally romantic but rather something that shows you've been paying attention, which if you think about it, is what we all truly want. Make a reservation at an elegant restaurant where the food is thoughtfully and perfectly prepared. It need not be super pricey, just a serene atmosphere with careful attention to detail. More than any other trait, this lady notices and appreciates detail, and the more you attend to the finer points of your courtship, the more likely you are to capture her heart for your own.

When the Venus in Virgo lady devotes herself to you, she goes all out to see that you're happy and well taken care of. That means scrubbing your back in the shower, knitting your socks by hand, and preparing all your favorite foods—without you ever having to ask. And considering that she's willing to take better care of you than your mother did, you ought to be able to put up with her occasional critical remarks—they're only aimed at helping you improve, after all. And she's willing to curl up sweetly in your arms at night, melting into a sensual, naturally sexy partner in bed, one who can meet you move for move until you're both sighing with tender satisfaction, so maybe you lucked out with this complex mate.

Whether you're a man or a woman, Venus in Virgo is discriminating, tasteful, cautious, and helpful, and will return affection prudently only after being sure that your feelings are genuine and true.

These celebs are among those with Venus in Virgo: Julia Roberts, Martha Stewart, Kim Kardashian, Blake Lively, Charlize Theron, Mila Kunis, Brigitte Bardot, Sophia Loren, Catherine Denueve, Gwen Stefani, Natalie Wood, Audrey Tatou, Demi Lovato, Sylvia Plath, Lil Kim, Lucille Ball, John Coltrane, Charlie Parker, Rober De Niro, Robert Redford.

The pristine romantic nature described by Venus in Virgo will be modified somewhat by the position of Mars—the planet of action.

Venus in Libra

Libra is an air sign, ruled by Venus, the planet of love. Because Venus in Libra is in the sign of its rulership, it functions here at its charming, relationship-oriented, romantic best.

Libra Sun sign people are among the most amiable of all the signs. They're always cheerful (even when they're low) because maintaining a pleasant atmosphere is so crucial to them. They like other people, crave company, and are experts at the fine art of compromise. In fact, when empowered as leaders of large groups, they decree that all members practice give-and-take in order to create an air of overall comfort and satisfaction.

Libras care about relationships of all types. They're very interested in romance, because to them the idea of the couple just feels like a normal way to live. The significant other is the one who completes them and who makes their life whole. They enjoy beautiful surroundings, graceful objects, pretty clothes, music, and art. They aim always to live their lives in a harmonious, balanced manner.

Libras dislike confusion of any sort. Emotional upheavals are as repugnant to them as is a garbage pile, so don't expect to find a strongly Libran individual in the middle of either one.

If your Venus is in this mannerly sign, you care very much about good taste. You have a certain image of life as it should be and you want to make your own life match that image. You're wildly romantic at times, and you want to fall in love with all your heart, as long as you don't do anything insane along the way. Without a mate, you really feel that something is amiss in your life. You seek love with someone who completes you.

The man with Venus in Libra wants a woman who is lovely, charming, and gracious. Like Ashley Wilkes in *Gone with the Wind*, he needs to feel that his woman embodies his ideal of beauty, grace, and harmony, that she represents something better than the mundane reality, for he wants this goddess to add beauty to his life. This is a very social man, and he requires a woman well schooled in the social graces. He's a charming host, an accomplished guest, and a considerate neighbor. He behaves in a way that could never make him the subject of unpleasant gossip, and in fact, the most unpleasant act he's willing to perform may be taking out the trash.

The Venus in Libra man considers his romance one of the most important areas of his life. He may be practical and hardheaded in other departments, but he idealizes relationships. Whether or not he's involved in a love affair, love is always on his mind, for he believes that it's through our relationships that we find our ideal selves. His fantasies may be more romantic than sexual, and he's definitely the type to send flowers. It would never occur to this man to be jealous or possessive. His concept of love is far more mental than visceral, and there's no nagging thought of the threat of abandonment that would prompt a jealous tirade; stormy, passionate scenes are just too messy for his taste. He prefers to follow a moderate course in every area of life.

Where will you find this genteel man? At a cocktail party, adeptly balancing a plate of dainty watercress sandwiches on his knee, on the board of directors of a cultural organization, or at an art gallery. He won't be the life of the party necessarily, but rather will be an attractive, pleasantly smiling individual, wearing well-cut clothing and engaging in congenial conversation. It's acceptable for you to go over to him in order to strike up a conversation, as long as your manners are good and your subject is tasteful. This is not the time to flirt with discussions of your drunken hookups.

Later on he may woo you at a charming bistro with good food and better atmosphere, which is what matters most to him. Ambience is essential. He's solicitous, attentive, and able to order for you without seeming like a chauvinist. If you return to his place afterwards, it will be as elegant as his budget allows, for Venus in Libra people can't bear to spend even a single night in a plain hotel room without immediate thoughts of how to make it pretty, cozy, and comfortable. His home is freshly cleaned and the fridge decently stocked, for being a good host matters to this man, and if you're a good guest, his interest in you will expand.

As time progresses, you can revel in the knowledge that you're immersed in a real romance, and even if the pace is rather slow, it feels quite delicious. If you end up together forever, you'll have many memories to share, and can look forward to adding additional sweet ones as the years go by.

The woman with Venus in Libra is friendly, charming, tasteful, considerate, and absolutely determined to create harmony and good cheer wherever she goes. She's the perfect hostess, the perfect wife, and a companionable friend. Her house is elegant, her clothing stylish, and her manner courtly and deferential. She can make you feel that your presence is a delight, and that you're truly an individual worthy of notice and attention.

Truly romantic, this lady lives for love. Having a good relationship may be her motivating force, and she can't help but go all out to make her paramour feel good. Her approach to love is mental more than emotional. It's the idea of the splendor of amour that enlivens her soul, not a passionate desire to couple gnawing at her loins. She's not given to jealous fits or to ill-mannered outbursts of any sort. Such indulgences are usually outside the range of her behavioral scope, but even if they were not, she would consider that type of conduct as an unfortunate reaction for an unthinking, ill-bred individual, someone completely unlike herself.

If you're interested in a Venus in Libra lady, stand in front of the mirror and give yourself the once-over. How's the cut of your suit—no synthetics, please. Are your eyes clear and is your jaw well formed? This lady may like you very much and even be drawn to you as a person, but if she doesn't consider you physically attractive, she'll shrug, call herself shallow, and tiptoe away. Arrive for your date clean and well-pressed. After she's known you for a while, you can relax a little, but not to the point of sitting around unshaved in your skivvies drinking beer in front a TV ballgame. You can downgrade from a suit to jeans, perhaps, but they should be nicely pressed. For this lady, dressing up is always preferable to dressing down. Buy her flowers, for this mate really appreciates all the old-fashioned courtesies, and indulging in them will not make her suspicious about your motives; she'll just conclude that your mother taught you well. And she'll accept any tokens of your affection graciously and with appreciation, not as her due.

The Venus in Libra woman likes to be taken out, despite the fact that she's so busy fussing over you from the moment that you enter her door that you might erroneously conclude that she'd prefer to stay at home. It's just her nature to be a concerned hostess even if you're locked in a neighbor's barn for half an hour, although being trapped in the storage room of a nightclub is definitely more her speed, for she's seldom the rugged outdoor type. A garden party may be delightful, but gardening in overalls while getting one's fingernails dirty is not.

Make reservations at a place you believe will please her. It doesn't matter if you suggest Greek when she prefers Chinese, for what will impress her is the time and effort you've devoted to the prospect of entertaining her. And it is, of course, obvious that drinking too much or making an ill-considered, sloppy pass will be met with great disfavor. She may exit smiling, leaving you unaware of your crime; such is her grace and social expertise.

If all this sounds like too many rules and too much work, you may be correct. This lady requires not only attention but also the right kind of attention, and if you're a real slap-dash person, she may not be for you. If, on the other hand, you're willing to devote some thought to creating this grand romance, you'll find your efforts well rewarded. You'll have a mate whom you can count upon for good cheer, good taste, and who is more than willing to spend a fair portion of her time focusing on you and your needs. She's the sort of mate who remains beautiful over the years and on whom it's easy to pin your fantasies of love, grace, and enduring devotion.

Whether you're a man or a woman, Venus in Libra is charming, sociable, considerate, tasteful, and assertive in its expression of affection, in a pleasant, genteel way.

These celebs are among those with Venus in Libra: Ryan Gosling, Will Smith, Jada Pinkett-Smith, Prince Harry, Beyonce Knowles, Emma Stone, Bill Clinton, Richard Gere, Grace Kelly, Claudia Schiffer, Rita Hayworth, Calista Flockhart, Anna Nicole Smith, Jenny McCarthy, Rose McGowan, Paz de la Huerta, Vanessa Minillo, Sean Connery, Pablo Picasso, Karl Lagerfeld, Kobe Bryant, Sean "P-Diddy" Combs, Lance Armstrong.

The elegant romantic nature described by Venus in Libra will be modified somewhat by the sign position of Mars, the planet of action and sex.

Venus in Scorpio

Scorpio is a water sign, ruled by passionate, intense, powerful Pluto. All planets in Scorpio operate in an emotionally intensified way. With Venus there, the drive to relate is strong, and the tendency is to forgo shallow, meaningless ties in favor of a very few supremely important relationships through which the participants can achieve growth and spiritual transformation.

Scorpio Sun sign people have received some bad press, primarily through misunderstanding. People who expect Scorpio to be sexy on cue and willing to leap into bed at the wink of an eye because of their astrological reputation are usually disappointed. So what's the real lowdown on those born in autumn?

Scorpios are passionate, intense, sexy, and very private. They have the uncanny ability to discern other people's feelings, motivations, and needs, and because they can do this so easily, they feel that other people might be able to do that to them, and so they are careful to keep their feelings guarded with all but a very few, very close loved ones. It's not that they have anything to hide; they just feel their emotions so deeply that they want to avoid sharing them with the whole world.

Scorpios are exceptionally loyal, and when they are on your side, they go to any lengths to help you. They make excellent confidants and good advisers about problems stemming from all kinds of human interaction. That's because they're the natural healers of the universe.

And yes, Scorpio is the sign most deeply involved with sex. To Scorpio, sex is the most intense form of communication possible between two people, and the transformations of the spirit that are possible because of this deep physical intimacy lend it an almost holy air. It's through sex that strongly

Scorpio people can reaffirm their oneness with God and all of creation. So, obviously, the casual fooling around that many people nowadays substitute for sex is rarely for Scorpio.

If your Venus is in this magnetic sign, you know that you possess a secret power—the ability to walk through a room and watch all heads turn in your direction. It's not something you do, but rather something you exude—like those pheromones the scientists—or is the it perfume people—are always talking about. You like this feeling because it means you can attract anyone you desire. What you want is the perfect soulmate, because then your life will feel complete. You want a real sense of trust and intimacy with someone, and then the whole world can fade away as you focus on each other, thrilled to your very souls.

The man with Venus in Scorpio is possessive, desires a woman who belongs to him alone, and expects her to have the same rules for him. To this devoted fellow, an open marriage is no marriage at all. His woman should be passionate, emotional, contained, and sometimes inscrutable. He expects restraint from her, and he doesn't want her to show her feelings to the world, nor will he delight in hearing her relate the intimate details of their life over the phone to a girlfriend.

This man is not casual—although he may seem very cool on the outside—and he's not interested in a great many superficial friendships. He cares totally or not at all, and he does everything with his whole being or not at all, and people who don't live their lives with this same passionate intensity bewilder and bore him.

No is his least favorite word, and because he's afraid that you might utter it, he may just insinuate himself into your consciousness to propel you along according to his wishes without ever discussing his feelings with you. But feelings are so complicated to him that mere words seem unable to accommodate them.

If you're interested in a man with Venus in Scorpio, first of all you must be certain that your interest is real. He will not look favorably upon anyone who wants to dally with his feelings. And, in fact, there isn't much you can do to entice him if he doesn't feel that instantaneous chemistry with you.

If he does feel that attraction, you may at first not realize the intensity of his desires. He'll chat with you, make a real effort to get to know you, and have a number of casual dates. When you're just about to conclude that everything you've heard about sex and Scorpio was wrong, he'll make an advance on par with the scene in Gone with the Wind when Clark Gable swept a transfixed Vivien Leigh into his arms and carried her up the stairs for a night of incredible passion.

The woman with Venus in Scorpio would like to be friendlier, but she feels it's her nature as a woman to hold back, being contained and impenetrable. Her thoughts and deep feelings are very private, and she feels that other people could be privy to parts of herself that she doesn't want to share if she's around them too much. She's completely loving to someone with whom she's involved, and can be very possessive even if she's secure in her man's feelings. When she's in love, she can become consumed with the desire to be around her mate to the point that he may begin to feel smothered.

This lady wants to be wooed by someone with whom she can have the total intimacy of sharing her deepest self, although she'd be hard-pressed to admit that she intends to open up quite that much. She certainly isn't going to talk about the prospect or about her feelings unless she's very sure of the listener, and then only rarely. Likewise she has only deep, abiding friendships, and only a few of those. She is not someone who travels with a pack of easily substituted gal pals.

This woman absolutely cannot be frivolous, and if you want someone frothy and light, look elsewhere. She likes serious music, deep colors, and the security of home. It's not that she loves entertaining—like a Libra—or that she dotes on taking care of others—like a Cancer—she just prefers to be surrounded by the comfort of her own, well-known home base. If you're beginning a relationship with a Venus in Scorpio lady, go slowly. As she's so closed with strangers, it takes a while for you to figure out how well you're doing, anyway. Ask her out to a quiet place with an intimate, candlelit atmosphere. The talk can be casual, like any meaningless conversation. It's the emotional subtext that she's listening to, and you can't orchestrate that. Gradually you may be able to tell by the warm light in her eyes when she looks at you that she's willing to open up. Or she may do something, such as letting her hand rest comfortably on your thigh, to make you aware of her desires. Be forewarned, however. The words, "To have and to hold" were written with this lady in mind, and no relationship entered into with her can ever be taken lightly.

Whether you're a man or a woman, Venus in Scorpio is passionate, intense, possessive, and serious in its expression of affection, in an emotional, sexually explicit way.

These celebs are among those with Venus in Scorpio: Leonardo DiCaprio, Demi Moore, Brittany Murphy, Kris Jenner, Chloe Sevigny, Jodie Foster, Naomi Watts, Condoleeza Rice, Alicia Silverstone, Serena Williams, Twiggy, Grace Slick, Sarah Silverman, Nia Long, Jim Morrison, Bruce Lee, Joaquin Phoenix, Tiger Woods, Ray Liotta.

The transformative romantic nature described by Venus in Scorpio will be modified somewhat by the sign position of Mars, the planet of action and sex.

Venus in Sagittarius

Sagittarius is a fire sign, ruled by expansive, optimistic, philosophically idealistic Jupiter. Planets in Sagittarius need to have a great deal of unrestricted freedom. They're social and friendly in a very nonjudgmental way. With Venus there, the urge to relate is very general, much more friendly than romantic, and the tendency is to go from partner to partner, rather than to seek a single binding relationship.

Sun sign Sagittarians always seem to be moving. You'd never expect to find them at home glued permanently to a couch. They like to keep going, free to experience anything they might bumble into. They have a restless kind of energy that needs to be expressed through physical action, or they get kind of twitchy, which is why they're often found outdoors engaged in athletic activity.

Sagittarians are idealistic, and they live according to their ideals more than the rest of us do. Honesty, justice, and morality are real issues to them. That's why they're so forthright in expressing their opinions. Tact strikes them as dishonest. They enjoy connecting on many levels and find the good in odd people and situations. Legendary for their wanderlust, they seek all manner of experiences and interact successfully with people far different from themselves.

If your Venus is in this adventurous sign, you're filled with enthusiasm for the many exciting aspects of life. You know how to have a good time, pretty much every day, even doing something small and insignificant. You're ebullient and affectionate, and you enjoy spending time with people who share your outgoing nature and happy approach to life. To you, love is seeing the wonder of life, reflected through someone else's eyes.

The man with Venus in Sagittarius is as warm and friendly as a puppy dog. He loves the world, and he suspects that just around the corner is someone new for him to discover, experience, and befriend. He wants a woman who shares his values and his philosophies, and who'll emphatically never think of trying to tie him down. This fellow is very reluctant to marry, and when he settles down, it will not be in a completely traditional way. Nine to five, a white picket fence, and apple pie every night would make him feel as uncomfortable as a stint in San Quentin. Before he makes the plunge, you can be sure that he's spent plenty of time playing the field, making friends of all the women he dates.

Once he does settle down, he remains friendly with old lovers, and makes new women friends, but he always attempts to remain faithful for ethical reasons, unless of course he's embraced some untraditional philosophy of open marriage, but this is probably unlikely. Instead he just makes the women of the world his pals, always coming home to the pal he married. It's easy to be interested in a man with Venus in Sagittarius. He's so friendly and outgoing that he's practically a walking party. Fun is his specialty, and you're likely to find him anywhere fun can be had in large doses. Go on up and chat. Waiting modestly won't impress him a bit, and in fact, he might not even notice you at all that way.

He likes women who have a healthy intellect and who enjoy communicating their ideas on a variety of interesting, possibly irrelevant topics. So walk right up and whisper, "what do you think about Plato's ideas on art?" Anything similar that really interests you'll do as well, but don't expect him to care about the rising prices in the supermarket. Plan a picnic or barbecue and invite him. Or visit the zoo together, as long as it's a wide open space, not the old-fashioned kind of zoo that cages animals. He can't bear to see anyone in prison, especially an innocent animal.

And if you decide to marry him, don't plan on getting an itinerary of his every move. He doesn't know himself. By the same token, he won't be angry when he arrives home one evening and discovers no dinner waiting for him. Obviously you had more interesting things to do. Why not round up a bunch of people and go out? The Venus in Sagittarius man wants a woman who'll roam the world with him, sharing causes and philosophies. He grants her the same freedom he demands, is never possessive or arrogant, and is the least sexist man in the Zodiac. He doesn't expect you to wait on him as his due, for he recognizes your individuality, and moreover, he knows that nobody enjoys being a slave to another person. He enjoys that you have your own interests and is your biggest fan as you develop your individuality to its utmost.

The woman With Venus in Sagittarius thinks of herself as a free spirit. Nothing and no one holds her down, and she may prefer to remain unmarried most of her life. If she does decide to wed, it's to a man who makes no traditional demands on her—someone who travels a lot, or a man who is a staunch feminist. She's not going to be anyone's little wifey, isn't going to fetch and carry, doesn't want to be a splendid hostess, and might be the type who likes to brag that she can't cook. If faced with a copy of *Little Women*, she'll say, "Yuck." Obviously the traditional feminine values are not the ones she embraces. She expresses her femininity through her ideals. She is what she thinks, an embodiment of her various philosophies. She is never shy, and she doesn't hesitate to discuss anything at all. Ideas belong to everybody, and we are all part of the cosmos. Playing the field feels normal and right to her, and she may be the one to proposition you, as long as there are no strings attached. She might like to wake up with one lover and retire with another in the same day. No one has any claim on her, and as long as she thinks what she's doing is okay, then it is okay.

If a Venus in Sagittarius woman has caught your fancy, go after her. She doesn't mind being pursued it all; it's being caught that scares her. Invite her out to a party, make reservations at a swinging nightspot, go horseback riding. She loves to be outdoors, and she's probably quite athletic. You don't have to beat around the bush. Tell her that you're wild about her, and that you want to follow her home. She might not say yes, but she won't be so insulted that she says no. If your interests encompass more than a night or an affair, you'll have a harder time. What you must do is impress her with your mind. When she meets someone with whom she shares cosmic interests, she's much more willing to consider a permanent tie. That doesn't mean that she intends to trade in her riding boots for an apron. This is one woman who always needs to express her individuality—and that's what attracted you to her in the first place, right?

Whether you're a man or a woman, Venus in Sagittarius is friendly, outgoing, and idealistic in its expression of affection, in a diffuse, field-playing way.

These celebs are among those with Venus in Sagittarius: Amanda Seyfried, Katy Perry, Jake Gyllenhaal, Nicki Minaj, Aaliyah, Parker Posey, Christina Aguilera, Tina Turner, Kim Basinger, Jane Fonda, Farrah Fawcett, Christina Applegate, Linda Lovelace, Angela Davis, Ann Coulter, Jimi Hendrix, Deepak Chopra, Jay-Z.

The exuberant romantic nature described by Venus in Sagittarius will be modified somewhat by the sign position of Mars, the planet of action and sex.

Venus in Capricorn

Capricorn is an earth sign, ruled by practical, hard-working, realistic, achievement-oriented Saturn. With the planet of love in this sign, it's difficult to be frivolous, because the strident Capricorn energy demands that everything be done with an eye toward achieving goal-oriented, practical results. This practical eye often turns itself on others to scrutinize them according to their ability to contribute something material toward success—and this hardly is compatible with the Venusian desire to love another just because he or she exists and, in existing, touches a special emotional chord within a beloved. Thus the Venus in Capricorn individual often eschews play in favor of work and, in choosing a mate, seeks to find a partner with tangible assets—such as money or social connections—rather than seeking a soulmate.

Capricorn Sun sign people are achievers. They work hard, and they like to point to the results of their work with pride. The larger social order is their natural milieu and they fit in perfectly, always willing to take their place in the pecking order of life, and always working to improve that position.

These serious individuals are always seeking practical results, and they have no time or energy for the more ethereal concerns on which many of us focus. Impractical dreamers earn only their scorn, unless those starry eyed folks conjure up something with concrete use (like the light bulb) during their musing sessions.

Dignified and austere, Capricorns are always aware of their public image, even when they're alone. You won't be likely to catch one of them making a scene for any reason, although they have no trouble at all taking the lead and being assertive. It's acting foolishly that they refuse to consider, and they're the slightest bit envious of the unselfconscious people who can throw caution to the wind in a bit of tomfoolery.

If your Venus is in this practical sign, you take life and love seriously. You don't understand the sort of people who are frivolous, and you disapprove of them. You're not here for casual good times, although you enjoy life as much as the next person. Instead, you want to be sure everything is going smoothly, that you're safe, and that your life is everything you want it to be. Serious gestures mean more to you than casual ones. To you, love means building a partnership with someone who provides a reliable support system and together you make a wonderful life, that is rich in everything that matters.

The man with Venus in Capricorn is a hard-working, no-nonsense kind of guy, and he wants a solid, substantial woman. When he settles on a mate, he chooses a partner who hails from a socially prominent family—preferably with that delightful anachronism, a dowry. She may be just out of the new crop of debutantes—if he has spent his early youth with nose to the grindstone, establishing his place and earning his fortune—or she may be a successful older woman who can help him make his way in the world while he is still a young, relatively inexperienced beginner.

His woman will be able to balance a checkbook without the slightest sense of trepidation (although it isn't likely he'll want to hand her the family purse strings even if she's a Wharton MBA). She's more than proficient at running the house with a capable, firm hand, whether it's a temporary cottage for two (only at the start, of course) or a mansion with a fleet of servants. She's his partner in life, she doesn't demand his money for jewels and other luxury items, and together they found—or continue—a dynasty.

Once the Venus in Capricorn man meets the woman who will bear his name and his children, he settles down as if he were born to be married. The fact is, he was. Living a steady, routine existence is what he was doing all along, and being married gives him the excuse he needs to stop attending the few social functions he was pressed into frequenting before his nuptials. His problem occurs during the "before" stage. Wining and dining are not his forte. Maintaining a controlled, reserved demeanor is second nature, and the joviality that is part of an early romance is often wholly absent in his courtship. He's thinking more along the lines of a merger, and if you're expecting something as incandescent as that described by poets of the Romantic era, you'll be severely disappointed. If, on the other hand, you seek a solid union with a man who wouldn't consider philandering, who always takes your physical needs into consideration, step right this way to sign on the dotted line. If a Venus in Capricorn guy has made your eyes sparkle, take a practical approach to your courtship. Show him you can cook, impress him with your clever mind, and be the down to earth sort of person who gains his admiration easily. You can be sexy as long as it's subtle, but a better approach is to consider this more of a job interview and use those same sorts of skills to make a good impression, just as you would in that situation.

The woman with Venus in Capricorn sees herself as an unemotional, no-nonsense person who can manage her life with no help from anybody, thank you very much. She's an ambitious workaholic who cringes at the word feminine. Practical, down to earth, and substantial, her clothes are as pristine as her spine is straight. No gallant gentleman ever drank champagne from her slipper, no matter how charming the swain or how dainty the foot.

It's hard for the Venus in Capricorn woman to believe in her own desirability as a female; she feels that it's her money or her status that attracts men to her, not her beauty or charm.

In a way that makes her like a successful man, for often that's how men see themselves—no matter how sexy they are. Likewise she seeks practical rewards from her personal alliances, and she may miss a number of wonderful friendships with people whom she fails to notice, simply because they do not offer her the money or status she seeks from relationships.

This is a woman who needs to lighten up, but that may be impossible because the people best able to teach her how are the very ones she scorns as undesirable. Instead, she prefers to spend her time with older, more successful people who can act as mentors. When she's older, if she has no children of her own, she may adopt as her protégé a young relative or trainee at work for whom she can perform the role of mentor.

This woman cannot be wooed with luxury items, although she may very well be interested in owning them. If you want to capture her interest, you must be someone who can offer her something real and permanent, and that means marriage. It's very doubtful that she'd ever be interested in casual dating or even a steaming affair. At least there's no need for mystery; lay your cards on the table (along with your blue-chip stocks and your pedigree). If she's interested, she won't hesitate to let you know.

Whether you're a man or woman, Venus in Capricorn is practical, materialistic, austere, and modest in its expression of affection in a controlled, unemotional way.

These celebs are among those with Venus in Capricorn: Brad Pitt, Justin Timberlake, Scarlett Johansson, Miley Cyrus, Portia de Rossi, Julianne Moore, Ellen Page, Tyra Banks, Britney Spears, Bjork, Cindy Crawford, Edith Piaf, Dolly Parton, January Jones, Ke$ha, Bette White, Janice Dickinson, Zsa Zsa Gabor, Molly Ringwald, Elvis Presley, Steve Jobs, James Dean, Paul Newman, Frank Sinatra.

The chilly romantic nature described by Venus in Capricorn will be modified somewhat by the sign position of Mars, the planet of action and sex.

Venus in Aquarius

Aquarius is an air sign, ruled by rebellious, freedom loving, individualistic Uranus. Planets in Aquarius operate in a way that is very social, yet they refuse to uphold tradition for its own sake. Planets in Aquarius gain personal strength through group ties. Although Aquarius is a strongly individualistic sign, it needs to feel there are others around to befriend and share a sense of mutual identity.

Sun sign Aquarians are often like the classic absent-minded professor, caught up in a vastly complicated mental world. They absolutely demand the right to express themselves, glorifying whatever quirks they may possess. Sometimes they like to flaunt their idiosyncrasies, just to shock the starchy. They're friendly and intelligent, and they adore meeting new people. They love to socialize and enjoy a lively exchange of ideas.

If your Venus is in this quirky, idiosyncratic sign, you have the urge to bond with a group of pals, rather than finding a single individual on whom to pin romantic fantasies. So you might exchange the Venusian drive for one-to-one intimacy for a broader based type of friendship. You love your friends very much, and feel a sense of camaraderie with them. Often you have philosophies in common and tastes that merge, and that gives you the sense that you're surrounded by energies like your own. If you do choose to marry, it's with someone who can be a best friend, who feels like a comrade as much as a lover. And then for you love is discovering how wonderful a group as small as two can be. You have an intellectual approach to pleasure. If something isn't good for you, you easily give it up. You never enslave yourself to desires, no matter what it might be.

The man with Venus in Aquarius seeks a woman who does

not necessarily embody the traditional feminine virtues, at least not to the exclusion of her own individuality. A soft woman who is content to stay at home in a gingham apron baking apple pies strikes him as singularly uninteresting. He wants a woman with whom he can share his ideas, and he expects her to have some interesting notions of her own. She ought to be doing something meaningful with her life, and she must be concerned with society at large.

The Venus in Aquarius man isn't eager to settle down. Intimate relationships make him a little nervous. He'd rather be pals with a number of nice women than have to deal with the deep emotional needs of only one. In fact, he'll never want a really emotional woman, for dealing with other people's feelings—and his own as well—makes him uncomfortable. When he does meet a woman he can truly think of as his best friend, he might consider marriage, as long as there isn't too much structure or the feeling that his freedom is challenged by making that commitment. In today's unstructured society, he may choose to live in unwedded bliss forever, or conversely, just to be different, may shock everybody by declaring himself a confirmed bachelor, then eloping—all in the same week.

It's easy for a woman to be jealous of her Venus in Aquarius man. He makes no bones about his interest in all your friends, and they find him fascinating as well. He's so reluctant to verbalize his feelings that it can be really hard to differentiate between the friendship he seems to feel for you, and the friendly gleam in his eye, turned on another woman. If you're insecure in relationships and need a lot of reassurance, or if you're inclined toward behavior that is even slightly possessive, you're with the wrong man. This guy will drive you crazy without ever meaning to. Probably the best gauge of his feelings is his actions. If you're the only woman he's coming home to—sleeping with—dating—then he cares for you and continues to find you exciting. Once that changes, he ceases to hang around.

The best way to interest this guy is with your brain. Home baked cookies may be nice, but they're no substitute for a lively conversation that challenges his mind. And if you have a group of friends who enjoy meeting for fun and intellectual stimulation, include him. A sense of community is the thing he most values in establishing a relationship.

Once he decides that the two of you make a good team, he's willing to enter into a marriage that's acceptable according to his anti-traditional notions. That may mean a sharing of the chores, separate bank accounts, role reversal, or even a traditional union. The point is that he should feel that the structure you establish actively reflects his point of view instead of conforming to some unchallenged norm.

So if you take an intellectual, slightly rebellious approach to life, you've found the man who will appreciate and encourage you—as long as your idiosyncrasies and his do not conflict—for he believes in being a one rebellion family. Together you can then seek out the other members of your society with whom you share a sense of community, and with them you can then go on to create the vision of a better world that first united the two of you.

The woman with Venus in Aquarius is determined to maintain the freedom to express herself and her ideas without being tied down by anyone else's structures, rules, or inhibitions. If this means spending most of her life without the benefit of a steady partner, then so be it. This is one woman who is not driven by the desire for home and family and, in fact, may prefer to avoid both. She loves to have new and unusual experiences, to meet different people, and she'd rather choke than submit to a life of boring routine. This lady plays the field, not because she's so sexually attracted to her many partners, but because doing so is both interesting and a way to avoid getting bogged down in one relationship that could be restricting.

This daring eccentric loves to shock the more traditional people she knows with her outrageous behavior. She wishes to create and maintain an image of unconventionality, and even when she shares the traditional values she is challenging, it's important to her to make a statement about who she is. As she grows older and more self-assured, she's less overtly rebellious, because her sense of freedom is challenged less.

First and foremost she considers herself an intellectual, so if you want to impress her, the way to do it is with stimulating conversation, not diamonds or pearls. She's involved in many group projects, and she makes her friends among the people who have the same view of a better society that she espouses. Feeling a sense of intellectual oneness is mandatory before any further intimacy develops. And the fact that you're interested in her mind and her ideas is far more meaningful to her than any physical attraction either of you might feel.

A socially significant play or movie followed by a party with a forward thinking group and a dinner featuring stimulating conversation along with the meal is a great opener. Then at a suitable moment you might murmur, "We have so much in common, I could trade views with you all night. How about coming home with me for some coffee?" Of course it had better be true. A guy who espouses opinions which are stupid could have the sex appeal of the top matinee idol, and he would still go home alone.

If she feels that she can maintain her freedom and your relationship as well, she may consider marriage, but it will probably be quite late in life. Unless, of course, she enters into a useful liaison as a rebellious way to escape domineering parents. For the most part, though, she does not see her destiny as aligned with a single other human being. When she marries, she continues to do as she sees fit. This may mean hiring a housekeeper and forgetting about children.

She's not the sort of woman who curls up in your lap at the end of the day and listens raptly as you discourse on the merger you just completed. She has far too many of her own concerns ever to focus that totally on you. She'll be home when she gets there, and whoever gets around to it will either cook or order dinner from a takeout place. Running a house just doesn't have enough aspects to challenge her mind completely, and you need never expect her to stop seeking those things in life that will. After all, if you wanted a girl like dear old mom, the intellectual sparkle that is so much a part of her personality would never have caught your fancy.

Whether you're a man or a woman, Venus in Aquarius is friendly, fraternal, and unemotional in its expression of affection in an eccentric, warm, noncommittal way.

These celebs are among those with Venus in Aquarius: Oprah Winfrey, Taylor Swift, Bruce Willis, Ashton Kutcher, Sade, Jessica Biel, Paris Hilton, Mitt Romney, Eva Mendes, Sharon Stone, Kate Moss, Yoko Ono, Heidi Fleiss, Gloria Steinem, Rashida Jones, Sienna Miller, Kim Novak, Janis Joplin, Aretha Franklin, Glenn Close, Kirstie Alley, Elin Nordegren, Diane Arbus, Quentin Tarantino, Stephen Hawking.

The freedom-seeking romantic nature described by Venus in Aquarius will be modified somewhat by the sign position of Mars, the planet of action and sex.

Venus in Pisces

Pisces is a water sign, ruled by mystical, illusionary, barrier-dissolving, inspirational Neptune, the planet of ego-transcendence. Planets in Pisces seek to reaffirm the connection to the infinite that is the source of all existence. It is this aura of limitlessness and of being a part of everything that is which often makes planets in Pisces operate as though they suffered from a sense of confusion about earthbound reality. With Venus there, it's natural to bestow affection on many people, for there is the ability to see the God-spark in all. Forming a close tie with a single other that is the Venusian goal is not so easy, however, because love is a more universal response than a personal one. That is not to say that Venus is not at its best in the dreamy, loving sign of Pisces, for Venus works very well here, and some might say that it achieves a level of ultimate love that goes beyond the mere romantic aims that the planet strives for.

Sun sign Pisces are dreamy, emotional individuals who are always willing to lend a sympathetic ear. Friendly and nonjudgmental, they can usually find something worthwhile in even those whom nobody else can abide. Often they can absorb feelings and negative energy from other people and from the atmosphere, so most Pisces require quiet time alone to clear their systems of this residual osmotic debris.

Social and creative, Pisces love to have a good time. They enjoy being invited to parties and happily host all manner of events without the slightest degree of tension. What happens happens, and if no appetizers are made, people can still have fun. Kindly and supportive, they make excellent, loving friends, and are always there for anyone they love.

If you have Venus in this loving sign, you're cuddly and sensitive. Lovers adore waking up with you because you snuggle them in a warm and tender way. You see the good in other people, and that can be very heartening for someone you love, for it provides confidence and security. You like to be around positive people whose energy is uplifting and who make you laugh. Often you don't need to talk at all, for you can feel the energy transferring between you, just by sitting close to each other. Love for you is finding that God-spark of divinity in the joyous feelings that pass between two people. The man with Venus in Pisces is filled with tender, romantic dreams. He goes around falling hopelessly and instantly in love, only to discover later that once again he's fooled himself. That's because he pins his own romantic fantasies on each new partner, without really getting to know her and actually discovering if she really is the woman of his dreams. He needs a woman who appreciates the beauty of romance and the romantic gesture, whether or not it has any relationship to reality. If he can lie next to her in the grass and plan a trip to Tahiti, then it's unimportant whether or not the tickets are ever bought, for the dream is the important thing. A hard-edged, practical woman who cares for nothing but success is no soulmate for this man, and it's nothing less than a soulmate that he seeks. He wants to look into the eyes of his beloved and speak volumes without uttering a single word. It's a magical union he desires, where all is known and all is understood without the agony of verbal communication that causes most of us so many snags. Of course, the beautiful dreams of this fellow are admirable, but he rarely is able to get the relationship he seeks, which is why so many Venus in Pisces people go from mate to mate unfulfilled. The problem is that relationships require the kind of commitment and hard work that erected the pyramids, and despite an occasional flaw in the blueprint or an unplanned mishap, what's needed is the determination to see the thing through to the end. With Venus in Pisces, instantaneous magic is the expectation, and as soon as a human flaw is spotted, instead of redoubled effort, the dream sometimes is abandoned. "I must have been fooling myself again," laments the poor fellow who is seeing his perfect love as nothing more than human. The challenge for people with this placement is to incorporate the practical demands of reality without losing the grand romantic inspiration at the core of it all.

The man with Venus in Pisces is friendly, giving, and helpful, and he is well-liked. It is tempting for him to be unfaithful, for he is quite susceptible to spur of the moment attachments. That, coupled with his expansive devotion to the whole human race, may make it difficult for his woman to feel that she is special to him. "After all, you love the world," she complains. "How can I feel like more than just one of the crowd?" Even a wedding band often isn't assurance enough. And if he makes a practice of devoting large quantities of his time to a number of ne'er-do-well acquaintances who need massive rescuing, he may be using his unselfish giving as a way of shoring up a shaky ego, and his mate is justified in her complaints of neglect.

On the other hand, there really is a tremendous amount of satisfaction to be gained from helping people make better lives for themselves, and you might consider joining in the effort. Afterward, when it's time to relax, retreating together to a safe harbor to divest yourselves of the day is a great way to renew the emphasis on each other and love. Share a hot bath and take turns recounting fantasies about the time when you were mermaid and merman frolicking around a luminous coral reef. Get out the hot oil, trade foot massages, and in general do your best to create a private world that only two lovers can inhabit. The ability to do this is the quality he most seeks in the soulmate he yearns for. If you marry your Venus in Pisces man, you have someone who can take you on a vacation every night simply by sharing the magical fantasies that waft through his imagination, someone who appreciates qualities in you that most people never even notice, and a giving and unselfish friend when you need one. Take heart, Cinderella, your prince has come.

The woman with Venus in Pisces sees herself as a dreamy, romantic, feminine creature. "It's bigger than both of us," is her philosophy of love, which explains in part why she may get involved with married men, or suitors unavailable to her in other ways. When she falls in love, her head often goes on vacation, leaving her heart and glands overworked in the extreme. Finding the ultimate, all-encompassing love is her goal, and it's a difficult task at best. Like her male counterpart, she seeks a true soulmate, and the rose-colored glasses worn by both cause innumerable bouts with heartbreak as potential soulmates are discovered to be unsuitable.

This lady has a terrific sense of romance and adventure, and if she tries at all, she can amuse you for hours with tales spun from her ample imagination. Having fun is one of her best skills, for she really enjoys people, and game playing of the best sorts. When she falls in love, she is capable of selfless devotion, of generous attention-giving, and of creating a romantic cloud of magic with which to envelop her mate. Even dear friends can be amazed by the degree of her generosity where they're concerned. What she seeks is a knight in shining armor who rides up in a cloud of dust and whisks her off to the land where they'll be happy forever after. In his eyes is the spark of recognition shared by lovers through the ages "It was meant to be," or, "I bet we were lovers in another life." For, more than anything else, it is magic she seeks.

So if you're wooing a Venus in Pisces lady, think romance. She doesn't want to grab a burger on the corner. Instead buy flowers, wine, some cheese and bread, put it all in a tote bag with napkins, a music player loaded with the most romantic ballads you can find, a cloth for the ground, and a candelabra. When you lead her to your local park and unfurl the trappings in your satchel, you should be well on the way to capturing her heart. When she recognizes the gleam of a kindred spirit in your eyes, she'll be ready to claim you as her soulmate forever. Then you have your own special fairy princess to keep you delightedly captivated by romance twenty-four hours a day.

Whether you're a man or woman, Venus in Pisces is dreamy, romantic, illusionary, and emotional in its expression of affection in an ego transcending, nonjudgmental way.

These celebs are among those with Venus in Pisces: Barbara Streisand, Kerry Washington, Michelle Obama, Diana Ross, Drew Barrymore, Kourtney Kardashian, Heath Ledger, Zooey Deschanel, Reese Witherspoon, Patricia Arquette,

Kirsten Dunst, Victoria Beckham, Cynthia Nixon, Laura Dern, Hugh Hefner, Marilyn Manson, Billie Holiday, Bettie Page, Benicio Del Toro.

The selfless romantic nature described a Venus in Pisces will be modified somewhat by the sign position of Mars, the planet of action and sex.

Mars in Aries

Mars in Aries is very strong, being in the sign of its rulership. Mars and Aries are totally compatible in the way they like to operate. Both are self-centered, action-oriented, aggressive, and headstrong.

If your Mars is in this sign, you're energetic and impulsive, quick to act, and quick to anger. You have no interest in power over other people and you're determined to make sure that no one has any power over you. Compromise and dishonesty strike you as having the same unattractively discordant ring. You would rather work alone or totally on your own than risk being in the position of letting anyone else dictate to you or complicate your progress. You're never slow, cautious, or prudent. And you can't imagine how anyone could see virtues in these qualities, anyway. The phrase life in the fast lane might have been coined for you, except even that sounds too organized for your tastes. It may be true that you get into a number of scrapes by being hasty and impulsive, but you also have many adventures that way, and the excitement is worth the risk.

The man with Mars in Aries is a soldier of fortune, a pioneer, and adventurer. He exudes a passionate air of aggressiveness that makes everyone around him yearn to be let in on a little of the excitement that is part of his everyday life. He's the kind of man who first decided to try making love in an elevator, or a closet, at a crowded party. Whatever his fantasies, he thinks nothing of acting them out. Reality and imagination mingle indistinguishably in his mind.

He likes to be the initiator in everything he does. He likes to sweep his partner off her feet (often literally), but even as self-centered as he is, he never deliberately hurts another person, least of all the lady he fancies. When a strongly Aries individual falls in love, it isn't with another person; as soon as she is loved, the woman becomes part of him in his mind. His wants and needs become hers, as he sees it. And although he may forget to consider her individuality, and sometimes he does tend to be rather a dictator, his intention is simply to follow his own course, expecting her to be a part of it. It won't occur to him to explain his actions or his whereabouts any more than it occurs to him to plan them in advance. Soldiers of fortune do not provide itineraries. And they rarely apologize.

If you love a Mars in Aries man, start by letting go. He doesn't want anyone breathing down his neck. If you like to be the initiator, be prepared for him to try to go you one better. Buy a new pair of sneakers so you can keep up with him during the day, and a fancy pair of shoes for dancing at night. Make your own decisions, and allow him the same courtesy, and if he seems to want his way too often, realize that's probably not going to change.

The woman with Mars in Aries is looking for an exciting, action-oriented man. A quiet, shy fellow with a timid, charming way is not the type to turn her on. She'd much rather deal with passion, even if she must forgo thoughtfulness. She likes fast cars, boats, planes, and she wants her guy to fit right in. In fact, she may be able to fix the car or pilot the plane herself. She likes hot night spots, exciting places where an adventure can start up without any notice. Like her male counterpart, she acts without thinking or planning, and is content to live life on the fly. When things go wrong, she makes new choices and tries something different.

This lady might sneer at that description of herself, and she might have been one of the founders of NOW, as long as no one expected her to hang around and work in a group. She's supremely aggressive and she wants a man she can respect. If other people think she's too assertive, then they're pansies and not worth her consideration. Either you're her equal or you're nobody at all.

These celebs are among those with Mars in Aries: Daniel Craig, Angelina Jolie, Steve Jobs, Russell Crowe, Clint Eastwood, Tobey Maguire, Paul Newman, Russell Brand, Kris Humphries, Larry Bird, Kate Hudson, Claire Danes.

Mars in Taurus

Do you hear "action," and translate it to "going shopping?" The Mars in Taurus individual never sees action as a goal in itself and often requires a mighty motivation to get moving at all, and acquisition of all manner of goodies is often the driving force you need. Of course, once you do start a project, not even an atomic explosion can deter you from accomplishing your goal. No one ever accused a Mars in Taurus individual of lacking stick-to-itiveness. A Taurus baby plays happily in the sandbox for hours, filling bucket after bucket with sand. Marathon TV watchers often have this placement, having all the stamina in the world but lacking the get-up-and-go needed to participate in an athletic marathon.

The Mars in Taurus man wants to own lots and lots of things, including his lady fair. It's not that he's possessive, exactly, or that he wants to restrict his mate's actions. He just wants her to behave herself according to his desires, just as his other belongings do. He never bickers or quarrels, preferring instead to hold in his anger until it erupts in a mighty explosion. How can you blame him, after all, when hardly anyone can key in to his moods because he always seems so placid?

This fellow probably has excellent taste, inclining to excess, if anything, and a free and open hand with his cash, especially if he's acquiring another worthwhile luxury. Then he might just turn around and act like a miser. Whatever choice, he makes it with determination and conviction. He sees himself as a strong man, the type of guy that everyone else can lean on, and he's probably right.

If you love a Mars in Taurus man, adjust yourself to his determined, deliberate pace. You can try to adjust him, but it could take a lifetime to get him to budge a millimeter, nevermind an inch. Be soft, feminine and cuddly, for he loves bear hugs and cozy good times for just the two of you. Let him cook for you, even if he's unskilled in the kitchen—he's also a great take-out expert. He'll have a good time playing Daddy and feeding you by hand. Buy him fabulous presents, wrapped in elegant paper. Anything of leather, precious metal or gemstone will do. After all, once he has committed himself to you, there's no doubt that he's your one and only forever after.

The Mars in Taurus woman is as stubborn as her male counterpart. Once her mind is made up about something, or a course of action is charted, nothing sways her. She is steady, reliable, down-to-earth, and she seeks a man with the same qualities.

She seeks a good provider, a strong man she can lean on, a committed father for her children, a partner with whom she can build a solid foundation. This woman is not looking for a jogger, a hippie, or a free spirit. She wants a house with a white picket fence, a nice yard, and a couple of kids. She wants a guy she can count on. It doesn't matter if he's not the dashing hero of anyone's dreams, as long as he is someone substantial, and someone who will stay in her life forever.

This doesn't mean she's dull or adverse to having fun. Far from it. Taurus' capacity for pleasure is legendary. Overeating, overbuying, overindulging in all forms of sensuality, including hours on end in the bedroom, are her idea of a good time. Just don't expect her to toss a football, attend a hockey game, or participate in a steeplechase. It's not in her makeup, and if you want her, it probably isn't in yours. But then, very few complaints are heard from men who are regularly treated to all-night back rubs and breakfast in bed, with a healthy amount of sex in between.

These celebs are among those with Mars in Taurus: Jennifer Lawrence, Kanye West, Bruce Willis, Mick Jagger, Michael Jackson, Adolf Hitler, Osama Bin Laden, Andy Warhol, Robert de Niro, Salvador Dali, Christian Bale, 50 Cent, Muhammad Ali, Chuck Norris, Fidel Castro, Tim Burton, Babe Ruth, Stephen Colbert, Vince Vaughn, Madonna, Jessica Alba, Keira Knightley.

Mars in Gemini

Mars in Gemini tends to work just fine. Because Gemini is reluctant to be tied down, and because Mars is the most supremely I-oriented planet, they are very compatible in expressing the ego energy of the individual. Mars in Gemini is super fast. If your Mars is in this sign, you may not be especially hot but you sure are fast. That means that it takes very little for you to get going, and you get things done quickly, although you may start many things that you never manage to finish because the urge to move on before boredom sets in is so strong. You probably have terrific reflexes.

You like to debate and argue, although you don't invest much of your ego in the discussion. Either side will do nicely, thank you very much. You identify yourself very strongly with your mental process. You love books and reading—anything where ideas are expressed is the way you love to spend your energy.

The man with Mars in Gemini is a super talker. In fact, he may be content to spend his time in the bedroom engaged in mental gymnastics rather than physical ones. He loves to talk, argue, debate, but don't worry—he doesn't mean any of it, really. He likes to move around, to travel, and take walks. He never wants to stay in any one spot long enough to be bored, so he has no time for prolonged phone conversations (although he may call you a dozen different times in a day) or for hours of gazing into each other's eyes. Don't expect him to help out around the house, unless he's able to perform a series of short tasks, such as running the vacuum (unless you live in a mansion with acres of carpet), taking out the trash (he may take off on his own for a while afterward), or telling stories to the kids.

If you love a Mars in Gemini man, plan on being free to roam or on being left behind. He won't want to accumulate a heap of useless possession that will make it difficult to travel or to move, although he probably owns many books. Plan on being interested and amused a lot. He thinks of himself as a wit, and he likes playing games and joking. Chances are he's plenty of fun.

The woman with Mars in Gemini wants to attract an intelligent man who's a free spirit. She wants a lively companion who's enjoyable intellectually as well as physically. She's quick on her feet and she demands that you be that way as well. Like her male counterpart, she likes clever books, witty people, and starting new things. She doesn't always care to finish them, for she too can be overwhelmed by boredom.

Talking is her favorite activity, followed by reading, although she may enjoy strolls along interesting by-ways, and speedy bike rides, as long as there's always a new path to take so that it remains interesting, and a companion who can offer enough clever comments so that her mental faculties are exercised as well. The man who wins this woman can never be slow, plodding, or dull, but then who would want someone like that anyway?

These celebs are among those with Mars in Gemini: Sean Penn, Al Pacino, Arnold Schwarzenegger, Daniel Day Lewis, Tiger Woods, Mike Tyson, Martin Luther King Jr., Sean Connery, Pierce Brosnan, O.J. Simpson, Tom Brady, John McEnroe, Bernie Madoff, Damon Wayans, Joseph Fiennes, Eva Mendes, Maria Sharapova, Barbara Streisand, Uma Thurman, Coco Chanel, Natalie Portman.

Mars in Cancer

Cancer is not one of the better places for Mars, because it tends to make it difficult for you to be as selfish and as aggressive as Mars is naturally. Cancer is by nature an active sign, but its pure emotionality conflicts with the way Mars normally functions most comfortably. The Mars in Cancer person tends to act on the basis of emotions and always likes to use energy to care for other people. With this placement, you can be shy, reserved, sensitive, inclined to moodiness, and disinclined to express anger or hostility unless absolutely essential. You love children, home, and family, and will expend your energy to affirm all the traditional values that encourage security and emotional well being.

With Mars in Cancer, you love to do nice things for other people. You're an enthusiastic cook and you enjoy treating a mate to breakfast in bed. Always thinking about the emotional needs of other people, you're a sensitive person who can be a terrific friend, because you intuit another's mood and can help cope with it.

People can hurt your feelings unintentionally, and because it's so hard for you to express anger, you let it slide, gnashing your teeth silently and preferring to get a stomachache than to speak up. Sometimes it may come to the point that you end a relationship because of a long-held grudge that was never expressed.

The man with Mars in Cancer has a gentle, sensitive quality, and when you look into his eyes, you sense that it's perfectly okay to communicate your deepest feelings because he'll listen and understand. He loves to stay at home, and he probably has a pretty nice place of his own (with a well-equipped kitchen) even if he's a typical bachelor. Don't be surprised when he prepares a dinner as good as anything your mother ever made. This guy will make a terrific husband for some lucky woman.

Be prepared to tiptoe a bit when he's in one of his moods. He feels like being alone to mope sometimes, and you might as well let him. At other time he may just withdraw into himself, and even if you ask if there's anything you've done or said, you may not receive a response. Thinking ahead is probably the best policy, followed by an understanding frame of mind and a high level of tolerance for unexplained moodiness. As long as you're willing to make allowances for the sensitivity of your partner, you'll have a man who wants to attend to your needs as much as his own, and that's a pretty rare creature, to be sure.

The woman with Mars in Cancer wants a modern man who can deal with feelings without feeling silly. She's not impressed by the caveman—she thinks that he's an incomplete clod. Her guy has to be as sensitive as she is. He has to love children and be good with them. The guys who are adept at managing a couple of noisy kids at the playground, and who obviously enjoy it, are the ones she thinks of as sexy. This lady wants a family man who'll make a commitment and settle down for life. She's far less interested in excitement and romance than she is in a solid, loving relationship where two people can be themselves, share the deepest parts of their feelings openly, and can raise a family that means more to them than anything else in the world.

If you're interested in a Mars in Cancer woman, you'd better be the type who wants a marriage partner, not a fling for the evening. It'll take her a while to relax with you, anyway, and the thought of a wild night with a stranger who has no permanent ties can make her very depressed. Relax and enjoy her TLC. No geisha ever did a better job of making you feel at home. With that kind of consideration, it's easy to let an evening turn into a lifetime.

These celebs are among those with Mars in Cancer: Ashton Kutcher, Ryan Reynolds, Halle Berry, Robin Williams, Miley Cyrus, Reese Witherspoon, Michael Phelps, Chris Brown, John Mayer, Keanu Reeves, Pablo Picasso, Wolfgang Amadeus Mozart, William Shakespeare, Stephen King.

Mars in Leo

Mars in Leo is steady, strong, and concentrated, imbued with strength, force, pride, and stamina. Like Mars in Aries, you need to be self-directing, but in Leo, Mars is much more aware of the other guy, so you're not likely to go off on a crazy tangent, oblivious to the rest of humanity. You're concerned with appearances and with making a good impression, so you do your best always to live up to your own high standards and those of the people you respect.

Tremendously brave and self-confident, you want very much to be a leader, and one who is admired. You have incredible staying power, and the ability and determination to stick with a task until it's completed. If anyone tries to interfere in your actions, you simply dig in more deeply and stick to your course. Because you're so determined to cut a dignified path and not to play the fool, you try always to be stalwart, sometimes preferring to appear impassive rather than allowing anyone to get a glimpse inside that might reveal your emotions and thus an Achilles' heel.

The man with Mars in Leo is stubborn and proud and won't stand for being made the brunt of any joke, no matter how innocent. Always determined to cut a dignified path, he is very self-conscious and hardworking. He cares very deeply about what everyone thinks of him, and tries his best always to be the sort of person worthy of others' admiration. He absolutely refuses to take orders from anyone, not because he's afraid of granting them power over him, but because he must be at the forefront of everything. Because his image of himself is of the admired leader, he can sometimes seem arrogant and domineering.

This is the kind of man you can absolutely depend on. Once he has pledged his devotion, it's yours forever, for like a

Boy Scout, he is steadfast, brave, and true. Ardent and truly generous, he loves to give of himself, whether it's his time, his money, or his heart. When the Mars in Leo man is in love, he goes all out. It's not that he likes to focus on you, or will intuit your feelings to any great extent. Instead, he's creating a romance, and he loves putting together a spectacle worthy of admiration. Thus he floods you with gifts, spends unlimited dollars on entertainment, and in general sees that you have a better time than at any point in your life. If you're his Cinderella, he'll absolutely be your Prince Charming.

If you're interested in a love affair with this man, just make an effort to please him. It doesn't really matter what you do, for it's the attention you're granting that makes him feel good. As long as he sees that you think he's the most wonderful man in the world, he admires your good taste and starts pursuing you. It ought to be that easy for us all!

The woman with Mars in Leo is looking for a bit of substance coated with a little flash. She wants a guy who loves her devotedly yet who doesn't wear jackets with patches on the elbows. She wants a fellow who makes a good impression, who's friendly, outgoing, lively, and loving. She likes parades, formal balls, and athletic marathons, and she wants a man equipped to handle the pace. Because she has so much drive and stamina, she needs a strong, forceful guy who can't be dominated or coerced. She must be able to feel as proud of him as she does of herself.

Basically the Mars in Leo woman wants a guy on the order of Prince William—a good catch, from a good family, able to provide a life of no little substance. If he doesn't have quite the looks of a movie star, no problem as long as he has the cachet. If you're ready to be this woman's royal swain, you may be ready to woo her. Getting yourself elected to an office for which people might throw a parade would be a good start. Invite her to ride beside you on your float.

If you can't quite pull that off, a seat on the dais of a charity function might be a workable alternative. Or even a night out at a swank nightclub frequented by celebrities. Whatever you plan, your Mars in Leo lady likes to go out where she can make an impression, although she might also respond favorably to a quiet evening in front of the fire, with you in your velvet smoking jacket and her in a silk peignoir—that is once you explain that you wanted to wrap her up in your arms, where she could be adored, savored, and appreciated—by you and you alone.

These celebs are among those with Mars in Leo: Channing Tatum, Harrison Ford, George Clooney, Beyonce Knowles, Mila Kunis, Cher, Michael Jordan, Serena Williams, Robert Redford, Frank Sinatra, James Franco, Conan O'Brien, Quentin Tarantino, Derek Jeter, Donald Trump, Ralph Fiennes, Ringo Starr, Leonard Cohen, Steven Tyler, Marlon Wayans, Lamar Odom, Neil Young, Jim Henson, Dennis Rodman, Jon Stewart, Salma Hayek, Brigitte Bardot, Hillary Clinton, Sophia Loren.

Mars in Virgo

Mars in Virgo is practical, detail-oriented, manually skilled, responsible, and very critical of the performance of others. If you have Mars here, you're very careful and organized in everything you do, and you may have quite a laugh at the expense of other people when you compare their efficiency level to your own. Whenever there's a job that must be done in the most efficient way possible—and even when some dawdling might actually be acceptable—you race to the forefront, gathering all your energies to achieve the utmost.

Although you appreciate praise and the respect of others, the one and only source of approval that matters is you yourself, for your own exacting standards are higher than anybody else's. Although it doesn't seem as though you're actually considering the feelings of others when you're pointing out the obvious (to you) imperfections in their work, nobody is more helpful and considerate than you are. You love to do favors for your friends, and anyone in a jam who seeks your help will be put in better order instantly.

The man with Mars in Virgo has all the patience of an accountant. No detail is too small or too insignificant to escape his steely gaze. He's one of the naturally hard workers of the world—the sort of guy who'd build a village on an unoccupied desert island while shipwrecked. He doesn't seek recognition; he's involved with work for the beauty of labor well done. Although he's not a leader in the traditional sense of the word, he's the type of individual who functions best when self-directed, because he's sure that his way is the only way to do anything—and he's usually right.

In his mind, love and service mingle indistinguishably, so if he's been reorganizing your files, straightening out your linen closet, or helping you get your life in order, it may mean that his interest is more than just mere friendship. He wants to see you happy, and it's impossible to be happy when your garage (or your career) are in shambles, isn't it? The Mars in Virgo man loves to give, but he's not the type to go to Tiffany and buy out the store. What use does all that jewelry have, anyway? If he wants to buy you something, he'll spend hours trying to decide just what you need and would truly be able to use. And if you're trying to settle on a super gift for this guy, take the same approach. Listen first and remember. He'll probably mention something he might like to make his life easier; it may not be glamorous or glitzy or even gift-like, but just buy it, and he will appreciate it deeply.

The Mars in Virgo man is, above all, a practical, down-to-earth human being. He's not carefree, wild, and idealistic, or even impulsive. He likes to think things through and follow up carefully. So if he's been spending lots of time with you, chances are you're far more than an idle flirtation, for as much as he enjoys the physical act of sex, it has to mean something for him to do it. This old-fashioned guy is not interested in one-night stands (who knows what you might catch that way?) or in casual sex. He loves to touch and to be touched, and as he sees it, sex is a meaningful way to express genuine feelings of closeness.

The woman with Mars in Virgo wants a man who's clever, well-organized, and self-sufficient. Men who're unable even to run a washing machine strike her as ridiculous, helpless creatures, not as virile, sexy types. How can a man unable to survive in today's world be sexy? This is a cool, efficient lady, and if she's not too busy working (or working miracles), she has the manual dexterity to give you the best massage you ever had. In any case, busy or not, she does love touching, and she probably puts in such a long day that she could use a good back rub herself now and again. So if you're the sort of guy who can run a household with a minimum of fuss and a maximum of efficiency, who can do a crossword puzzle, balance your checkbook effortlessly, and assemble a child's one-hundred piece toy without swearing, you're almost her equal and may have the potential to be a permanent mate.

She couldn't care less about flash; what turns this lady on

is substance and quality, and that's what she's looking for in a man. Invite her to your office. If it's a model of cool efficiency and you shine in a position of respect, she'll be more impressed than if you'd invited her to share your coach in a tickertape parade. Just relax and be your totally wonderful, absolutely perfect self. It's not so hard, really, for with her around, you have someone completely able to point out your every flaw so you can alter anything not up to snuff. The flip side of that coin is that she will also be able to point out your every virtue, in the most minute detail, and when this lady gets finished listing your wonderful qualities (many of which you didn't even realize you possessed), even you will be convinced of the fact that never in the history of the planet has there existed a more perfect man.

These celebs are among those with Mars in Virgo: Britney Spears, Ben Affleck, Matt Damon, Sarah Jessica Parker, Barack Obama, George W. Bush, Blake Lively, Johnny Depp, Hugh Jackman, Mikhail Baryshnikov, George Michael, Will Smith, Jeff Buckley, Ernest Hemingway, Stevie Wonder, Jeff Bridges, Evel Knievel, Idris Elba, Cameron Diaz, Gwyneth Paltrow, Audrey Tatou, Charles Manson, Alicia Keys.

Mars in Libra

Mars in Libra can be forceful, aggressive, and dominant. It can also be hesitant, changeable, and hard to pin down. Often there is a combination of these qualities in every individual with this placement. You want to be aggressive, yet you always feel compelled to consider the wishes of the other guy. Sometimes the net effect is to become locked into combat-type situations with significant others. If so, it's because you're learning about the forces of aggression and the right of everyone to be self-assertive.

Although Mars in Libra is traditionally considered weak because it's in the opposite sign of Mars' rule, it can be good for analytical action, such as in the military or even a chess game. Because it's so natural to think about the other guy and what's right for him, it can give an edge in knowing what an opponent might do, and thus the upper hand. Mars in this courtly sign does tend to be changeable, however, and it can be frustrating for intimates to deal with all the stops and starts that go with this placement.

The man with Mars in Libra idealizes courtesy, and he sees himself as a chivalrous individual. He may very well be the last man on earth who opens a woman's car door for her, and he might do this while in the middle of an ego battle to the death. You have to admire such good manners! He's the model of graciousness, good taste, and civility. He attends to your needs whether you're home or out, seeing that your glass is refilled, that the room is comfortably warm, that your vantage point in the movies is good. He never makes plans without consulting you first, nor does he ever do anything likely to embarrass either of you, no matter how small. He can never assert himself without being aware of how his actions might affect you or anyone else.

Consider offering suggestions about what activities to

share, for he may not want to take the lead. If you suggest his favorite activity, or prepare his favorite meal, he's visibly pleased and remembers your gesture long after you feel it's relevant. As the evening winds down to a close, it's okay to lean against his arm. He may seem endlessly patient, but really he's debating with himself about whether or not he should go ahead and make a pass. This is one guy who'd never just wrestle you down to the bed, for he's far too civilized. Of course, once you make your desires known, there's nothing to stop him from indulging you in hours of passionate lovemaking. This man is determined to please you—anything else would make him less than a gentleman.

The woman with Mars in Libra really feels incomplete without a partner. She's a team player (even a team as small as two), and she knows it. Sacrifice her freedom to be tied down in a permanent intimate relationship? For her it's no sacrifice—it's her heartfelt desire. This woman wants a man with good manners, good breeding, and a well-developed sense of social savvy. The Borats or Stanley Kowalskis of this world hold no attraction for her at all. She wants someone like the characters portrayed by Fred Astaire or Colin Firth—elegant, smooth, and suave. She has a great many ideals where her potential mate is concerned, and most of them can be summed up by the phrase *well schooled in the social graces*.

If you're interested in a Mars in Libra woman, you could begin with a careful study of an etiquette book, but it would be far better if those skills came by you naturally. If you're a prizefighter, a plumber, or just a simple rough-and-tumble guy, you're probably not her cup of tea. A dance instructor, a judge, or a diplomat is probably more along the lines she'd seek, but what really matters to this lady is that you're a human being who never loses sight of your basic courtesy, civility, and good breeding.

These celebs are among those with Mars in Libra: Alexander Skarsgard, Zac Efron, Bill Clinton, Kobe Bryant, Nicole Kidman, Jessica Simpson, John Lennon, Elvis Presley, Bill Gates, Eminem, Abraham Lincoln, Winston Churchill, Nelson Mandela, Alfred Hitchcock, Pamela Anderson.

Mars in Scorpio

In Scorpio, Mars operates with force, passion, intensity, and determination. Although Scorpio is a water sign, its emotionality becomes a powerfully magnified force for the expression of Mars' ego energy. Mars was long believed to be the co-ruler of Scorpio, along with Pluto, the universal force for breakdown and transformation, and thus in the sign Scorpio, Mars is very powerful. If the thrust of Mars in Aries can be likened to thermal energy, in Scorpio that energy becomes thermonuclear.

If your Mars in this dynamic sign, you're the most persistent person in the world. As you stay firm, you manage also to undermine psychologically an opponent's base until he no longer feel secure and he yields. To say that you're stubborn and used to having your own way is to put it mildly. That's because you invest your total self in everything you do, think, or feel, so any challenge to your actions is a threat to your very ego that you cannot tolerate.

As with Mars in the other water signs, you have a hard time releasing anger. That's because you tend to hold your feelings in, concentrating them until you can't avoid a powerful explosion. When angry, you can be a frightening sight to someone less intense, or, in fact, to anyone at all. If you do decide to enter into a fight, heaven help your opponent, because fighting to the death is the only kind of battle you recognize. Your physical energy can seem limitless to those who know you. That's because your stamina is challenged only by your own belief in the course you have set. Obviously this can result in some very impressive sexual statistics.

The man with Mars in Scorpio exudes a powerfully magnetic sexual air. He is absolutely confident about his prowess and his ability not only to satisfy a woman but also to wear her out. It's clear from the first minute you meet that he expects to be the winner in any contest, by sheer virtue of his staying power if nothing else.

Remember Scorpio's strong feelings about sex; they never take this, our most powerful positive energy, likely. This man is no belt notcher. He makes love only with a woman he cares for deeply. Any other form of behavior is unthinkable to him. After all, he's an all or nothing kind of guy. If you're interested in a Mars in Scorpio man, you might as well just relax. The only way to get his attention is if he's interested in you. If a cinematic sexpot rang his bell and waited for him with open arms, the only chance she'd get to ring his chimes as well would be if he felt a visceral attraction to her—and physical beauty has nothing to do with it.

It might be wiser to ask what a girl can expect when a Mars in Scorpio guy is interested in her. First of all, she'll have to learn to say yes—a lot. Not that he's inconsiderate of her feelings—all people who have Mars in water signs are experts on the feelings of other people, and they are always reluctant to hurt anyone. This guy just feels that he knows her intimately enough to discern her deepest desires, and he may be right, even if she's inclined to protest. Despite his stubborn persistence, the Mars in Scorpio man is caring, sensitive, and determined to please his partner sexually. And there is nobody more able to do so.

The woman with Mars in Scorpio enjoys a man who is able to dominate her, and this is a tall order indeed, for she can sometimes seem as frighteningly intense as her passionate male counterpart. This is no shrinking violet, and although she may be well reserved, one always senses that she has the power and determination to accomplish any of her goals easily.

She wants a man who sweeps her up into a relationship of passionate intensity. She expects him to be possessive and a bit jealous, and if she becomes involved with a man who doesn't act this way, she feels that he really doesn't care for her. A thousand bouquets of flowers won't give her the same message as one "Where were you last night?"

She expects to discover hidden layers of herself through an intimate sexual relationship, and a man whose approach to sex is casual or intellectual isn't for her. She wants a guy who understands the potential for merging of souls inherent in the act of making love, for nothing less will do. And just because she requires intensity, don't assume that you can grab her, pull her to you, and grind your mouth against hers after the first hour. She may well slap your face, sneer at you without uttering a word, and disappear into the sunset. Of course, it's okay to do just that after she's made it clear that she's willing. After all, Scorpio is the most perceptively sensitive of all the signs, and that is exactly the quality she will demand of you.

These celebs are among those with Mars in Scorpio: Leonardo Dicaprio, Oprah Winfrey, Taylor Swift, Joaquin Phoenix, Dylan McDermott, Jennifer Aniston, Jude Law, Mel Gibson, Bruce Lee, Bill Murray, Howard Stern, Kurt Cobain, Joseph Stalin, Charlie Sheen, Mark Zuckerberg, Benicio Del Toro, Usher, Deepak Chopra, Bobby Brown, Martin Scorsese, Frank Zappa, Dr. Phil.

Mars in Sagittarius

Mars in Sagittarius is energetic, idealistic, flexible, and free-spirited. The Martian drive for unhindered expression of the ego is quite compatible with the Sagittarian drive for freedom. Although in Sagittarius, Mars is motivated by unselfish ideals, the very individualistic manner of implementing them is in perfect harmony with the me-first philosophy of Mars. If your Mars is in this flexible sign, you're determined to behave honorably at all times. And although your ideals have everything to do with the philosophical ABC's of the universe, you're a loner when it comes to action. Coordinating your energies with those of other people is painfully limiting, and the restraint of a fence of any kind is intolerable to you.

You need to be free in everything you do, and this drive to remove limits is almost a physical sensation. When you've been cooped up (even philosophically) for too long, you want to leap out a window and run away. That's why you're probably very athletic, and if you're not, you fidget far too much. People with Mars in Sagittarius need to get outdoors regularly for some exercise. Even a strenuous daily workout in the gym isn't enough if you don't go outdoors. There's something about the open air that restores a feeling of limitlessness that you need to function happily.

The man with Mars in Sagittarius is a cowboy at heart. He wants to be outdoors, riding the open range on horseback, blue sky above his head and a lariat in his hand. At the same time he feels personally connected to the moral issues he embraces so strongly. His unwavering honesty has earned the respect of countless friends; all the while they feel like choking him for being so restless and hard to pin down.

He has an infectious kind of enthusiasm that can be

invoked instantaneously in response to an idea you fancy. "Let's do it!" he says, oblivious to the details, ramifications, and practical realities. Whatever moment he's involved in is the one that's important, and he knows that another moment may bring a change that he'll want to respond to. So not only does he hate to be tied down by anyone else's structure, but also he refuses to tie himself down, which is a problem when it comes to giving RSVP's. He may have lost the occasional friend because of an unwillingness to commit to advance plans. The spur of the moment is not everyone's favorite way to live, and dates who're faced with his hesitation to make plans can sometimes feel hurt and discounted.

If you want to lasso this guy for longer than it takes to share a kiss, you may have a problem. Even if he adores you, he may want to move along. Obviously the only thing to do is to want the freedom to move along yourself. The less he feels entrapped (committed to more than an hour hence), The less compelled he'll be to escape. So unleash the reins, throw a steak on the grill, get the camping gear ready, and prepare for a lifetime with your idealistic cowboy.

The woman with Mars in Sagittarius wants a man whose moral standard she can admire and who never tries to tie her down. Her guy is someone who innately recognizes the validity of the women's movement—someone who never had to be reformed because it was natural for him to treat women with equality all along. She wants a man who likes to spend time talking about his thoughts, and that doesn't mean reminiscences. Her guy likes to discuss ideas, philosophies, and the way the world works ideologically. He doesn't spend hours sharpening his pencils or cleaning out closets. He's not the sensitive, emotional type, although he has a stake in seeing that justice is done.

She doesn't expect to be at home by five, with hearth warm and dinner hot, not unless she feels like it, anyway; and she won't tolerate a man who assumes that such activities are her duty. She doesn't want a father figure or a man who believes in allowances for wives. The woman with Mars in Sagittarius will settle down only with the man she considers her philosophical counterpart. She'll commit to one man only if she finds one whose enlivening presence is so wonderful that together they're both more fulfilled individually than either could ever be separately. So don't worry about where you make the reservations, if you're buying flowers or candy, or the wine you're drinking (though you could check her Venus about those details). Who you are is more important than what you do, and that's something you have already decided.

These celebs are among those with Mars in Sagittarius: Jon Hamm, Kim Kardashian, Joe Manganiello, Ryan Gosling, Bradley Cooper, Lil Wayne, Javier Bardem, Jules Verne, Guy Pearce, Michael C. Hall, Ted Bundy, Dick Cheney, Arsenio Hall, Billy Dee Williams, George Takei, Louis CK, Rihanna, Mariah Carey.

Mars in Capricorn

Mars in Capricorn is controlled, disciplined, and, above all, ambitious. Even though Mars is the planet of unplanned, self-centered action, and Capricorn is the most controlled sign, the energies of the two combine well to produce an individual who is determined to succeed at his goals and inspires the trust and respect of those he encounters. Mars in Capricorn likes to say, "I set my goals and I work hard and efficiently until I achieve them. Then I set new goals." Inertia is never an issue for people with Mars in this sign; they are always going somewhere, and they know where that is. Even during recreation, this Mars is ambitious, bestowing the feeling that one should always be doing something—repainting the bathroom rather than lying around in a bubble bath.

If your Mars is in this practical sign, you're a master of organization. You leap out of bed in the morning, a list of the chores you need to accomplish fresh in your mind—or in your very capable hand. And even if other parts of your chart give you an overwhelming lazy streak, you inspire confidence in others—they just naturally expect that you'll accomplish whatever you attempt, and this constant vote of confidence goes a long way toward creating the positive results you envisioned initially. At work, this quality helps you gain promotions, and it's likely that you'll ultimately be in a position of leadership for you're as capable as you seem. Getting others organized for team success is as easy and natural for you as managing your own affairs adroitly.

The man with Mars in Capricorn has had his act together since before he knew he had an act. He's practical, hard-working, down to earth, and he knows what he's doing. He's the epitome of the strong, silent type. Nothing throws him—not a malfunctioning appliance or an earthquake. He has the inner confidence to know that he can meet whatever challenge comes his way. It takes a lot to ruffle this guy's feathers. He's not given to tantrums, loud outbursts, or even an occasional rude word. He prides himself on his self-control, and giving in to the urge to temperamental behavior is allowing another to have power over him. Being the master of his own fate is important, not because he can't bear to take orders from anyone, like Aries, but because he has more confidence in himself than anyone else.

Somewhere in between hard-working and workaholic, the Mars in Capricorn man has much trouble seeing himself as fun-loving, and unless his Venus is in a very social sign, he may never want to party. So instead of inviting him to a formal bash, you may have better luck asking him over to help you put up a shelf. Afterwards he appreciates a good, home-cooked meal and simple conversation where you both can share your goals. You're falling for the type of old-fashioned, solid, substantial, value-conscious man often played by Gary Cooper in the 1940's. Buy him a shiny new tool chest, pop some muffins into the oven, and let him organize your life.

The woman with Mars in Capricorn doesn't want the sensitive, artistic type; the emotional "new man" often strikes her as a wimp. She wants a man who has his life in order, who's going somewhere worthwhile, and whose bank account is solid. She wants a guy like her father, someone of the old-school who believes in strict discipline at all times; often she is attracted to a military man.

This lady wants a serious mate, someone who is a doer, not a talker, and usually he's her senior by a number of years, but if he is her own age, he somehow seems older by virtue of his demeanor or his position in life. She wants to be able to point to her man with pride, not only in who he is but also in what he's accomplished. Of course there's always the flip side of this story. The woman with Mars in Capricorn may decide to be the strong figure in the relationship and allow her man to be the lesser partner—assuming her Venus is in a sentimental sign.

The woman with Mars in Capricorn wants a man who is

schooled in the social graces—he should be able to order in a restaurant, and taxis should stop obediently at his command. This is not because, like Libra, manners are the essence of life to her, but rather because she likes a man to be able to make his way in the world with assurance and finesse, just as she herself can do so easily. If his manners are not all they ought to be, but he has the promise of being someone with whom she could build the kind of life she desires, she'll easily forgive what he lacks (unlike Libra, who'd be long gone).

So stand up straight, make sure your life is in order, your three-piece suit pressed, and get tickets to a play. Some traditional wooing is right in order here, but don't forget the traditional goal of courtship—marriage—for that is her goal as well.

These celebs are among those with Mars in Capricorn: Brad Pitt, Christina Aguilera, Sharon Stone, Julia Roberts, Robert Pattinson, Ewan McGregor, Taylor Lautner, Woody Allen, Walt Disney, Marlon Brando, David Bowie, George Harrison, Jim Carrey, Jake Gyllenhaal, Shia Lebeouf, Tom Selleck, P-Diddy, Jerry Seinfeld, Mark Ruffalo, Samuel L. Jackson, John Wayne, Lady Gaga, Catherine Zeta-Jones.

Mars in Aquarius

Mars in Aquarius is stubborn, magnanimous, group oriented, and determinedly nonconformist. In this sign, Mars has plenty of energy and plenty of stamina. Here it seeks a group connection, in order to align its energies in a synergistic way to promote and realize personal ideals. It is through this group bond that the Mars in Aquarius person validates individuality and transcends it as well. The whole goal is to see the self as part of a much larger "we," and thus be selfish and unselfish at the same time. The greater society Mars in Aquarius envisions and works so unselfishly for is, after all, no more than extension of its own narrow self. This can be as large as being a player on a football team or as small as owning a business with a few family members.

If your Mars is in this sign, you're determined to do things your own way. Often you rebel from the established norm just to be different, whether or not what you're doing makes any sense. Clearly this may not have worked in your favor as a child, or your parents' favor either. As soon as you heard the words, "Just do it," you were like a bull spotting the red flag. Often boys with this placement are such a worry to their parents that they're forced into the army, where they do so well that everybody is amazed. Once they feel part of the team, they dig in and pull their weight more than willingly, although they may continue to enjoy displaying a few quirks from time to time.

The man with Mars in Aquarius is sure that he knows what everybody needs. Of course, everybody doesn't always need the same things, but he rarely looks at life from that point of view, even though he's determined to go his own way at all times. He works hard to come up with a perfect plan for everybody, and seeing the brilliance in his perfect creation, he then tries to ram it down people's throats, feeling that somehow they're just not connecting with his ideas, and that if he can make them see, they'll agree.

Often the result is a no-win situation. But being an idea man is his singular identity, and if you love a Mars in Aquarius man, be prepared to have him act according to his thoughts, with little or no concern for practical reality or emotions—his or yours. He has a certain way he sees the world, and everything must conform to that vision.

He always takes the lead, and assumes that he knows best, and if you're determined to change his mind, you'll have to go about it with a great deal of evidence about why he should do what you think is right. It's like one of those situations where the husband refuses to look at the map or stop for directions, and the wife keeps insisting it's one block to the left, and he keeps turning right. On the plus side, he has a great deal of stamina, and is usually willing to keep at a task until he gets it done. That may be a good thing where sex is concerned, but it doesn't lead to new choices. He does tend to repeat the same actions because once it feels comfortable, he does it again. If you enjoy repetition, such as finding that sweet spot and hitting it frequently, then that will work for you as well. But if you want a little innovation, he's not unwilling to try something new, if you make it interesting.

The woman with Mars in Aquarius wants a man who can dazzle her intellectually. A clever mental approach to life is number one on her list of requirements for a mate. To her, communication is the same as action, and her man must be ready with fascinating thoughts and remarks if he wants to keep her interest. She wants a man who is willing to give his time to good causes that will make a better world. She, herself, is probably a hard-working member of several committees whose purpose is to improve the community in some way, and she is likely to be very attracted to a man she works with in this capacity.

She likes eccentric behavior and unusual people, and the guy mother picked out for her is probably the last man on earth she'd marry. Instead she probably delighted in parading a number of high school rebels through her parents' living room and enjoyed registering their emphatic disapproval. Once they feigned disinterest in her dates, she was content to end the contest.

Her ideal man is an idiosyncratic genius, and she doesn't care if he can tie his own shoes as long as he has the brains and clarity of vision to invent a new material from which to manufacture them. This is one lady who is almost impossible to win over to your side. Either she sees something in you that attracts her, or she does not, and all the champagne suppers and love letters in the world will not change her mind. The thing in you that she must see is the embodiment of her ideals. A thousand hopefuls can pass her by, but when she meets the man whose life is an example of his beliefs, and who can see beyond the narrow framework of his own ego, she has no trouble at all aligning her destiny with his.

These celebs are among those with Mars in Aquarius: Mark Wahlberg, Scarlett Johansson, Sarah Palin, Michelle Obama, George W. Bush, Adele, Alec Baldwin, Justin Timberlake, Justin Bieber, Kristen Stewart, Gerard Butler, Jay-Z, Tupac Shakur, Cary Grant, Lance Armstrong, Gary Oldman, Axl Rose, Ang Lee, Hugh Hefner, Howard Hughes, Elijah Wood, Sacha Baron Cohen, Justin Theroux, Rush Limbaugh, Karl Rove, Kim Jong-un.

Mars in Pisces

Mars is the planet of ego expression. Pisces is the sign of ego transcendence. Obviously there are some problems combining the two modes of existence. It is not the job of Mars to worry about anyone other than you; feeling justified in being selfish is the purpose of Mars, and without it we'd all be at the mercy of the winds. Of course, Mars in Pisces can be most effective by using energy, not for its own ego gratification but unselfishly, by focusing on the needs of others. When the recognition of this ability to be of tremendous help to others is made, Mars in Pisces comes into its own.

If your Mars is in this sign, you probably express both of the qualities of covert action and unselfish devotion to others, for in daily life almost all of us have to be self-assertive at some time or other, and it's just more difficult for you to do so because it's hard for you to acknowledge the supremacy of your individual self and individual needs.

The man with Mars in Pisces need some reassurance about himself as a human being. He's so used to thinking in universal terms that it's hard for him to concentrate on the personal. And he needs someone there to back him up when he's forced to be assertive, because he always feels guilty, even when he's right. Whether he's the local shoulder to cry on or a major philanthropist, he's always involved in some form of good works or other. And people who care nothing for others may receive his friendship, but they do not earn his admiration, for he knows that making a contribution on a larger scale is really what life is all about.

This unselfish humanitarian needs a good deal of breathing space, and some time on his own every day to meditate, daydream, or just relax. He has the ability to absorb energy from the atmosphere that other people don't even perceive, so if he's been in an environment in which a great deal of negativity was projected, he feels grouchy and a bit negative himself. Thus he needs time to renew himself and to wipe his psychic slate clean. So if he habitually retreats to a closed room without you, don't feel neglected. He knows that not until he refreshes himself will he be able to give you the attention you deserve.

If a Mars in Pisces man interests you, remember that you have fallen for the sensitive, emotional type, not a rough and tumble chauvinist cowboy. This man isn't likely to drag you out of the living room, throw you on the bed, and make love savagely. Instead, he may be a little reticent and almost shy where sex is concerned. To have sexual interaction always carries a heavy emotional price tag, so he is rarely casual about relationships. It's not that he can't be seduced, he just prefers to avoid meaningless one-night stands. He enjoys quiet, peaceful, relaxing times in which two people share their thoughts and are lazy together. A picnic packed for the beach is the perfect way to spend an afternoon. And we all know that perfect afternoons often lead to perfect nights.

The woman with Mars in Pisces wants a sensitive man who's able to relate emotionally. She may sometimes be attracted to alcoholics or drug users who need to be rescued, but eventually she learns to use the positive energy of this placement and to avoid those people who refuse to take responsibility for themselves. She's a concerned, helpful person, who is more than willing to devote herself unselfishly to a good cause, and the man she marries must see the importance of doing good works. A venal, grasping businessman who cares for nothing but the dollar doesn't impress her a bit, although she may need help where finances are concerned, because going out and bringing home the bacon is rarely one of her strong suits.

This is seldom a terribly aggressive woman. She isn't likely to arm wrestle with you in a spirit of friendly good cheer, nor is she going to engage in a battle to the death ping-pong game. The kind of guy who goes on safari or takes his woman along into the jungle isn't her ideal. Her man loves kids, animals, and poetry. He lies awake in the moonlight spinning pretty stories to transport them both into a magical wonderland. And if he never makes it to work the next morning—so what? Isn't it more important to share your soul in the moonlight than to grapple for the almighty buck at dawn? It is to her.

It's difficult for the Mars in Pisces lady to win an argument. If she's right, she just feels too guilty about asserting herself, so she usually backs down. Feminine wiles come in quite handy here, unless, of course, she's dealing with an Aries who'll just tromp all over her. She needs a good deal of practice (with some encouragement) to become more assertive, and often she enters into a traditional marriage in order to have a man to fight her battles for her.

This soft and cuddly woman likes to stay at home, taking catnaps and protecting herself from the intrusions of the world at large. She delights in your company, but she is rarely up to discoing until dawn. She needs her beauty sleep. Inefficient and a bit untidy at times, she nevertheless is a kindly, sympathetic, and very human woman who seeks a mate who, like herself, has the ability to connect with the rest of humanity and who takes the time to appreciate the intangibles of life.

These celebs are among those with Mars in Pisces: Elizabeth Taylor, Marilyn Monroe, Josh Brolin, Tom Hanks, David Beckham, Denzel Washington, Paris Hilton, Christina Hendricks, Heath Ledger, Ralph Nader, Steve McQueen, Lebron James, Vincent Van Gogh, Michelangelo, Keith Haring, Bob Dylan, Christoph Waltz, Ray Liotta, LL Cool J, Michael Cera, Juliette Binoche, Tina Turner, Kim Cattrall.

Venus-Mars Combinations

To many people, astrology is a collection of bits and pieces of information. The hard part is putting it all together. As you've already learned, Venus is the planet of love, and Mars is all about action and sex. Your own love style results from the combination of these two planets and how their divergent energies combine—or clash. Each combination is like a fortune cookie truth—the heart and soul of you. They represent what you need from love and what you're willing to do to get it. Who are you deep in your heart's core? Your Venus-Mars combination tells you in detail.

Venus in Aries-Mars Combinations

Venus in Aries with Mars in Aries

This is an intensely active, headstrong combination which refuses to allow even the tiniest interference from anyone. You want to do what you want, when you want, and anyone posing a threat to this philosophy is in for a struggle. You like to do things quickly, with a minimum of time spent in preparation or preplanning. Aries-Aries is the combination of the caveman. He sees what he wants and he charges in and drags his conquest back to his cave where she fulfills his desires for as long as he desires her. Her needs are never taken into consideration. Of course some women (and men?) like the feeling of being overpowered by a strong, dashing heroic caveman/woman. If so, great.

You innately concentrate on your own personal needs; it feels so natural just to leap along, focusing on your own inclinations rather than a mate's. In love, this can lead to a good deal of surprise and heartbreak, for ultimately a partner will decide to be assertive, and you may be left alone and bewildered. "But we loved each other so," you wail.

The lesson to be learned is that always concentrating on only yourself creates a lack of awareness and a communication problem in relationships. It's a hard lesson for you, for it requires taking the time to notice somebody else, and the wisdom to realize that mere love does not join two individuals into one entity. The problem is, of course, that the one entity you desire to be is you—and your lover is supposed to merge into it, which many people don't enjoy because they feel it robs them of selfhood. If you can create that one entity of two souls, it has to be an equal melding of both parties and by doing so each is changed by the other.

Your Aries-Aries lover is exciting, and possesses the self-centered determination to create an atmosphere of untethered passion. Nothing is forbidden, too shocking, or unthinkable in bed. Midnight visits, without even a warning phone call, are not unusual. And nothing you can do will be considered unsuitable—at least not in bed.

Let the Aries-Aries person take the lead. Relax, and enjoy the feeling of going on an exciting roller coaster ride. Don't be pushy or demanding, unless you want to say goodbye before you've even said hello. Retain your independence but also be willing to lean on this lover, who likes to be in charge. Expect a few intensely angry words now and then, but don't be shocked when the anger evaporates as quickly as it's expressed. No grudges will be held.

Go out, play, have a fun time doing exciting things. Aries-Aries can teach you everything you ever wanted to know about excitement. And you must be interested in the that type of living or you wouldn't be reading this paragraph!

Venus in Aries with Mars in Taurus

This can often be a difficult combination to live with because of conflicting urges. You desire much freedom and you like to make snappy decisions, particularly where love is concerned, but you aren't always so quick to carry out your own wishes and you seldom afford your partners the same space in relationships that you demand for yourself.

Self-centeredness and stubbornness are often the qualities that a potential lover will complain about, and although you might take offense at this description of yourself, it's frequently difficult for you to express your anger in a reasonable way, waiting instead until you blow up to blow off the accumulated steam. And in this case, the complaints may be justified, so it's hard to mount a rational defense.

You like to be unburdened and fancy-free, but often you buy on impulse and later regret being overwhelmed with an excess of possessions. Love affairs can sometimes take the same turn. You become impulsively involved with a partner who allows you to be as possessive as you'd like, then when he or she acts as though you're a team, you realize that you're stuck in this relationship that feels disturbingly permanent, you get nervous because you don't like the feeling of being bogged down, and you want to bolt.

The problem is that when you find someone who likes the kind of stability you need, he or she usually seems too dull to hold your interest, or you feel smothered. The carefree types whom you find terribly exciting can be great for the short haul, but they refuse to put up with your stubbornness and they seem too insubstantial for you to rely on. Obviously a balance is needed. You can modulate your energy—which you enjoy doing—so that every whim isn't acted upon instantly, and that gives you the chance to learn more about a potential mate. By going slowly, you form an attachment only after you're assured there's a degree of compatibility. Then you can remain committed for a long time.

Your Aries-Taurus lover likes to be the innovator of shared pleasures that often include a combination of excitement and sensual good times. He or she likes to touch and be touched. In bed, this lover wants to be impetuous and speedy but is more likely to be slow and sensuous. Aries-Taurus finds pleasure in owning nice things; she might adore a present of jewelry, he an elegant gadget case made of very fine materials. Although your lover might enjoy the idea of going off on a helter-skelter adventure, chances are that the follow-through might be lacking. Going out to an elegant restaurant where you both can enjoy some fine food might be a better bet. Finding someone who's flamboyantly exciting as well as emotionally and materially stable is the challenge for Aries-Taurus, and if you're that sort of person, then you've met your match.

Venus in Aries with Mars in Gemini

This is a highly cerebral, swift, and changeable combination. The Aries-Gemini person likes to begin things very much, but completing them is often another matter. If you're Aries-Gemini, you're extremely hard to pin down. It's not just that you demand your freedom (you do) but also that you're so mercurial in your actions, you hardly ever stay put long enough for anyone to be able to challenge your freedom.

It's also not that you tend to be unreliable, but rather that you find boredom hard to handle, and relationships get boring quickly, mainly because the catch of the day is so much more enticing than leftovers. Stability is not your forte and you don't want it to be.

You might be just as happy to spend your time creating stories of excitingly romantic adventures that take place in many faraway locations, as you would be actually living those adventures. After all, thinking is your favorite activity, and anyone who believes talking with a fast-thinking pal isn't an exciting way to pass the time of day isn't someone who appeals to you

Your Aries-Gemini lover is fast to act, and you might discover you've been seduced before you even realize that you're being led down that infamous primrose path. This firecracker likes things (and this includes sex) quick and exciting. Why live for tomorrow when today can be so enthralling? Unless other factors predominate, settling down with this individual is hard to pull off, and if it's your goal, you might actually get that wedding band but discover along the way that your spouse is very often flirting with someone else.

If you can tolerate some free love, then wanting to reel this mate in might work out. If having fun is important to you and Carpe Diem is your motto, then you're in for a grand time. Aries-Gemini never drags you into a cave. Instead you're propelled into a book-lined chamber with clever mind games and infectious verbal charm. Laugh and have a good time with this sparkling individual. Enjoy matching wits and sparring with mind-tingling puns. It doesn't matter, really, which side you take. Just don't belabor your point or have a slow, dull mental process. But then, if you did, chances are that this individual would hold very few charms for you and vice-versa.

Venus in Aries with Mars in Cancer

How do you remain an independent, untethered individual when you like to use your energy caring for and meeting the needs of other people? This is the dilemma of the Venus in Aries, Mars in Cancer individual. You demand the freedom to be your own person, free from the dictates of anyone else, yet you just naturally like to mother everyone you meet. You like to prepare cozy dinners or breakfasts in bed, yet you wonder why you're bothering to pamper people, when you know they should be pampering you. It's enough to make you mad, if it weren't such an awful feeling to be angry, that sometimes you just hold it all in until you get an awful stomachache or develop a permanent grudge against the other person.

You're inclined to be moody, and there's no reason for you to keep those moods secret. You want what you want, and sometimes you become so quickly enamored with someone that you just overwhelm them with your passion. It doesn't feel to you like you're smothering, because really you're not, and often you lose interest and want to move on. But why is this other person claiming you made promises you didn't actually make? Chances are it's because your interest is so intense at the start that the lover you lavish with your attentions feels *wow, this is forever*. You'd like it to be forever, but you can't help it if it doesn't work out.

You feel a bit sad if a relationship ends, but then you bounce back, romantic and cheerful and on the prowl—again—for your one true love. Yes emotions are messy and embarrassing, but you're an intense and passionate person, which is much better than being clueless and wooden.

Try to take better care of your Aries-Cancer lover. Even if he or she turns around and insists on being in charge of the care taking, the efforts will still be appreciated. If you have a large family that's noisy and exciting to be around, share them. A lovingly wrapped box of delicious chocolates will be consumed with pleasure. A trip to the beach, a visit to the zoo or the aquarium, or a meal prepared by you'll go over well.

Relationships are a problem for Aries-Cancer, for hostile situations with romantic partners seem to develop frequently, causing misery and guilt. He or she usually remedies the situation by buying a present and hoping everything is forgotten without ever thinking to work at communication, which is what really would help.

In bed this lover can combine the best of tenderness with excitement, turning you on in the shocking ways that have always been a part of your fantasies—and you thought nobody knew what you were dreaming about last night! That mind-reading ability is really just an awful lot of sexual ESP, and that's a quality which makes it easy to put up with a touch of moodiness.

Venus in Aries with Mars in Leo

This is a confidant and courageous combination, which can sometimes seem self-centered and arrogant. You want to be a leader but never feel truly at ease meshing into any group. Your impulsive urges to action are tempered by a strong sense of pride, which endeavors to maintain a dignified appearance.

You're not what anybody might describe as overly emotional. In fact, you're much more interested in the image you project, and that any romance in which you participate has a quality of splendor. Hearts and flowers are not nearly as beguiling as pomp and circumstance. Yet you're full of genuine love for anyone with whom you become involved, and your feelings are always expressed honestly.

You like to be the center of attention in any situation, and that includes amour. Your mate must always be someone of whom you can feel proud and who enhances your image of yourself. Sometimes you've been accused of treating a mate as an accessory, and you admit it's occasionally true. You're not the sort to want a sentimental relationship in which every thought and feeling is shared by the partners. That would feel far too heavy for you. Instead you want fun, excitement, and a good deal of glamour in a partner, and the person you marry should be well able to function independently, as long as you remain the boss.

Your Aries-Leo lover delights in having an admiring audience that encourages true self-expression at all times. Give elegant parties as a showcase for your mate. Make sure that your admiration is genuine, and express your sentiments often. It's obvious that no one else is as radiantly exciting, and naturally you agree or you wouldn't be so love-struck. Be content to follow a few paces behind this fiery leader—well metaphorically speaking. Never try to interfere with his or her plans, or you'll be met with stubborn resistance and redoubled determination. You may find yourself being courted at an embassy ball, in a palace, or on a yacht. Not even Cinderella could resist that! In bed Aries-Leo wants to recreate the splendor of Cleopatra and Mark Antony floating down a barge on the Nile and beguiling each other with the magical intensity of a newfound passion.

Each night you spend together is an unmatched romantic interlude, and this can go on for years without the slightest diminishing of either magic or pleasure. As long as you share that attitude, it's pretty easy to fall under a romantic spell in which you relinquish authority with a sultry, "Take me—I'm yours."

Venus in Aries with Mars in Virgo

With this combination you want to be free to express yourself and are willing to attend to the details that will allow you to do so. You may be a little bit impetuous emotionally, but your every action is deliberate and well planned, with careful attention to details and consequences. You can seem a bit headstrong and are often sure that your way is the only way to do anything. You're not dictatorial, but you do like to see things done to your specifications, and you want your high standards to be met.

You like good times that are tasteful as well as exciting. You're not overly flamboyant, but you're definitely not stodgy. Meeting your responsibilities is necessary before you'll allow yourself to cut loose and have fun. Relationships can be a problem because often you just have other priorities. Yes, you fall in love, but there are other elements to your life that are just as important.

Some people with this combination tend to be real loners. Often the excuse is that they can't find anyone who meets their standards, but in reality they feel uncomfortable in relationships and are concerned that a permanent commitment will restrict their freedom to an unacceptable extent.

Your Aries-Virgo lover wants to be adored as much as anyone; just be sure you give some thought to the details of your seduction. Setting up a beautifully appointed table with perfectly prepared food, designed specifically to delight, is a good beginning. Pay careful attention to what pleases him or her and then do it, adding little embellishments of your own. People with planets in Virgo are always impressed when others care enough to get the scoop on them.

In bed, Aries-Virgo usually takes the lead, and this lover has the ability to be exciting and the patience to take the time to notice what really turns you on, and to concentrate on the little details of love that make all the difference. There's nothing wrong with voicing suggestions of your own, but in sex, as in everything else, this perfectionist feels that nobody does things better, so be prepared to follow orders or to turn a deaf ear to the criticism that results when you don't. Just because he or she insists you're doing something stupidly doesn't mean that you're being called stupid, although it does mean that your lover is being tactless (again). If you're willing to learn new ways of getting things done, your Aries-Virgo lover might teach you some titillating tricks you never even dreamed of.

Venus in Aries with Mars in Libra

You always have to choose between your desire to be an independent operator and the fact that you feel much more comfortable acting in conjunction with another person or a group. "I want what I want, if it's okay with you," could be your motto. You do want to have your own way but not at the expense of conflict with the other people in your life. Relationships are very important to you, and in fact, the need to create a harmonious relationship picture may be one of the all-important themes in your life.

Thus the urge to act impetuously is usually tempered by

the inclination not to act until all possible consequences are weighed and considered. Often you may feel that you're far too indecisive, and much too concerned with the other guy. Although you may feel that healthy competition can be fun, harmony is very important to you, so much so that you may have a difficult time expressing anger, and may even feel guilty when the urge to complain and quarrel hits you.

Your Aries-Libra lover is as interested in creating a pleasant relationship as anyone you'll ever meet. This individual wants the two of you to merge into a happy, harmonious unit, in which everyone is contented, and sometimes that means your partner makes choices that don't quite feel personally comfortable, all in the spirit of compromise. Obviously that's good for you if you're the teensiest bit selfish.

Don't pressure this well-meaning individual. Allow your mate plenty of time for decision making, and don't balk at multiple about-faces. Play classical music. Send flowers. Make an effort to please and the favor will be returned. After all, how often do you meet someone so interested in having a beautifully smooth relationship that the individual puts all of his or her energy into creating it. Yes, some of your mate's` ideas of perfection may not be precisely what you'd want, but you have to admire the spirit behind the gesture.

In bed, as in other areas of life, Aries-Libra tends to charge right in, then hesitates, wanting not to be too hasty. It's your responsibility to offer encouragement, and sometimes to take the lead. After all, it takes two to tango, and sex is nothing more than the dance of love.

Venus in Aries with Mars in Scorpio

This is one of the most intense, most passionate combinations in the Zodiac. You have a smoldering quality that can either be quite exciting or a little scary.

When you decide what you want, you pursue it with fierce determination, and heaven help the individual who stands in your way. *No* is a response reserved only for yourself. A lover's quarrel can be an incredibly exciting event, whether you choose to blow off the steam immediately or let it build into a powerful explosion complete with cutting remarks and hurled crockery. You may continue to seethe for a week, but when the fracas is over, you desire a reconciliation that will possess and consume your mate.

Weak people inspire your contempt, and you can truly respect only someone whose strength and passion match your own. A terrific friend or mate, you're totally loyal to a pal or partner, and will do all in your power to help solve a crisis or provide moral support in general, although you do tend to take charge a great deal, which can either be comforting or annoying. You just can't stand the idea of doing things half way. Either a matter is worth the total commitment of your heart, soul, and mind, or it isn't worthy of any consideration at all.

If you're interested in a relationship with a passionate Aries-Scorpio person, be prepared for intensity and excitement. Don't expect smooth waters, for you'll rarely get them. A healthy amount of unwavering devotion and frequently expressed admiration provides a good beginning— but make sure it's genuine, for your Aries-Scorpio mate demands total honesty from you and is better at reading you than you might think. Remember that this is a highly sensitive, emotional person, although you may never see profuse weeping. Be wary of what you say. Even if you're only returning tit for tat in a lover's quarrel, your remarks are likely to remain smoldering in your lover's mind long after you've forgotten what ill-advised comments or behavior prompted them.

Be prepared to be overwhelmed with passionate advances on very little notice. If you like the idea of being plucked from your television program, being thrown on the floor, your clothes removed (or torn away) to become involved in a steamy interlude that's more exciting than anything ever written in a blue novel, then you're in the right place. If not— beware. Your Aries-Scorpio lover is never going to wait for you to dry the dishes or light the candles. But with a lover who provide fireworks twenty-four hours a day, who needs candles?

Venus in Aries with Mars in Sagittarius

You need to be free at all times, in whatever you do, because you know you must be able to express your urges and ideals, which are numerous. Whether you want to be outdoors throwing a football (and you're likely to be one half of the couple who sneaks off in the middle of the game to make love under the bleachers), or whether you want to be at the head of an organization to free hostages, promote freedom, or promulgate a particular philosophy, you refuse to allow anyone to interfere in your freedom.

In your mind, you're an easy going, fun partner, someone who loves a good time and rarely makes demands on anyone else. That's just what you want from a mate, but often you feel smothered rather quickly and find a way to part company, usually on good terms, or at least you hope it's on good terms. You don't like being hemmed in, fenced in, or held back. It just seems wrong to you because life is so filled with exciting possibilities and interesting people that you want to be able to follow your fancies at a moment's notice. That makes you a lot of fun, but it might not make you the world's most stable or reliable partner. If you can find a mate who isn't that rule oriented and with whom you keep on having fun, you might extend the relationship into the realm of forever.

If you're interested in an Aries-Sagittarius lover, you may be a little bewildered about how to capture him or her. What's the best strategy? Forget capture! This lover is a total cowboy—or gaucho if we're being chic—and every gaucho retains an essential part of his or her freedom; even the critters roped and tied at the rodeo are ultimately liberated. Your best bet is to seem a little bit unavailable yourself. If you want a good time more than a secure commitment, you seem more appealing to this partner, and making the chase interesting helps keep it going. Act as though this very minute is the only time frame that matters, and that tomorrow may find you who knows where—ready to resume your own footloose and fancy-free status in a blink.

Enjoy outdoor activities and outdoor sports. Have fun. Play, and consider playing an important part of your life. You can't be super serious, but don't for a moment maintain a shallow mental attitude. Your Aries-Sagittarius lover has a highly philosophical, probably liberal bent, in which it's very important to create a better world for all sorts of people. You might find yourself gazing into your lover's face by the light of a campfire, your horses grazing on a nearby plain, as you snuggle farther down into a double sleeping bag. Whether or not the liaison is permanent depends on your ability to keep a loose hand on the reins and a twinkle in your eye.

Venus in Aries with Mars in Capricorn

"Everybody to the rear of the line, behind me." Chances are that everyone in your life has heard this phrase and has complained about it at one time or another. Your Aries independence is combined with Capricorn orderliness and practicality, along with a palpable desire for status and achievement. In fact, your single-minded drive to achieve a measure of authority and prestige probably has landed you in hot water in your love life at more than one point. But then, making your way in the world is much more important to you than any relationship.

You may feel that love is frivolous, and a deterrent to achievement. Although you like sex well enough, you may have a hard time relating with the opposite sex in a harmonious way, and in general, relationships seem natural to you when there's a fair amount of friction. If you're in a permanent liaison, it may be with someone who never interferes in your life but who provides you with a measure of increased status through the association. For you to be willing to allow a partner to make much of an impact on your behavior, that partner must have a hold on you—a relatively greater amount of social prestige or the ability to aid you in your career. Obviously this is no way to encourage a serenade of violins. But then you aren't much interested in violins—unless it's your orchestra.

Does this mean that you're an avowed single for the rest of your life? Not at all. You just want your love life to work within the framework of your life as a whole. Until you're with the right mate, you're content to go it alone as a freelance romancer. And sometimes a night of blazing passion here and there is all you need to feel content until the next one comes along.

As you already have deduced, your Aries-Capricorn lover is going to present quite a challenge if you want any kind of romance at all. Unless you're his or her patron, employer, or are quite high on the social register, your gentler emotions may go unheeded for a long time.

In bed, Aries-Capricorn is definitely in charge. This mate tells you where to put your head, where to put your feet, and what to do with every part in between. "Hey," you might protest, "Now it's my turn to conquer you!" Humor is a good way to deal with this autocratic behavior.

Be a patient and unselfish friend who's willing to listen to problems, to help at mapping out the routes of success, and be full of praise and admiration when a problem is resolved or success achieved.

Be ambitious yourself, for mutual respect is mandatory in a relationship with Aries-Capricorn. In return, you get a relationship with a high-powered achiever who's at the head of the class, the top of the ladder, the peak of the mountain.

Venus in Aries with Mars in Aquarius

You're more of an individualist than everybody you know, and often you do something just to be different. You may be original in the best way possible, a true future-thinking pioneer who can blaze new and much-needed trails.

Although you may not be a favorite of your mate's parents (at least not before the wedding), you can be a lot of fun to be around for all sorts of partners who like a touch of unpredictability in romance. Because you have a kind of universality to your appeal, combined with a devilish twinkle in your eye, you may be able to find a common ground with many vastly different people—sometimes simultaneously, to a mate's dismay.

You bring merriment with you wherever you go, but you're still a determined and stubborn individual. A lover who tries to subdue or manipulate you meets with the same success that your parents had when giving orders, or the high-school principal had when issuing a command—none. You make your own decisions and you follow your own star, and that's just the way it is.

Your Aries-Aquarius lover never just takes you to the movies. Be prepared instead for a visit to a political lecture in which you're in the center of the storm, or if you do end up in the movies, expect a new-wave art film and don't be surprised when you hear "Want to fool around?" Aries-Aquarius delights in the forbidden and the unconventional, so this mate is one of the best friends you ever had, as well as a lover who delights in dreaming up new ways to please that might shock you just a little at first.

Forget sitting around together drinking tea with your mother, unless your mother is a legend. You can relax about your appearance, ignore the dust on the furniture, send out for dinner. Aries-Aquarius couldn't care less. In fact, your unconventional disregard for socially acceptable behavior might just win you a permanent mate. And you'll be getting someone who never asks you to do the laundry, take out the trash, or serve breakfast in bed—unless you can request a return of favors.

Venus in Aries with Mars in Pisces

With this combination, you may feel like acting in a self-assertive way, but often you're just too sleepy to carry it off. Somehow you want to believe that your own desires are the most important, but you're too emotionally involved with other people and their needs to be really effective at being selfish, no matter how you might like to try. Often the only solution to this dilemma is to retreat alone for a nap or a session of meditation.

You like exciting people and tend to draw to you lovers who are quite a handful, which seems thrilling at first but ultimately can be difficult to manage. You don't always mind when relationships end, because you're friendly and outgoing, and you sense that someone new will be right around the corner. Love isn't meant to be a buffet, you know that, but still it often feels like it is. When you're honest with yourself, you admit that you sort of like it that way.

People often seem to come to you with their problems, revealing more of the private details of their lives than you might like to hear. It can be difficult to have a lover who expects you to be a psychiatrist, or at least a sympathetic ear. And it's hard to get your own relationship going when potential lovers seem to think of you as a helper rather than a partner. On the other hand, you're able to put your needs aside a good deal of the time in favor of very helpful, unselfish behavior.

Your Aries-Pisces lover may not be a ball of fire. Instead of going out, you're more likely to spend peaceful hours together in front of the fire, drinking wine and listening to romantic ballads, sharing quiet talk of dreams and fantasies that you may never get around to acting on. With this mate, action often takes a verbal turn rather than a physical one. Enjoy hearing the most exciting fantasies and be enthralled with his or her wonderful imagination, but don't expect as much action as talk, no matter how your lover seems to want to, for something just holds him or her back.

The Aries-Pisces combination has a lesson built into it— and that is the fact that there are far more ideas to capture our fancies than we need to give life to physically. And, in fact, when we don't leap off into the sunset at every notion that strikes us as wonderful, there is much more time to dream and create even more beautiful dreams.

In bed, Aries-Pisces doesn't always choose to act out high-energy, fantasy-inspired sex. Instead he or she tends to talk of exciting things and to settle for more cuddling and coddling than actual lovemaking. Snuggling in together under the covers and sharing the events of the day as you take turns tickling each other's toes is one way to spend the night. Your Aries-Pisces lover is always exciting yet sensitive, and not everybody can find a partner for whom the magic of fairy tales is as real as the latest sporting event.

Venus in Taurus-Mars Combinations

Venus in Taurus with Mars in Aries

You have a terrifically sensual nature, and all the energy in the world to act on it. In fact, you may be acting on it all over town, in every boîte, bistro, and bedroom that still allows you entrance. When you take a fancy to someone, you charge right over to overwhelm him or her with new worlds of sensual pleasure, available immediately, thank you very much. You may be a fine artist or craftsman, and at the very least are excellent at conjuring up a very erotic atmosphere. You like your pleasures and excitement in equal doses, and as such can be an incredibly enjoyable person to have around, as long as your partner is in agreement with your desires. If not, you can be quite persuasive.

You love to spend money on yourself, acquiring all manner of finery as it strikes your fancy. You often bemoan your tendency toward impulse buying. Certainly anyone supporting you will. Although you do pride yourself on your ability to satisfy a lover, you may tend to be a little too self-interested to want to satisfy anybody on his or her terms. Why should you when your own terms are so decidedly superior?

You want a love that lasts, but it must be one that remains exciting. In your heart you believe in faithfulness and longevity of relationships, but sometimes your senses take the rule, and you become overwhelmed by a new attraction to someone who isn't your mate. Obviously this is something you can control, particularly as the years pass, and as long as you're with the right mate, you can remain content—and committed.

Your Taurus-Aries lover will sweep you off your feet, but it's more than a mere cave to which you'll be dragged. Actually, this passionate individual may start the sweeping long before the cave is even reached. Having a good time, now, is uppermost on this mate's mind. This means lots of the best of everything, brought forth at a moment's notice.

Comfort, pleasure, and excitement will be dispensed in equal proportions. And you never have to be patient while more important concerns come first. To Taurus-Aries, having a good time is the most important concern. And who wants to complain about that?

In bed, Taurus-Aries is a driving pleasure machine. Every exotic delight discovered is no more than routine for this highly skilled lover. Sensual and passionate, he or she knows how to walk the fine line between arousal and consummation, and you're likely to be swept along, quivering with delight and open to realizing new discoveries of your own erotic potential. If this is the outer limit, you'll surely line up for more.

Venus in Taurus with Mars in Taurus

With this combination, you seem slow, placid, earthy, and above all, easygoing. For someone to light a fire under you, he would need a blowtorch. You love to have good times, and if you seem too slow or too lazy for other people, that's their problem, not yours. Whatever you do, you take your time. And that includes sex. More than any other combination in the Zodiac, you're likely to be the one who spends whole weekends at a time in bed.

You're very attached to your possessions. You can't really be happy without having lots of nice things around you, and lots may be not quite enough. You like to indulge yourself in every way possible, whether with luxuries, food and drink, good times, or physical pleasures.

Although you seem calm, often it means that you're simply refusing to express your anger until it builds into a mighty explosion. Unless a partner knows you well, your actual feelings may be difficult to determine. You're calm, and you often refuse to quarrel or be budged, but it doesn't mean you're not seething inside.

Your worst fault as a lover may be your incredible possessiveness. Everyone loves to be adored, but hardly anyone wants to be owned. You need to temper the urge to regard people as just one more (albeit important) item in your inventory. This is essential not just because it's the right thing to do, but because you desire a secure, committed relationship, and it's easier to keep one going when everyone is happy.

Your Taurus-Taurus lover will spend as long as it takes to satisfy you, even if you need hours of warming up. Persistence is a quality invented by the Taureans of this world. In fact, this lover may still be working on satisfying you long after you'd rather be in dreamland. A quickie is not in the Taurus sexual vocabulary. Be prepared to spend long, long, lazy hours doing the kind of things that brought many ancient civilizations to a close. In fact, your modern-day reveler may have made quite a few improvements since the days of the Romans. Plan on being wooed lavishly. Don't be either weight-conscious or gain-proof, for with this lover, you'll be plied with lavish delights from morning to night. Add rich gravies, fancy sauces, superb wines, and the most luxe of desserts—you get the idea. A Taurus-Taurus lover is not on your Weight Watchers plan.

Go ahead and nag. Try to get him or her to change to suit your specifications. Start as many quarrels as you want. Taurus-Taurus may hear you but will continue on a chosen path with unflinching determination. Your best bet with this guy or gal is to love and accept your mate—as is, because this lover will very likely remain that way for a lifetime, and that is a kind of insurance we rarely get nowadays.

Venus in Taurus with Mars in Gemini

You would love to indulge yourself in all manner of sybaritic revelries, but you just can't sit still long enough to be a full-fledged hedonist. Anyone who probes your mind, however, discovers a flood of ideas about self-indulgent pleasures. The best way for you to work out your conflicting urges for relaxed decadence and inconstant action is to engage in much verbal fantasizing. For you love to think and to communicate, and no interaction would feel quite comfortable to you without a good measure of verbal banter.

You need to be physically active, and you must feel free to get up and go with a moment's notice. Almost any routine at all feels stifling to you, no matter how enjoyable it might be. That applies to relationships as well. Although your affections remain constant for a long, long time, you often feel the urge to move on and experience new people, sometimes on the spur of the moment, and for a never-repeated quickie. It takes a special lover to realize that your feelings haven't changed a bit even if you're unfaithful. It was probably a Taurus-Gemini who first instituted an "open" marriage.

What's the best way to sustain a relationship with your Taurus-Gemini lover? Be flexible. Enjoy whatever you're doing while it's happening, but be prepared to take off and try something new before you've stayed too long. Don't be possessive, although your mate may not always grant you the same consideration. And if he or she does seem uninterested in tying you down or tracking your whereabouts, chances are that you're only picking up on the kind of treatment your partner expects in return.

Buy lavishly illustrated books of erotic art, and don't be surprised when your lover suggests that life can imitate art—right at home. While you're in bed exploring each other's minds, hearts, and fantasies, be prepared for quick, frequent bouts of sensual lovemaking that provide many teasers. Taurus-Gemini can get to the point quickly, and can then be in the mood to try again.

With this lover you share a desire for comfort and luxury without ever feeling that you're a slave to your possessions or that you have to be tied down in any way at all. Your relationship might feel like a vacation at a luxury resort, interspersed with many lively flights of fancy, and nobody ever got bored with a combination like that.

Venus in Taurus with Mars in Cancer

Nothing is more important to you than having a comfortable home where you and your family can live happily and remain well taken care of and well fed. Food can be a real way of life to you, whether or not you've ever been in need, so you're determined always to have at least enough of everything. If you're inclined toward overeating, more than just pleasure is the issue—you feel a real urgency to nourish yourself.

Your feelings are easily hurt, and because it's so difficult for you to express anger (and other negative feelings), you often hold it in, letting the feelings fester, creating a stomachache or other physical manifestations. After an emotional scene you may withdraw alone to console yourself with an unhealthy dose of sweets.

You can be a terrific partner, lavishing on the object of your affections everything you ever wanted for yourself. This can extend to sex as well. Few other partners in the Zodiac have your ability to know what would please a lover in bed, as well as the sensuality to carry it off. Unfortunately, you may often feel that you're doing far too much giving and not nearly enough receiving. If that's the case, it's important to learn to speak up and make your wishes known.

Your Taurus-Cancer lover so appreciates your efforts to please that it almost doesn't matter what you try, as long as you have the right spirit. Think back to the last special occasion (it may well have been yesterday) in which you were feted. Chances are, clues to what would please him or her are strongly in evidence in what was offered to you. Turn the tables.

Try to remember that this mate doesn't always feel as unselfish as you might expect, so being extra careful not to take advantage will go a long way to maintain harmony and positive feelings.

Pleasurable activities that include the whole family are high on the list of favorites. A vacation to a seaside resort where you can lie on some cool, clean sand, soak up the sun, listen to the waves, and drink exotic tropical drinks while the children splash about is ideal (even if the children aren't your own—yet). Just remember that the Taurus-Cancer person isn't interested in a momentary fling or transient good times. Your relationship is too important. This lover wants to establish a family, and when that's taken care of, you'll share his or her favorite holiday—Christmas—every day of the year.

In bed, this mate is the perfect combination of sensuality and ardor. Often food is involved, and if you enjoy being lathered with treats that are slowly licked off your skin, this is your chance. Taurus-Cancer is willing to listen to and attempt your fantasies, try any position that's your favorite, and snuggle you for as long as you need afterwards. Clearly, this could lead to a lifetime of bliss.

Venus in Taurus with Mars in Leo

Although you desire the best that life has to offer and make working for it a priority, you also seek a relationship with a mate who can love and satisfy you—for the rest of your life. You like the idea of security and a long-lasting romance because you know that as time goes by, it's very satisfying to share mutual memories with someone who was there all along the way.

You don't really enjoy quarrels of any sort, and lovers' quarrels are perhaps the most draining to endure. What you don't get is why they happen at all, but somehow you do seem to be at odds with a mate more often than you'd like. It can be frustrating when you end up spending quite a bit of your time in ego battles and defensive arguments in which no one is the victor.

Nevertheless, you can be a genuinely generous, loving partner, as long as you feel good about yourself. This warmth and pride in yourself and anyone you love can provide quite a contrast to your sometimes selfish, possessive behavior. Your goal is to live a balanced life in which you can be mellow and happy with the right person always by your side.

Your Taurus-Leo lover knows how to live. "Only the best" is his or her motto, and it extends to you as long as you're a pair. You're always wooed lavishly, as befits the consort of this deluxe individual. Being served the finest champagne aboard luxury yachts, hobnobbing with the stars on a movie set (and your Taurus-Leo may be among the most stellar on the lot), and greeting millionaires with aplomb is your fate with this individual.

Your lover's home may truly be a castle, for this can be a very wealthy combination. And in this humble mansion you're treated as well as you might wish, for stingy is not in his or her vocabulary. If you're the kind of person who can read the more tender sentiments into a lavish gesture, then you'll fare very well. If not, you can try to explain your need for tenderly articulated verbal declarations of love—offered with sincerity and a single long-stem rose. The next morning you might waken to find a giant horseshoe of flowers adorning your lawn while an orchestra of tuxedo-clad musicians plays *I Love You Truly.*

In bed, this lover spends hours engaging in sensual, sybaritic pleasures. Jacuzzi for two followed by slow, sexy explorations of each other's erogenous zones—and trying to set a record based on newly discovered points of pleasure—is only the beginning of the evening. This is one person who really does everything to the hilt, and that most emphatically includes sex. Few other partners have the stamina and sensuality of Taurus-Leo. Even if you're too exhausted to participate equally, your lover just carries you along to greater heights of physical pleasure. You may moan, "Stop," and "Don't stop," concurrently, but you'll surely moan!

Venus in Taurus with Mars in Virgo

This is a very earthy combination. You love to touch and be touched, and you can think of a thousand detailed ways to accomplish this. Your sexuality is a naturally expressed part of your everyday life. Your surroundings are quite important to you, and you probably have excellent taste, filling your home with many finely crafted items made of only the finest materials. Perhaps you created some of them yourself.

A permanent relationship is very important to you. Being with the right person makes all the difference in a happy life—not to mention a fulfilling sex life. Although you feel that you could find satisfaction with pretty much any lover who's willing to spend more than a few minutes at the act—you know that chemistry makes a difference and you want to be with that person with whom you're compatible. Just looking into each other's eyes and sharing mutual desires and tastes is what it's all about.

Your Taurus-Virgo lover seeks a serene and companionable relationship. It should feel easy when you first connect, as though you've known each other all your lives. You laugh at the same things, have compatible points of view, and just feel comfortable together. If you meet and instantly sense that this could become something real, then you're on the right track. You don't have to be coy or alluring—just be your warm, natural, appealing self, and chemistry will do the rest.

In bed, Taurus-Virgo is very careful in attending to all the details of your affair or marriage, whatever the case may be. Nothing is spared to create an atmosphere in which you can experience sensual good times. The air is fragrant, the sheets luxe and perfumed, the candles lit and softly glowing in a beautifully appointed room. Setting the scene is just the beginning. Might you enjoy long, lazy hours of tender caresses? Do you want a back rub, a champagne bubble bath for two, a woodland repast in a serene corner of a very lush forest?

Sex is so easy and natural to this sensual individual that you begin to wonder why other people ever make such a fuss. Bodies merging in a symphony of pleasure is no more than we all might expect as beautifully natural. Your Taurus-Virgo lover discovers every combination of pleasures, from A to Z and back, that are the very essence of lovemaking, not just for everyone, but for you in particular. And that's a really wonderful way to live.

Venus in Taurus with Mars in Libra

Relationships are very important to you and you care deeply about your connection with a significant other. You're sensual and passionate and you want to connect with the perfect mate so you can have a long-lasting relationship. Sometimes this works out, but sometimes you become enamored, or distracted, or simply you change your mind. When this happens it feels frustrating, because your heart seeks constancy, and even to be able to possess a mate. You want what you want and you hope the other person will give it to you.

The question is, whose side are you on? Sometimes you yearn to be adored selfishly without worrying about the other person's needs, but you realize that's the sort of love for which you have to pay, and which ends when the evening does. You know there should be compromise, but that also feels uncomfortable. So early on you realize that the key to happiness is in finding someone with whom you can have the perfect rapport, someone whose values match your own, whose desires mirror your own, and who wants what you want when you want it. Nobody can dispute that as a recipe for happiness and success, can they! You like your pleasure in an elegant atmosphere and a tasteful and tasty lover.

Your Taurus-Libra lover can present a number of challenges. It can be confusing to deal with someone who wants to be allowed to be selfish but is guilty for feeling that way. On the other hand, this mate believes in love and romance wholeheartedly, and wants a commitment that lasts a lifetime. That's positive going in, if you want the same thing, for at least you know you're not dealing with someone who wants an evening, not the morning after. Share beautiful meals of fine food, soft lights, lilting music. Dance, allowing yourselves to melt into each other's arms. The trappings of romance are very important to this mate. And install a Ping-Pong table so you have an acceptable way to work our your competitive urges. Sometimes a healthy dose of competition goes a long way toward promoting harmony and peace.

And don't forget sex, either. A lively, well-animated sex life has kept the boxing gloves off more couples than all the diamonds in the world. Taurus-Libra loves sex but sometimes feels a little hesitant about making the first move. He or she'd rather respond with a quiver of excitement, once you provide the stimulus and attention. Go ahead and try it—make a pass. Lavish your lover with the physical evidence of your affection. Not only will he or she love every minute of the experience, but you'll be adored more than ever for caring so much, and that's better than any Ping-Pong game either of you might win.

Venus in Taurus with Mars in Scorpio

With this combination, your life can be a violent seesaw of passionate assignations and impassioned quarrels. Although you're aware as much as anyone of your need to have a relationship, having one doesn't always come with ease. It requires hard work and much compromise, and that is often your greatest hurdle.

You're stubborn, willful, as well as passionate and sensual. You go after what you want with persistence and determination, and you aren't often swayed from your goals before they're met.

Sex is one of your favorite pastimes, for you love the indulgent sensuality of lovemaking as well as the passionate melding together that is a part of sex as you see it. Probably because you're so sexy, you can get away with all sorts of unreasonable behavior that would end anyone else's relationship.

You want to possess your lover, body and soul, and the way in which you do it can be a totally enthralling experience, so much so that you may not get the chance to learn much-needed lessons of live and let live that are implicit in this placement. Although on the surface you may not seem as formidable as other people do, there is an air of emotional intensity about you, a sense of power seething far below the surface that all but the most casual of acquaintances will sense. Obviously this makes seduction a relatively easy prospect, but in fact you seek constancy and devotion more than conquest, and want the mate you can hold in your soul as well as in your arms.

The person who loves a Taurus-Scorpio must be totally loyal in every way. Even harmless flirtations are out of the question. This is the type of person who might become jealous and tie you to the bed, which might not be so bad, but he or she would likely leave you there—alone.

You need to learn to walk a tightrope. Find a way to combine the qualities of the innocent ingénue (so your lover can have fun overwhelming you) with your own perfectly apparent inner strength (so he or she never loses respect for you). Find ways to cater to your partner's needs, both sexually and physically. Plump up the pillows, give a refreshing foot massage, prepare favorite treats. Share your erotic fantasies and be ready to act them out.

Your Taurus-Scorpio lover provides you with many hours of the most impassioned interaction of your life. Once you're accustomed to this intense brand of relating, other people may seem dull.

These are the mates who refuse to speak to you for a week (after a slight you may have forgotten), then turn around to spend a night overwhelming you with passion. Tender caresses followed by sharp bites, pinches, and scratches are just the beginning. What choice do you have but to acquiesce? But then, if a calmer style of loving was what you sought, you would have fled long ago.

Venus in Taurus with Mars in Sagittarius

Having a nice body and doing physical things are very important to you. When you're participating in athletics (particularly outdoors), you feel good about yourself and about your body. Sports and outdoor activities give you the outlet you need to express yourself and maintain a feeling of freedom that is essential for you to be happy.

You want to have a permanent liaison, since your feelings for your partner are strong and durable, but often you find yourself at odds with this desire for stability in a relationship versus your acknowledged need for unfettered freedom. As soon as you begin to feel obliged to behave in a prescribed way, or sense that you're in any way becoming fenced in, you take off, although you may feel as badly as the lover you leave behind.

Dating and trying on new people is almost a hobby—in your youth, but eventually you realize that you want to settle in with someone, as long as it's the right person, someone who shares your passions and your ideals. You recognize that sometimes you have itchy feet, and your sensual nature does lead you astray, so if you can find a mate who's willing to forgive an occasional transgression, you'd prefer it.

Your Taurus-Sagittarius lover presents an interesting combination of earthy sensuality and fiery idealism. He or she may try a first bid at seduction as you sit outdoors under a tree sharing idealistic interests. Suddenly Taurus-Sagittarius notices how nice your body is and then reaches over casually to stroke whatever part has captured his or her fancy. One thing then leads to another.

Taurus-Sagittarius prefers never to feel tied down, but don't be surprised if this freedom-loving individual needs to feel totally secure about your affections. "Where were you last Thursday night," your lover inquires casually, as though it doesn't matter in the least. You can bet that it does matter—a lot. This mate just isn't really sure how to act jealous and how to deal with those feelings, unavoidable as they may be.

Go fishing together. Prepare a delicious picnic for the two of you to share on some grassy knoll. Make sure the blanket you pack is extra thick so you'll be comfortable engaging in post-picnic passion. Being outdoors just naturally arouses this individual. But then, you must be a bit of a woods sprite yourself, or you'd be barking up some other tree.

Venus in Taurus with Mars in Capricorn

With this combination, you may be determined to acquire all the material goods you ever desired, and you have the discipline and determination to achieve this goal. The accepted social order is plenty good enough for you—after all, it never prevented deserving individuals from becoming millionaires in the past, did it?

Wealth and status are important criteria to you, and you want a mate who shares this ethos. Obviously you're interested in love and sex, for who wants to go through life alone—going on a luxury cruise is less fun without a partner. And a good sex life not only is the best possible recreation, but the perfect way to release those workday tensions. You like the idea of being in a committed relationship, of having that mate on whom you can always rely, who will always be there for you. And it's nice to have another income too.

As you see it, you want a partner and together you'll be in harness—pulling the cart of your life and achievements together. You enjoy and appreciate chemistry, but what you seek is someone who fulfills your needs in every area of life—a true helpmate who's essential to the multi-dimensional, happy life you seek.

Your Taurus-Capricorn lover is earthy and sensual in bed. He or she delights in the physical expression of love and can be quite adept at providing a memorable sexual experience for any partner. This mate loves to touch, and to be touched, and will probably enjoy sharing a satin-covered bed with you. The sheets alone cost a thousand dollars. The bon bons beside the bed cost a bundle. As did the designer throw pillows. Isn't it all wonderful?

This mate sees that you have every material pleasure the world has to offer. You receive jewels, silks, and the finest of everything, as befits his or her partner. Your children attend the finest schools, your house is impressive...you get the idea. But what about tender sentiments? As sexy and sensual as this mate can be, often he or she sees the expression of affection in terms of things—gifts—so if you can translate that into *I love you*, you're all set. Order an in-home massage as a prelude to lovemaking so you both feel relaxed and happy. The more physical intimacy you share, the more it enhances the total lifestyle this mate wants to build of beautiful luxury shared with someone who appreciates the good life.

Venus in Taurus with Mars in Aquarius

You'd like a beautiful, warm relationship, but often it doesn't seem to be something you can manage, possibly because the concept, however lovely, is just too old-fashioned for someone as trendsettingly modern as yourself. It's not that you lack for sexual partners. You're warm and friendly enough to attract many potential mates.

You can be incredibly stubborn and fixed in your behavior, partly because you're determined to go your own way. Sometimes you just want to be different, period. But sometimes your motivations are to find a new way to be and to act that will enhance life for everyone on the planet. It's just that other people sometimes have difficulty in recognizing this about you. They usually like you, however.

You like to engage in sexual activity in improbable places and at odd times. For you, it's a lot of fun to be a little unconventional and a little shocking. You want to make it fun, beyond the ordinary. In your heart of hearts you'd like something stable and long-lasting, and if you can find the person who gives you space yet wraps you up in love, you might just sign on the dotted line.

Your Taurus-Aquarius lover wants to be surrounded by nice things and to relax enough to be really sensual. It's just that the idea of doing it seems so boringly conventional that it's rejected automatically. If a group of people were engaging in an orgy to promote world brotherhood, that would be another matter.

If you can come up with an intellectual reason to justify ordinary revelries, then your partner is not as likely to protest. So what if your home is outrageously luxurious, your bed delightfully soft, your body fragrantly perfumed in anticipation. Simply point out that, after all, the new style in sex is a quick grapple. Nobody has the oomph needed to engage in sexual marathons any more. And that's why there's so much war.

"No kidding, I can see your point," says your paramour as he or she rapidly peels off layers of clothing and steers you toward the bedroom, ready to make love for hours in the interest of world peace.

Venus in Taurus with Mars in Pisces

With this combination, you may often feel like snuggling down into your cushy nest, pulling up the covers, and having a sugary snack. You love people, and they often like to confide in you, but it feels so good to be at home that you really prefer they come to you. Did I say you were lazy? Of course I'd never be that mean, but other people might, for your tendency toward indolence is legendary, something that can be very nice when you're enjoying a weekend in bed.

You're very sensitive, and if one of the people you love has a problem, you just seem to absorb it, which can be helpful for him or her, but really tiring for you and the reason why you enjoy those solitary naps—they clear your heart and restore your spirit. When you really love someone, you want to take care of that person, to share your delicious food, to provide good company in your lovely home, in general to help make your beloved feel good and happy. If you can find someone who will return the favor, you're in heaven. A relationship of mutual tenderness and nurturing is what you seek and you can picture yourself happily devoted for decades, growing old together, smiling, and taking care of each other.

Your Taurus-Pisces lover is a quiet, good-natured soul who needs to be around calm and sensitive people who won't take advantage of a kind heart. He or she loves for you to demonstrate your affection by buying presents or making treats. Obviously this mate requires persuasion to come jogging with you or to go bike riding. Instead, you might choose to languish poolside, if the day isn't too hot or the place too crowded. Outdoor activity is the perfect restorative, but sometimes this mate lacks the get up and go to want to participate—unless you make it sound enticing.

The same is true of sex—this is a sensual lover who isn't necessarily dynamically physical. You won't be swinging from any chandeliers, and as sweet and totally tender as this mate is, the kind of sex that leaves the partners too physically exhausted to speak just isn't his or her style. Instead you'll make love in slow motion. Lots of cuddling combined with long, luxurious caresses, and plenty of kisses may sometimes be enough. No matter whether he or she wants the full experience or just the foreplay, this mate will work very hard to please you in any way possible, for Taurus-Pisces is very giving.

Have faith in this mate, be sensitive to tender feelings, lend an understanding ear to difficult problems, and offer lots of soothing foot massages. Your bird in a gilded cage needs as much from you as he or she always gives back.

Venus in Gemini-Mars Combinations

Venus in Gemini with Mars in Aries

This is a very restless, highly fidgety combination that will not easily incline you to a committed relationship or to a long one, not without very strong indicators from other planets in your horoscope. In your world, it's more about the fun, right now, this minute. You're a friendly, fast-paced individual who loves to be first to experience all kinds of new things. You won't allow anyone to tie you down, hold you back, or set the pace, because chances are things will go agonizingly slowly with anyone else at the helm.

You love a spirited debate involving art or intellectual issues, and you may be infamous for your ability to blow up in an angry storm of words and then to cool off again before anyone realizes what hit you. You're definitely not a team player, even a team as small as two. Although you need and enjoy company and social interaction very much, you hate anything that can complicate your life or threaten your freedom.

You love dating, as long as it's not limiting in any way. You may often find yourself starting several relationships within the same time frame, and then moving on to start others. As soon as you sense routine (or the specter of permanence) setting in, you're off, like TV's Zorro, who charged in, made his Z, and got out.

Your Gemini-Aries lover enters your life in a flash of speedy action and sparkling conversation. You spend the evening in a fast car, engaged in fast repartee. But unless you're as much of a singleton as this swift-of-foot individual, you're liable to be left with nothing more than melancholy memories. How do you get this person to settle down? Easy. You don't. The Gemini-Aries people desiring permanent liaisons can be counted on the sixth toe of your third foot. Well, it may not be quite that bad.

Say you feel really uneasy about the prospect of a white picket fence, daily battles with dirty diapers, the same face across the breakfast table morning after morning. You're in the right league. You can stop feeling guilty about the fact that normal people have to grow up sometime and assume day-to-day responsibilities. Some normal people prefer to be vagabonds, hitchhiking across Europe, visiting every interesting spot, and meeting all the people who might never wander into a fenced-in yard. Some perfectly normal people maintain relationships for years, although they don't always live together the whole time or feel the need to remain faithful. The point is that it's normal for them as long as they feel happy about it.

Gemini-Aries demands a life of freedom and changeability, and as long as those are your needs too, you have the chance of establishing a tradition-free relationship with an exciting person who'll never be staid, boring, or commonplace. And if there are more sensitive factors in other parts of this mate's horoscope, perhaps it could endure longer than a blink of the eye.

Venus in Gemini with Mars in Taurus

There are many incompatible elements in the way you like to relate. You want to be free to move on, to experience new ideas and new people, but you don't always have the physical hastiness and speed to enact this inclination. Oftentimes, you might prefer a cozy evening for two with good food, good wine, and soft music, but somehow this seems so boring that you can't quite enjoy it.

In love and in life, you don't like to feel tied down by people or possessions, yet you just seem to acquire more things than feels logical. Perhaps you have an enormous book collection. Whatever your indulgence, sometimes you feel as though you're burying yourself in things, when what you really care about is ideas.

In your mind is the idea of the grand love affair, the connection so profound that it's possible for it to endure, because you each strike such a chord of fascination in the other that years pass and you never tire of looking into each other's eyes. That to you is the ideal, and you hope to find it one day. Of course it also helps if the person you adore doesn't mind when you're off flirting with someone else for a while.

Your Gemini-Taurus lover needs a lively atmosphere with fascinating people and stimulating ideas. A cocktail party with interesting guests, a good movie, and a book of light verse are all things that are appreciated and help contribute to the stability of your relationship. For although this man or woman seems steady, he or she demands the assurance of plenty of freedom before making a commitment to settle down with you.

You need to be able to walk a tightrope of freedom versus stability. Can you seem unavailable and at the same time devotedly his or hers? Can you project a mental sparkle without having to roam the world on foot? Can you be super fast and super slow simultaneously? That's the enigma of Gemini-Taurus, and living with it can present quite a challenge.

In bed, Gemini-Taurus is often at odds. This mate might enjoy hours of lazy sex, but he or she often seems mentally or emotionally distracted part of the time. What results is some coitus interruptus. You make love for a while, take a break to watch TV or to talk, and then resume the physical activity. If you're the kind of lover who can maintain your passion during the sexual pit stops, then you might discover that this style of loving is guaranteed to keep you turned on twenty-four hours a day. If, on the other hand, you like to finish what you start in an orderly progression of foreplay, sex, and afterplay, then you may be ready to look elsewhere. It's all up to you.

Venus in Gemini with Mars in Gemini

This is the fastest, most fleet-footed romantic combination in the Zodiac. The problem is, you're probably not very interested in relationships, not the traditional ones, anyway. You dislike anything that smacks of gooey emotionalism, and even sex may be too prolonged and too intense for your tastes. You might prefer porn to actual human interaction, phone sex to in-person sex, or fantasy to reality. That doesn't mean you don't like people or the sparkle of romance, but rather that you never quite could buy into the happily ever after part of the story, for that is the part where the humdrum sets in.

You're smart and have a wonderful way with words. Your jokes can keep us all laughing, and your light verse may well grace the inside of a number of greeting cards. Because you demand so much variety to keep yourself from getting bogged down or bored, you frequently leave many things unfinished, and amorous adventures are no different. It's not that you're unfriendly, you just need variety to survive. You're content to date someone new every day of the week. You like beginnings way more than middles and the ring of familiarity feels more like a noose than something you want to settle into comfortably.

In you have more security-seeking elements in your horoscope, it's your challenge to find a way to have permanence in your love life without feeling smothered by it.

Your Gemini-Gemini lover will seldom promise you forever, and even tomorrow afternoon at five P.M. is highly doubtful. He or she may adore you (in an intellectual, unemotional way), but the response to a request for a definite date may sound a lot like, "Don't fence me in." This individual isn't really romance oriented, and to him or her, hearts and flowers may well be just a design motif. This mate may be eighty years old, but still feels the urge to move along and check out new points of interest.

In bed, you may often talk rather than make love, for he or she is just not that sensual. And if you are, then you must find a way to acquaint your lover with the pleasure possibilities of his or her own body, or you have to feel free to have physical relations with somebody else. That's okay, for jealousy is just a word to Gemini-Gemini.

The only way to survive with a lover like this is to be someone who likes variety in your own life. Being a casual swinger who wants to experience a great many people will help you maintain your cool when your partner refuses to heat up. Or heats up and cools down at a rate that is too fast to provide you with satisfaction. This person invented the quickie. So even if you both choose to spend time with other people, as long as you each keep discovering new and interesting facets of the other, there will always be a reason to get together.

Venus in Gemini with Mars in Cancer

It's sometimes difficult for you to reconcile your needs for lightness and frivolity with your very emotional nature. It's as if you wish you could manage a pleasant flirtation but someone keeps messing things up with heavy emotionalism, and that someone is you. You can be very moody at times, and when you're in one of your lows, it's hard for you to sparkle and crack jokes, even if you really do want to. At other times, you confuse yourself with the intensity of your own feelings. It somehow seems out of place.

You like charming, intelligent people who enjoy expressing ideas and having fun. The problem is that sometimes, without even thinking, someone will make a casual remark that unintentionally hurts your feelings. Either you feel too silly to say something or you just ignore the slight because you don't enjoy expressing anger. When you're integrating your outgoing self with your sensitive self, you have the ability to combine your chatty intellectuality with a great deal of emotional sensitivity, which can make you a terrifically interesting partner. You just always know the right thing to say to make a mate feel better.

Your Gemini-Cancer lover needs to have a rewarding relationship and to feel free from the boredom of being tied down. Although he or she may seem a bit fickle, in fact your mate truly needs the security of a home and family to feel happy.

Be supportive while you're being scintillating. Invite your lover to family gatherings, the bigger the better. Go to the zoo or visit a playground. Gemini-Cancer loves to communicate with children. Be flexible. Be sensitive without seeming gooey. Be patient when this mate gets into one of those emotional phases that he or she actually despises. Buy Gemini-Cancer a cheering book of clever love sonnets and offer a little TLC.

In bed, this mate can be lots of fun, and you should have a

good time as well. You giggle and play games like hide and seek under the covers, and have tickling contests. Your lover thinks sex should be a really good time as well as a process of deep emotional sharing, combined with heavy doses of ego-massage, which it's your pleasure to provide. In return you get a lover who likes to amuse you with a clever turn of phrase or a witty remark, and who has the emotional sensitivity to pay real attention to your needs. And that's a mate who's worth keeping.

Venus in Gemini with Mars in Leo

This is a highly unemotional combination. You aren't pining at home for the lack of a lover, nor are you likely to go out with your violin to serenade a prospective mate. Instead you like to be at the center of a lively gathering, enjoying yourself around people who interest and respect you.

You seek a mate who is both interesting and worthy of the notice and respect of the other people in your life. You want friends and family to give a resounding thumbs up to any prospective date or mate.

As much as you enjoy socializing and people in general, you demand the right to express yourself as you see fit, and refuse to be tied down by anyone at all. It's easy for you to maintain this posture, because establishing a permanent relationship with those matching wedding bands isn't your number-one priority. In fact, avoiding one may be if you have a busy social life and many friends with whom you regularly hang out.

You have a great deal of intellectual pride, and you love expressing your ideas, particularly to an admiring audience. You may write for the theater or teach children. Whatever you do, you're at your best when in front of an interested audience, as long as it cannot constrain or restrict you in any way. That's not to say you disbelieve in marriage or permanent commitment, for you have the ability to offer devotion within a stable connection. You just want to make sure the person will hold your interest for as long as it lasts.

Your Gemini-Leo lover is lots of fun to be around. You go out frequently, socializing and enjoying yourselves. Lying around at home watching TV is no way to spend a Saturday night, not with this firecracker mate.

In bed, plan on much fast-moving excitement that centers on your lover. This combination is likely to love the idea of having a harem, whether male or female, so beware! He or she may like to go to swing clubs or to have sexual encounters with multiple partners, all of whom focus on him or her. If it's just the two of you, some spice is needed to keep it interesting in an ongoing fashion, that is if you're determined to share fidelity and a one-to-one relationship, so make the effort to be spectacularly enthralling and to vary your approach. Dressing in costumes, acting out fantasies, and reading sexy books together in bed (then playing out the parts) are good ways to begin.

You must be serious about the way you treat this mate. Although he or she loves witty repartee, avoid teasing or jokes at your lover's expense. This individual refuses to be bossed or dominated. You'd be far better off to follow his or her lively lead than to try to take the helm of this relationship. Gemini-Leo tries hard to live up to your every expectation, so as long as you have a high opinion of your lover, and chances are that you'll be rewarded with behavior that justifies your positive feelings.

Venus in Gemini with Mars in Virgo

With this combination you're both fast and careful about details. This ability allows you to do painstaking work both quickly and well. You're probably an excellent artisan, or a craftsman of no little ability. Although you like to be free to avoid emotional entanglements, you want to be a very responsible individual, and you usually try to finish what you start.

In all sorts of relationships, even those uncomplicated by romantic issues, you may have a measure of difficulty in connecting in a harmonious way. First of all, you're not particularly emotional or relationship-oriented; and secondly, you can tend to be critical and intolerant of others, no matter how well you like them. When sex is involved, it complicates things further.

When involved in a romance, you need to find a mate who can maintain your interest without overwhelming you, and then you might be willing to settle down. The only real question is do you want to do it, or are you happier enjoying casual social interactions as they're presented to you. Sometimes it feels happy just to pursue your own interests independent of a mate. But if you become enamored with someone quick and clever, who is also smart and reliable—basically the counterpart of yourself, well, it could work.

Your Gemini-Virgo lover is smart, no question about it. He or she has clever ideas and careful techniques in implementing them. This can extend to your relationship as well. Long before boredom sets in, your mate comes up with inspired ideas to put some new sparkle into your romance.

In bed, this individual likes to keep things light, but earthy as well. Your lover may be willing to tickle your back, give foot massages or just snuggle while chatting. Gemini-Virgo likes to touch as well as talk, and doing favors for loved ones just comes naturally, so you can be the beneficiary of much physical TLC. Your partner goes to great trouble to please you and keep you interested as long as you're never too intense, emotional, or demanding. He or she may buy you a handmade book, a fancy new digital device, or a recording of love poems—or limericks. You might consider returning the favor. A thoughtful indication of your affection is appreciated, particularly when the presents are interesting and useful. Those may well be the bywords for Gemini-Virgo. Where else could you find a lover who can type ninety words a minute while offering suggestions about how to reorganize your home office?

Venus in Gemini with Mars in Libra

You love to be around people, talking and socializing. It's so much fun for you to be with your friends when everybody is having a good time. It's important for you to feel that there is harmony in your environment, that nobody is restricted to anybody else, and that everyone is free to enjoy the activity. The basic atmosphere of unfettered socializing indigenous to a cruise ship is the one you'd choose full-time, if you could.

You're an easygoing individual who has no desire to be involved in a relationship that seems heavy, overly intense, or in which one partner dominates the other. You'd much rather be part of a happy, fun-filled group, where everybody is fond of each other and is cheerful to be around.

Although you can reach for what you want, you never seem assertive, but rather gentle and sparkling. You do enjoy collaborating with someone else, because cooperation is so important to you. However, that other person should be mellow and easy going, because you don't want anyone's emotional garbage heaped on your head.

Your Gemini-Libra lover is artistic and literary. He or she may be a poet, a writer, or a social director, for this individual always has something charming and interesting to say and can provide any gathering with pleasant companionship and good conversation. Always fair and friendly, your lover is interested in seeing that people are well treated and enjoying themselves. Never one to be possessive or domineering, he or she prefers to keep any relationship light and harmonious.

If you're hoping for a long-term relationship with Gemini-Libra, you probably want a pleasant companion who likes to have fun and wishes to get along peacefully with you and everyone else. A passionate, intense lover who sweeps you off your feet and engulfs you forever, you haven't found. But not everyone likes to deal with overwhelming intensity. Go with Gemini-Libra on a tour of art museums, attend gallery openings, and go to theater previews. Buy beautiful art books, theater subscriptions, French lessons. Being wooed in French can amp up the passion in even the most bland romance, which yours certainly isn't, but this single step can soon have you both saying, "Vive l'amour."

Venus in Gemini with Mars in Scorpio

It's easy for you to connect with others, and you can do it in any number of ways. You enjoy verbal interactions and those around you appreciate the way your conversation sparkles with wit. To those less communicative souls, you can be magical, alluring, and very sexual. It's all in the flexibility you bring to every encounter.

You feel social interaction is very valuable, in part because it provides you with new levels of knowledge about the universe and yourself. This is why you need so many people and so many types of involvements. Though others may dislike your romantic flexibility and say that you should make a commitment and stick to it, you recognize that your life is not just a series of one-night stands for the purpose of fun and games. You're making real progress through your involvements, and sometimes a relationship does not need to last forever to be satisfying, meaningful, and important. You also recognize that it's possible to maintain a number of very rewarding ties with different partners at the same time. Whatever you share is important to you both, and it is not diminished in quality or meaning because it isn't the only relationship in your life.

Does this mean you're unavailable for a permanent tie? Of course not. You're basically a steady person, and being connected and committed feels relatively natural to you. You just also enjoy flirting—a lot—and you like the idea of seeing that look in someone's eyes when you've been particularly enchanting and seductive. Whether you act on it or not depends on how attached you are to a partner who might be a one-and-only.

Your Gemini-Scorpio lover can be a lot to handle, particularly if you're looking for single-minded devotion and forever after. While it's possible that you may forge a bond with this individual that remains vibrant and satisfying for the rest of your lives, it's unlikely that it's the only relationship in his or her life, so if you're prone to possessiveness or jealousy, another mate might be a better fit.

If, on the other hand, you're open to all sorts of experiences and growth that multiple involvements, many partners, and unchallenged variety can provide, stick around.

This partner often seems to be more than one person. Some nights you're treated to no more than good conversation in bed. Then, when you've concluded that such an asexual person could hardly be the gadabout described above, your lover decides to get physical.

Then you may be amazed to discover the number of tricks, techniques, and thrills that this mate considers routine in bed. It all depends on your relationship and what the best way to communicate with you is in the current moment. So if you enjoy surprises and are never tempted to learn where all this expertise was acquired, this is one partner you can count on never to bore you.

Venus in Gemini with Mars in Sagittarius

Nobody knows better than you the necessity for compromise in relationships. You've spent much time pondering the philosophical implications of relationships of all types, and you understand the principle of give and take very well. The only problem is that it's so restricting. And everybody knows that there's no such thing as compromise—not without giving up much of your freedom much of the time. And while you may be a great expert on the nature of relationships, you may well have concluded from all your studies that they're just too much trouble and too personally limiting for you.

You want to be free to meet everybody who interests you, to talk with all sorts of fascinating people, and to get to know their ideas and their philosophies of life. You love to experience new things, and having one permanent partner puts severe limitations on your ability to experience the richness and variety of the ever-fascinating human race. You love travel of all kinds, and you're truly at your best when outdoors, whether you're having a good discussion, a picnic, or competing in a sporting event.

Impulsive, you're the kind of person who could start out

on a walk through the woods and end up on a cross-country hike. The important thing to you is to keep moving. Being bogged down or hemmed in is the worst thing that could happen to anyone, and you're determined to see that it doesn't happen to you.

Your Gemini-Sagittarius lover is probably a better friend than a permanent mate. Permanence is not in this individual's vocabulary, for it is just too stifling a concept. You may have been regaled by your lover at one time or another on the subject of monogamy and the numerous ills caused by that dreaded custom. So if you want to keep this idealistic dreamer around, keep it light. Maintain your own individuality and your own interests. Don't even suggest buying sleeping bags that can be zipped together.

Obviously he or she believes in maintaining the freedom to sleep with anyone at all. In bed, you have fun, and the one-night stand holds no evil connotations for this determined explorer. Sex should be fun, light, relaxing, enjoyable communication between two people, but just because you enjoy sleeping together, there's no automatic assumption of any commitment at all. Gemini-Sagittarius can't understand all the heavy, serious sentiments that often accompany sex. Why complicate the issue?

Go hiking, camping, and to political rallies. See movies set in exotic locations. Have fun—while it lasts, and if you're the same freedom-loving type of individual, you may well have met the only "friend" you'd want to keep romancing day after day for as long as it feels new and interesting to you both.

Venus in Gemini with Mars in Capricorn

You may be quite reluctant to enter into close relationships for fear that the other person will introduce complications into your life and prevent you from concentrating on your goals. You're an ambitious, achievement-oriented individual who really gets involved in work.

You love to socialize, but tend to be disciplined enough to

enjoy a little free-wheeling chat at the water cooler and then back to work you go, even if everyone else is still gabbing.

Sometimes you wish you could just settle down with someone interesting so that when you have the urge to interact, there would be someone suitable available. You don't like being alone all the time, and although you don't mind dating, for it's fun to meet new people, it does often seem like a time waster. A commitment would be a good thing, but then you think about all the needs you might have to meet, and all the heavy emotions that could be thrust upon you, and you shrug and go back to work. It seems easier to concentrate on work full-time and your social life in brief little installments. If only you could find someone as ambitious and as clever as yourself, you'd settle down, and that's your goal. You know that's a good plan and some day you plan to make it your reality.

Has a Gemini-Capricorn caught your eye? Perhaps it was the way this individual started with something small and built it into something substantial. Perhaps it's the responsibility you sense below that friendly exterior. Maybe your potential lover is attracted to you, is friendly far beyond mere politeness when you meet by chance at office parties. But how do you get a date, and possibly a mate, when this object of your desires converses and retreats behind closed doors to work overtime?

You start out with a good idea that can increase productivity and interest at work. Submit it and suggest that the two of you can work on implementing it together. As the time passes and your project is working splendidly, the two of you become better acquainted. As you work late, night after night, you could suggest a post-work supper, ostensibly to discuss office matters. Eventually you might invite him or her to your home to review a project. Obviously it takes some planning to woo this individual, but the more time you spend together, the more appropriate it might seem for your all-business relationship to segue into romance.

What a surprise! Who would have guessed that this friendly workaholic would be so interesting in bed, with all that touching and those cute little remarks? Who would have thought that sex could be so earthy and so uncomplicated at the same time? You did, or you wouldn't have gone to so much trouble, would you!

Venus in Gemini with Mars in Aquarius

What you want far more than a husband, wife, or lover, is a friend who is there to share many good times with you and who never tries to tie you down or restrict you in any way. Actually you want many friends, for you're a group person, being far more at home when in the company of many friendly people who share your willingness to be exposed to all sorts of new and ground-breaking ideas.

You're happy to live in the moment and to share good times with anyone who happens to be in the room. You don't mind a quick tumble and you never quite get why people put so much strain onto the idea of sex. It can be so much fun— and darn good exercise, so why shouldn't people just live, love, and enjoy life.

You think about marriage and wonder is it for you. Having a roommate you like can be pretty nice on every level and it's possible that such a situation could turn into a romance, just because it takes you by surprise.

Your Gemini-Aquarius lover possesses a lively kind of verbal sparkle, and may well be the most interesting conversationalist you've ever met. Of course, there's more to love than a good chat, but you're not quite sure this mate is all about the romance.

Being intellectually enthralling as well as slightly unavailable piques the interest of Gemini-Aquarius. Be a pal. A good buddy. That's a far more comfortable format for romance with this mate.

Of course, romance may be nothing like what you're experiencing, as I hinted above. You go to political meetings. To cocktail parties to raise money for good causes. You overthrow governments, fight dictators, install world peace. Or at least you talk about doing all those things. And if that is your idea of romance, you've found the right partner.

In bed, you may never get around to making love. Sex isn't the number one priority of this individual, so it's up to you to plant the idea if you're interested in fireworks more often (and more personal) than what's in the sky on Independence Day. Gemini-Aquarius fantasizes often, so talking about sex may be a good first step. "Darling, I want to tell you about the most fascinating dream I had last night. I'm sure it must mean something, because it was so erotic. I just can't stop thinking about it. You were so different—so passionate, so intense, so sexy...." You get the idea. Fill in the blanks as you choose, and no, it doesn't have to be a real dream. Sometimes made up dreams are the best kind of all, and that's really something to which this mate can relate.

Venus in Gemini with Mars in Pisces

You're probably the best storyteller around. You may write poetry, film scripts, or at the least can invent the most fascinating fairy tale a child ever heard. You're so verbally creative that almost everyone is willing to excuse your mood swings and occasional physical languor. You don't like overly aggressive people, and you're glad not to be one. In your opinion, it's far better to stay home and keep to yourself when a dark mood strikes. At other times, you're thrilled to go out to a party and be a delightfully fun guest.

When it comes to romance, you prefer to be with someone who is easy going and cheerful, although you're not always available for a committed relationship. You get much satisfaction from casual, friendly interaction, and the alone time you have feels restorative.

If you do find a best friend who seems like someone with whom you belong, you're willing to make a commitment and see how it goes.

Your Gemini-Pisces lover is not always interested in a permanent relationship. Instead, this individual likes the closeness of the moment and, surprisingly, can move on, flowing with the changes of the environment and the people in it. If you want more than a romantic fling, be prepared to share. This guy or gal believes firmly in experiencing the moment as it presents itself and with whatever fascinating person comes along.

That goes for sex as well. He or she can easily be led down the primrose path by a new partner, so if you tend toward jealousy, beware. Sometimes casual socializing is enough to satisfy this mellow mate, so if you want a relationship that's more deeply erotic, be willing to orchestrate it. Setting the scene is the best way to start.

Organize a party by the sea in which everyone must dress up as his or her favorite character from literature. At the end of the evening, take your lover's hand, lead him or her gently around the corner to your own private sand dune, toss a handful of rose petals down on the sand for a blanket, and start writing sonnets of your own—with your bodies. For as long as Gemini-Pisces is enchanted, he or she is likely to hang around. And with all the effort you're putting into the magic that you're creating together, your lover simply won't have the energy to explore that primrose path with anyone but you.

Venus in Cancer-Mars Combinations

Venus in Cancer with Mars in Aries

You're a sensitive, nurturing person who nevertheless demands the freedom to act as you see fit, free from interference from anyone else. You're a high-energy individual, a born leader, who can set the pace for others without losing your sensitivity or emotional awareness. To you, life is complicated and you want richness in all dimensions. You need your freedom, but without someone special to come home to, what's it all worth? In your mind, the ideal is a happy, boisterous family, with two fun-loving parents at the helm.

When you choose a partner, the most important quality you seek is the ability to understand you and give you what you need. You don't want to be in a situation where someone is always having to compromise, although you mind it less when it's someone else making that choice. It just makes more sense to be compatible and to keep the quarrels to a minimum so that everyone enjoys life. You do know an occasional spat is likely and that's okay, for it can lead to some pretty exciting make-up sex.

You admit to being rather emotional, even tempestuous at times, but in your mind that just makes you exciting. Other people think so too, even if you are a bit of a whirlwind. Everything to you is a bit larger than life, and that makes it all way more fun.

Your Cancer-Aries lover can be simultaneously emotionally sensitive and excitingly independent. Despite the occasional attempts at bravado, this mate never loses sight of a sentimental interest in a home and family. Be prepared to provide much pampering and TLC and sometimes the favor will be returned, sometimes not.

He or she can find ways to make even the most ordinary pleasures sparkle with fun and excitement, and is naturally adept at bringing out the best in children. When Cancer-Aries looks for a partner, the goal is to find someone who wants to have good times yet who wants a family as well. Someone who loves adventure but also feels cozy at home is ideal. So pack a picnic and go on a motorcycle ride into the country. Toast marshmallows in front of your fireplace, or go to a family reunion. It never hurts to put a little excitement into ordinary pleasures.

And that's exactly how this mate feels about sex. You'll never forget just how adored you are, yet there is no lack of tremendous physical excitement. Cancer-Aries wants to swoop you up into a timeless time of tremendous passion and loving communion of two devotedly adoring lovers. The rest of the world is forgotten totally while the two of you are making love, for each time you do, you're reaffirming the commitment that bonds you together eternally.

Cancer-Aries wants a secure relationship in which two people share totally without either person ever having to sacrifice a bit of his or her individuality. And with devotion to romance that complete, you'll indeed share the kind of love that endures into eternity.

Venus in Cancer with Mars in Taurus

You're one of the most security-conscious, family oriented people around. You're sensitive, careful, and cautious, and absolutely everyone knows what a super parent and mate you are. Your home is the hub of many family (and perhaps neighborhood) activities, with you the radiant center. You're generous with your children and work hard and save to see that they never want for anything. People who are casual and callous about their offspring never cease to bewilder you.

You like to take your time where decisions are concerned, preferring to weigh all the options before you take action. Once you begin a project, you apply steady determination and careful effort, seeing that it almost always gets completed. You're possessive and jealous of the people you love, wanting to be sure that nothing interferes with their feeling for you. Sometimes this can be a problem with a partner, but it is likely that you attract the kind of person who desires a close relationship with very little need for independence of action or unquestioned freedom of movement.

You see a committed relationship as truly essential, for you desire the security of knowing that the person you love will always love you in return and be there to provide tenderness and nurturing.

Your Taurus-Cancer partner loves home, and particularly the kitchen, where you may find him or her cooking or eating twenty-four hours a day. You know the people who make love on the kitchen table? They're not always the sexual innovators; some are just homebodies with a love of hearth and home cooking. This calm and sentimental individual loves to smother you in gravy and home baked cookies. Luxuriate together in comfy sofas and chairs, cozy window seats, a porch swing, all placed to create that *Home Sweet Home* atmosphere. In order for the calm to remain, watch your tongue, for hurt feelings are not infrequent with this combination, but expression of anger is a mighty difficult thing for Cancer-Taurus.

Your lover is an ardent acquirer. Shopping is so much fun for this mate, and holding onto everything just seems prudent. There's no such thing as drowning in stuff to him or her. If you're the beloved, there's a bit of a sense that you too are a possession. It's just this mate's way of showing love. Buy a present, for as you surmised, Cancer-Taurus loves things. A framed portrait of the two of you together is a wonderful offering. A picture book of adorable children, a carefree movie, or a batch of treats that are (or taste) homemade are all approval-generating gifts.

Invite your prospective mate home for a cozy evening (you'd be crazy to consider this cuddly family type as anything other than a future husband or wife no matter how splendid the fireworks between the sheets). Relax and enjoy the family atmosphere you create together. You'll never fly off to breakfast in Paris at a moment's notice, but who can complain about living in a recreated version of Ozzie and Harriet in these fast-paced, hectic times.

In bed, things are slow, luxurious, and sensual. You may spend the entire weekend enjoying foreplay, or reading one of those tantric sex books and trying them out. This is a sensuous, physical lover, and together you explore all the many dimensions and delightful complications your bodies can offer.

Venus in Cancer with Mars in Gemini

You care about your home and family, but you need to be free to come and go as you please, because you hate to get bogged down. Just because you don't always feel like staying home, doesn't mean that you aren't thinking about your partner and family, for you take happy thoughts of them wherever you go. You recognize that sometimes people get bored, and even that it's easy to be tempted to dip your toe in another pond, but if you're happy and in love with a mate, you try not to do that. Although you need variety, you need security in equal measure and you hope to build a relationship that gives you the best of both.

Fun is a part of your nature, and you'll always be joyful and playful. You want to share good times with a mate and to enjoy each other's little quirks. Perhaps you love children so much because your inner child is so vibrant and lively, and you'll always be that way. Romance to you isn't something heavy with annoying violins playing as they do in all the clichés. Instead it's about people who enjoy each other's company bringing out the best in one another and in the moments they share, day to day.

Your Cancer-Gemini lover is a lot of fun. You'll enjoy hearing amusing stories about people you both know, and going out with a bunch of close friends or family to have a good time. A vivacious mental sparkle enlivens all this individual's conversation, including the clever little phrases, stories, or limericks made up for the amusement of kids, or people with youthful mental outlooks. This guy or gal can be eighty years old but will always radiate a quality of youthful good cheer. Such ingenuous ways can be charming and delightful even to people who are blasé sophisticates.

If you want a permanent romance with Cancer-Gemini,

take the time to get to know his or her interests and avocations, and see what appeals to you. Go on lots of outings, buy picture books, build sand castles, and read mystery stories together. Before you know it, you'll be taking pictures of your own kids and packing for Disneyland.

In bed, your lover is the same as everywhere else— sensitive and interested in having a good time. You'll be regaled with little jokes and share laughter and puns in between the hugs and cuddling. Forget a deep, intense melding of souls when you can feel that you're sharing the most exciting ride at the best amusement park around. And he or she never for a moment forgets to take your needs into consideration, despite a natural hastiness about sex. If you need more time, your lover might be persuaded to slow down until you catch up. Communication is the key.

Venus in Cancer with Mars in Cancer

You're a highly emotional person, and you need to feel security and love in order to be happy and able to act effectively. Your family is the most important thing to you, and you work very hard to see that they're happy and well taken care of. You love romance and pretty dreams, and can be a wonderfully giving partner. Because your intuition is so keen, it is easy for you to discern what would most please your lover, and doing all sorts of nice little (and big) things for a mate gives you unlimited pleasure.

Children are your favorite people. The idea of yourself as a caring, nurturing human being, and especially a parent, is one of the most basic components of your self-image. You long to have a good marriage and to start a family, and nothing will deter you from this goal. In fact, you may have scared off a few potential mates on the first date by asking if they liked children, but to you that's just fine because you know what you want and eliminating the losers early on saves time.

Being single feels sort of sad to you and as you look around and see friends who love the dating scene and enjoy all those one-night stands, you can't imagine how that is a positive means of living. To you, it's all about finding the soulmate who will become part of you, like a picture in your heart, permanently there, providing a foundation of love and security, someone you can cherish for the rest of your life. Not until you connect with that person does it feel as though your life has truly begun.

Your Cancer-Cancer lover is one of the really special people in the world. Careful never to hurt your feelings—and you should return that favor, for he or she is very sensitive— this mate loves to take care of you, whether during the flu or on long, cozy evenings in bed together, where your every desire is happily met.

Although this sweetie loves to have you come over for quiet evenings in front of a fire, turn the tables sometimes. Make an effort to please by preparing a home-cooked dinner, breakfast in bed, or planning a nice evening of dinner and a movie. Although a swinging disco is not a big favorite, Cancer-Cancer does love to be out in the world with a special someone. Bring your lover along to your family gatherings. The fact that you can provide an even larger network of devoted relatives for this family person makes you someone he or she cherishes even more.

In bed, Cancer-Cancer always concentrates on you, and is quite adept at discerning just what you need or want. Soft and sensitive, gentle and tender, no one combines sex with TLC so effectively, and if you love being the adored center of attention, this is your chance.

Venus in Cancer with Mars in Leo

You have the ability to combine the best of strong, self-confident leadership with emotional sensitivity. You feel that it's important to maintain high standards, and to uphold the expectations of your family and the other people who are close to you. You respect your parents and hope that they will respect and admire you, and these desires extend to your children as well.

Within your own group, you're the unquestioned leader, providing a sunny hub of energy about which everyone else can radiate. Although you do like to be a figurehead of strength, you never lose track of your feelings, nor do you wish to ignore the feelings of others. You seek a partner who supporst you in your efforts, without interference or questioning. Together you work to build a secure and pleasant home of which you can both be proud.

You just want to love and trust someone and feel that you're in it together for the long haul. Security and commitment are important to you, and you're willing to give a relationship your all in order to build a foundation for happiness that can last all your life long.

Your Cancer-Leo lover is thoughtful, kind, and generous. Occasionally domineering and stubborn, but more often displaying sensitivity and unwavering emotional involvement that temper these flaws substantially, your lover takes his or her own feelings seriously, and you would be well to do the same, for Cancer-Leo will not respond well at all to teasing or being made the brunt of someone else's jokes. A lack of respect on your part is the surest way to provoke anger. When you first start going out, Cancer-Leo woos you with a resolve that can be a little intimidating to anyone less used to ardor combined with determination. No expense is spared in making you feel special and appreciated.

Throw a party for your new love interest, so that you can show him or her off to friends and family. This partner loves being fussed over. Cancer-Leo also loves kids and enjoys any gathering that features interactions among the generations. Be prepared to enter a romance with a goal: marriage and children. In today's world of one-night stands, beware, for you may find yourself standing in line to win the heart of this energetic family person.

In bed, this terrific lover combines the best of emotional sensitivity with physical endurance. You feel special and very loved for hours and hours every night. Pleasing you pleases your partner, and being good in bed is a point of pride, so be ready for the best time of your life.

Venus in Cancer with Mars in Virgo

You're a gentle, emotional person who likes to take great care in everything you do. Your family is your greatest joy, as well as your most serious responsibility. But then you tend to be a serious person who regards meaningless frivolities as valueless. You like to feel that you're a person of substance.

It's hard for you to want to go out and have fun because so many activities that other people enjoy strike you as a waste of time. You'd rather combine fun with group activities—like a family project of some sort which promotes togetherness while it accomplishes something.

When you fall in love, you can sometimes idolize the person you care for, noting every detail that you like, down to the tiny hairs on his hands or her toenail polish. Sometimes you fall for someone who reminds you of one of your parents. The point is to find your one, perfect soulmate, nothing less. You don't want just a partner, you want *the* partner, the one person with whom you were meant to share a lifetime, someone whose destiny merges with your own, and who is just right to be a part of the perfect life you envision.

Your Cancer-Virgo lover wants to see that you're happy, down to the last detail. He or she tucks you under the covers, making sure that your feet are not crowded in, adjusts the channel to your favorite late-night movie, puts a beautiful handmade bowl filled with warm popcorn next to you, and cuddles up happily to keep you company. Popcorn not your favorite? Whatever is, don't worry, for it will be on hand and presented momentarily. Like having your feet tickled or your back rubbed? This is one lover who loves to focus on you.

Obviously that can mean many very pleasant hours in bed. Good sex is something we all need to make us feel happier and more willing to get on with our lives. Have a favorite position, fantasy, or routine? Cancer-Virgo discovers it easily and makes sure that it is incorporated into your sexual repertoire. Taking care of others successfully is a well-developed skill, so you can be sure that you've found a treasure—in and out of bed, a mate who will make you the center of attention.

Cancer-Virgo loves nice things that are tasteful as well as useful, and anything with those qualities is a good bet to please. It's nice to try to take the lead with someone like this, because it comes so naturally to your lover to take care of all your littlest needs, that it is sweet to remind him or her that you care enough to turn the tables.

Venus in Cancer with Mars in Libra

You want a loving, harmonious relationship in which you and your partner can establish a comfortable kind of closeness that allows for total cooperation. *All for one and one for all* is your motto, and you do your best to actualize it. When you have trouble creating this best of all possible realities, you become angry and can feel a bit hostile toward your partner. Having the kind of relationship you want seems as though it ought to be much easier than it actually is for you, and it's difficult to determine why that's the case.

You need to be free to express your feelings, even though sometimes you feel that doing so is a messy, inelegant process. When you're with a partner who accepts this part of you, you feel happier, and make an effort always to be gracious and charming. Because having a good relationship is so important to your sense of emotional security, you need to try to attract a partner who is good for you and who shares at least some of your ideals. Chances are that you're able to do this after a few false starts early in life.

Your Cancer-Libra lover is a real softy, despite the occasional angry outbursts that occur. Despite occasional unfocused agitation from time to time, you have a partner who really wants a nice relationship. Like receiving flowers? Cancer-Libra likes to send them, so you're in luck. You go out often to restaurants that have lovely décor and pleasant atmosphere. Wining and dining are a specialty of this elegance-loving mate. Soft lights, lovely music, and quiet conversation are more than just the accoutrements of romance, they're a way of life with this individual, and some say they can be quite habit forming.

Cancer-Libra wants a good relationship that lasts, so you know going in that you're with someone who hopes to be there for the long haul. To gain this mate's attention, you need a little sparkle and a nice demeanor. He or she appreciates people who put some effort into love. Little gifts that you tuck under the pillow are deeply appreciated and can be something as simple as a locket with your picture, or something with a monogram. You should be sentimental, but not sloppy.

You won't be overwhelmed with selfish or inconsiderate behavior in or out of bed, for this mate is more than willing to try to accommodate your desires. If you're the type of person who works at communicating your needs, your lover will be receptive to you and your desires.

Venus in Cancer with Mars in Scorpio

This is such a highly emotional combination that almost everything you do is done because of feelings, passion, and emotion. You seldom think before you act, at least not in love, and you're not one of those people who weighs the pros and cons of every possibility before making a move. Instead, you operate on a kind of emotional automatic pilot. You're possessive and intense, and you don't care about flings, one-night stands, or meaningless sexual interludes. That's because you invest so much of your total being into any relationship that you can't bear to lay yourself on the line casually, and you need to know that the one you love returns your feelings in equal measure.

Heaven help the lover who incites your ire. Because you often choose to withhold expression of anger until it erupts, your wrath is a frightening experience for anyone unused to such passionate intensity. When you do get mad (admittedly infrequently), you're inclined toward the sort of lovers' quarrels and attendant reconciliations that blue novels and songs are written about. Usually, though, your emotions and your sexuality are an innate part of your life, and they function in a smooth, natural way, with little conscious attention on your part.

Your Cancer-Scorpio lover is tender and gentle, as well as passionate and intense. He or she wants to assure your happiness, in bed or out. Feeling depressed or anxious? This mate probably already has intuited your feelings, their cause, and the cure for your blues. Go ahead and talk it out. You're involved with a terrifically insightful and sensitive listener.

Cuddle up for a cozy evening at home by the fire. Cancer-Scorpio loves to entertain you at home, where you both can feel happy, secure and totally focused on each other. No halfway measures satisfy the romantic impulses of this highly emotional homebody.

Sex is the best way to communicate to each other and to share the deepest, most personal parts of yourselves. There is no act too intimate, no passion unsuitable, no desire beyond fulfillment. Not as long as you're totally in love, that is, and totally in love is the only way to be with this partner, for anything less feels like nothing at all.

Venus in Cancer with Mars in Sagittarius

You're a loving person who has a hard time in relationships because they always seem to tie you down to an unacceptable degree, and you wonder why you gravitate toward these clingy mates. The type of closeness you had with your family in childhood was probably ideal—you were loved and felt close, yet no one put many unbearable restrictions on your comings and goings. If you could find a romance with that kind of balance, you'd jump at the chance, because your heart is quite tender and you yearn for love. Your ideals and philosophical values are a real and important part of your everyday life, and one of the things you idealize is the family unit.

You may have had many relationship that left you disappointed. If you become involved with someone who can love as deeply as you do, he or she also wants to tie you down and sometimes to cling. People who are more free spirits never seem to bring to a relationship the depth of emotional involvement that you do. It's a problem that can be frustrating but which becomes less prevalent in your later years. Past partners may not have been able to understand that although you need to be free to move on, your feelings for them remain unchanged. With maturity you learn to communicate your level of commitment as well as your need for avoiding clock-punching, and then you can find a mate who gets you and loves you for all your truly special qualities.

Your Cancer-Sagittarius lover needs a wide berth within a relationship. If you can make your loving feelings clear without seeming to want to restrain your mate's actions, so much the better. Spend time together outdoors. The person who invented the picnic probably had this combination. Things that combine the security of home with the freedom of the great outdoors are favorites. Go fishing, go hiking, barbecue often. Invest in a tent and a backpack and go on a camping trip. Making love under the stars (or a sunny blue sky) is a big turn on.

By maintaining a sense of freedom within the atmosphere of togetherness, and sharing passion fostered by your cozy outdoor trips, you may find that you've achieved a big accomplishment—getting Cancer-Sagittarius to stick around long enough to have the kind of relationship he or she wanted all along.

In bed, this mate combines sweet tenderness with playful athleticism. Whatever you want to try is fair game and he or she will enjoy anything new, outrageous, or even goofy. The point is to share happiness, and this mate wants to see you enjoy yourself during this, the best of all possible playtimes.

Venus in Cancer with Mars in Capricorn

You want to have a good relationship, and you're willing to work to create one. More than most people, you're aware of the need for compromise, and you regularly do so willingly. That's because you take a serious view of relationships. No matter how lightly other people regard human interaction, you know that substantial work is always the main component of any successful relationship. A stable family life is important to you, and marriage and family—rather than mere fun or sexual gratification—are always the end you seek. You want to create a whole lifestyle that you and others can point to with admiration and respect.

Having money and security are significant issues for you, and you're practical and hard working so that you can earn a good living and take care of your family. You look at life through a broad lens and know early on that it's not just about romance but where it leads: marriage, home, family, mortgages, burial plots, and all the memories you can cram into the years it takes to build all that. You want a mate you can love and be proud of, someone who works willingly by your side to achieve essential goals that create the financial success and happy family that mean so much to you. Your mate must care about his or her profession and share your ideas from the start or you're unlikely to offer a second glance, no matter how attractive or sexy the person is. You're in it for the long-term and you don't have time to waste on frivolous applicants.

Your Cancer-Capricorn lover can sometimes appear too money-and-status-oriented. Yes, your mate is all wrapped up in a career, but he or she would never neglect tenderness or loving feelings. Success is just one way to guarantee happiness for both of you. This is a very grounded person, and you must be as well to earn his or her notice. Cancer-Capricorn wants you to be happy and cheerfully sits to discuss any problems you're having as you brainstorm together to vanquish them. Relationships are created through effort, as he or she communicates again and again.

In bed, your lover is both tender and controlled. Sexual expertise is important, and like everything else, no effort is spared to achieve it. Sensing your needs and then trying hard to fill them are just part of the combined emotionality and earthy sensuality that he or she expresses.

Cancer-Capricorn loves to surprise you with presents that show a thoughtful awareness of your needs and interests. You happily cuddle for hours, having your back tickled and sharing intimate conversation. You work side by side in any home or family project that you undertake.

Just remember that this individual is serious about your relationship and really only wants to be involved with you if you're serious as well. Love and romance are great as far as they go, but for this mate, the security and stability of a well-organized family life are the ultimate goal of any romantic involvement.

Venus in Cancer with Mars in Aquarius

You're a very family-oriented person, and because of these personal feelings, you're able to extend your caring to the world at large. With a little more involvement from all of us, and the recognition that we're all connected in a brotherhood of love, the world would be the wonderful place that by rights it should be. It's this love for others (and often for others you don't even know) that motivates you to reach out and make connections with those around you.

You seek close and nurturing ties in your immediate circle, and you then want these people to join you to branch out and to reach others for additional support and closeness. Intimate partners may resent this universal quality of affection, for they sometimes feel that you're too involved with the abstract world of caring and not available exclusively enough to them. You're happiest when your personal expression of love can incorporate some of your universal ideals, and a partner who shares this feeling is perfect for you. For example, if you marry and then adopt some displaced orphans from another country, you share your brotherhood and good deeds in a personal commitment to love and support all through the giving you do to those specific children. You make the world a better place through love, which is your ultimate goal.

Just because your Cancer-Aquarius lover is so available to the rest of humanity, don't assume that he or she undervalues your importance or your relationship. This mate needs you very much, and the more you share, the stronger will be your bond in life.

Yes, you may become involved in many more group activities and do-good projects than you would want, but you find your life enriched by the demands of this relentless humanitarian. In fact, you may grow closer more through the good works you perform side by side than through the intimate moments that bond most others.

In bed, Cancer-Aquarius wants to be tender and loving, but it may sometimes be hard for this individual to do so. Whether it's a family history of emotional confusion or a succession of partners who just couldn't respond, you may have to go out of your way to provide a supportive emotional environment. Once your partner realizes that you're there for him or her on all levels, you'll receive as much devotion, TLC, and attention to your needs in bed as you'll see him or her lavish on the cares of the world. It's all in pointing out that, after all, you two are a microcosm of the world at large, and as much intense devotion is needed within that small circle as in the layers without.

Venus in Cancer with Mars in Pisces

You're so emotional that it's almost impossible for you to do anything based merely on reasoning. Sensitive and sentimental, you're often so flooded with emotional responses to all sorts of stimuli (and other people's responses, which you seem to attract like a sponge) that you need to spend some time in solitude, meditating and clearing your head.

You'd like to have a peaceful, self-possessed lover who spends quiet moments at home with you, cuddling, sharing your dreams, and taking catnaps. It's sometimes difficult for you to find that, however, not because it's unavailable, but because you can't always be certain of your precise desires and your right to have them met. As much as you love people and want them to respond to you, it's hard for you to be as assertive as others are. People admire your softness and gentleness and like turning to you in times of need. Although people adore you, sometimes it feels that you're always a friend, never a lover.

Why not take some time to consider your true heart's desire where love is concerned. Visualize the sensitive and nurturing bond you want to forge with an intimate partner and the sort of mate who could give back to you all the tenderness and love you lavish on him or her. As you keep doing this, the right person will cross your path and then you can have that affectionate and secure love that you crave.

Your Cancer-Pisces lover needs much devotion, calmness, and solitude, although it may never be directly requested. Because your lover is as unselfish a person as you'll meet, you must take the initiative in consideration, and in doing the little things that say I love you and I want to take care of you that he or she so selflessly does for you. Sex can be a terrifically intimate way to communicate and to relax. You spend hours reaching each other, touching, saying tender words, and sharing sweet kisses. It's not about being physically swept off your feet, but emotionally flooded with love, and this mate's heartfelt expressions of devotion can touch your soul far more profoundly than a firecracker sexpot might.

Try a trip to the sea where the pounding of the surf can work its magic on you both. Buy a book of fairy tales that you can take turns reading to each other. Magical fantasies seem as real to Cancer-Pisces as they do to any child. Get a long feather and tickle each other's toes unmercifully; your sensitive, emotional lover, badly needs someone to interject a note of fun and frivolity into day to day life.

Venus in Leo-Mars Combinations

Venus in Leo with Mars in Aries

You're a ball of fiery energy, excitement, and passion. Decidedly independent, impatient, and aggressive, you allow no interference in anything you do—your word is law. In any group of one or more, you must be the leader, the authority figure, and the one at the forefront. In fact, you're so determined to be number one that you may sometimes lose track of your followers.

You're totally unwilling to compromise, and you're not much on cooperation either, but you're so sexy and attractive that your friends and lover are willing to go along with you without complaining. If they won't, you're perfectly content to love them and leave them, even though your affection never wavers, for you must be true to yourself above all.

A more honest individual never drew breath, and if you declare your love, the recipient can be sure of dedicated devotion for as long as the two of you stay together. How long that is depends on your partner; a mate who remains exciting and unrestricting is liable to be a part of your life forever.

Your Leo-Aries lover is warm and generous while simultaneously acting unfeeling and self-centered. As long as you recognize these two vastly different dimensions, it's safe to read on. Do you want a tender companion who senses your every mood, shares every tiny feeling, and revels in your revelations of intimacy? Someone who cuddles you during the long winter night and whispers love sonnets in your ear? If so, advance to the Pisces-Cancer chapter and don't look back.

Leo-Aries is not big on sweet nothings. Instead, this mate is liable to spy you at a party, advance with swift and fiery determination, sweep you off to a waiting Maserati, speed you away to his or her bedroom, and engulf you in molten kisses, passionate embraces, and uncomplicated coupling. You said no? He or she probably refused to hear it.

The next morning you may be smothered with affection then abandoned without a word while your lover is off to chase excitement yet again. Although this mate wants to be able to settle down with one partner, it might be easier to have a friends with benefits situation so that there can be fewer complications and more freedom.

Venus in Leo with Mars in Taurus

You're careful and slow, sensible and cautious, and you care very much about what people think of you. Nothing but the best is your motto, and part of that means having a showy image as someone with plenty of money and the finest possessions. The things you own mean more to you than just luxury—they seem to say something about who you are, deep inside. Status symbols are important to you and you attempt to have the ones you feel are significant.

You can be possessive about people as well as things, and they, too, can be the providers of reflected glory for your self image. Because you identify yourself so closely with the people in your life, you care very strongly about what happens to them. You want them to be well provided for and well taken care of, and work very hard to accomplish this.

Harmonious relationships seem like a challenge to you, partly because you're so absolute and stubborn, and partly because you don't see a problem with this. A little anger smoldering below the surface seems normal to you to a certain degree. Often you feel that quarreling is the best way to express yourself with a lover and that friction below the surface also seems acceptable. This may give a sexy sizzle to your personality and the opportunity to have any number of passionate reconciliations in the bedroom. Part of the problem may be that when you're mildly annoyed you do and say nothing, burying your anger until it boils over and then, like a volcano, you erupt. Decide instead to deal with the issues as they arise, and there will be much less stress in your life and love life.

Stability is quite natural to you, and you try to maintain a relationship forever. Even if things have devolved, you tend to want to stay. If you still feel the spark is there, it's quite possible that you can fix anything causing a problem and hit that fifty year mark with your love intact.

If you're involved with a Leo-Taurus, there's ample evidence of the extent of your lover's devotion. You're lavished with gifts and attention as you've never been before. This is one of the most materially generous combinations in the Zodiac and is likely also to be a well off individual easily able to afford to be as generous as he or she might like. You enjoy evenings in luxurious dining spots, with the best of everything to eat and drink. The music is perfect, the atmosphere deluxe, and you're at the center of it all—right beside your glittering mate, who has no problem accepting all this attention.

Later on, you share hours of passionate, sensual lovemaking. This mate has all the ingredients necessary to become the sort of romantic partner honored in sexual marathons. Fantasies galore, the desire to live up to high standards in which your pleasure is the yardstick, and the stamina to keep going, possibly even after you collapse in sated exhaustion, make Leo-Taurus a lover worth celebrating. So if that sounds like your ideal recipe for romance, pay lots of attention, prepare delicious meals (or go out for them), and be prepared to become a beloved and pampered possession.

Venus in Leo with Mars in Gemini

Even though you like to be free to go where the wind blows you, your affections remain constant, and you always have good feelings for the people you love. Sometimes you can be involved in more than one love affair at a time, and although this ability bewilders even you, you manage to love both the objects of your affection. It's just that you tend to make fast decisions, getting yourself involved in situations that a slower approach might disallow. You can't help being curious and naturally interested in all kinds of people, and it might just be easier if your affections were as inconstant as your actions.

You like to be part of a lively group of elegant people who have interesting minds and active lives. You probably know many actors and writers, and you enjoy regular get-togethers with your friends to socialize and exchange ideas. In fact, perhaps you find yourself drawn into threesomes or even free love situations. In your heart you want one true love, but sometimes your inclinations lead you in other directions. If you find a partner who continues to interest and satisfy you, you're content just to flirt at parties and remain faithful, but always in the back of your mind is the thought, hmm what would *that* be like.

Your Leo-Gemini lover is as friendly and warm as a puppy dog. Always interested and interesting, you may never meet another individual as genuinely involved with whatever you happen to be saying. Any number of fascinating hours can be passed together, strolling through nice areas locally, driving down pretty streets, or just talking about everything.

If you want to begin a relationship with a Leo-Gemini, be gorgeous and interesting. Have an impromptu party with all manner of fabulous people—with you and your lover the most fabulous of all—naturally. Host a screening of short subjects, for this individual loves movies but hates to be tied down with any one thing for too long. You shouldn't have any trouble making the moves toward some more intimate private moments. In fact, he or she will probably make the first pass at you with an approach to sex that's natural, open, and swift. Meeting desires as they arise is just part of such an easygoing sexual style. And although you may often be propelled into the bedroom for a quickie that's aimed more at your lover's satisfaction than your own, the excitement and fun of the moment make up for an occasional itch he or she neglects to scratch.

Just remember that you're not planning the love affair of the century, for this is one partner who doesn't like life to get too heavy. Better to keep things frothy and elegant, as in one of those timeless Astaire-Rogers romances. As long as the glitter sparkles, it feels fun, and you remain interesting, you can be assured of a place in this mate's heart—and bed.

Venus in Leo with Mars in Cancer

You're a friendly, caring individual, and it's easy for you to like everyone, and for people to like you in return. When you care about someone, you care deeply, because loving relationships matter so much to you.

You're terrific at taking care of other people. You like to see that your loved ones are well dressed and well fed, and you're a determined family person, whether you're still part of your parents' family or if you've begun one of your own. Because you're so giving, people can sometimes take advantage of you and be unaware that you secretly wish to be the person everyone else fusses over for a change.

You're proud and ambitious; being someone deserving of respect and admiration is important to you, as well as having enough money to buy what you need and what you desire. You love things and may in fact own far too many of them, but even if you recognize this fact, it isn't likely that you'll divest yourself of some of them, because possessions mean far too much to you and you can't seem to release those sentimental attachments to pretty much everything in your world.

You seek a mate who appreciates the good life and who wants to share it, but you'd never choose just a gold-digger or boy-toy. You want someone who wants to have a beautiful life, someone who loves you equally and with whom you can build a level of happiness that you can clearly see in your mind.

Your Leo-Cancer lovers is much more sensitive than you might think, so be careful not to tease or hurt those very fragile feelings. If you're just starting out, be sure to introduce your family. Leo-Cancer loves to be in the middle of a happy gathering of close clansmen. Go out to a really fine restaurant where not only the food is superb, but the atmosphere as well. Write poems, buy special little presents, pay devoted attention, give sensuous backrubs, and tickle your partner madly, for this is one guy or gal who loves to have a good time, but will also never forget the more sensitive areas of courtship.

In bed, Leo-Cancer wants both of you to be satisfied. Part of your mate's lesson is to learn to balance the desire to be the center of attention versus an innate ability to care for others— and the bed is the ideal forum in which to work on this life lesson. A literal you-scratch-my-back-I'll-scratch-yours approach is a good beginning. We all need to learn to express our desires in bed (although some have internalized this knack far too well already). If you can take turns at playing lover and love object, your mate learns to balance those conflicting urges. Ideally, during lovemaking each person should give and get equally, and both should be completely satisfied.

Your Leo-Cancer partner is someone who loves you forever and who never casts your feelings aside. Your needs are always as important as his or her own, and together you can start a family as cheery and beloved as anything you might find on television. It's all about finding the joy in life and sharing it, and what's better than that.

Venus in Leo with Mars in Leo

This is a hot and magnetic combination, and you have no worries about your love life at all. Why should you worry about chasing a mate when everyone you know is chasing you! You're stubborn, determined, and you try to be as unemotional as possible. Heavy emoting and tender moments feel a little awkward to you, as you prefer warmth and friendly love to sentimentality.

Because you know just how appealing you are, you can sometimes be a bit arrogant and self-centered. On the other hand, nobody was ever blessed with a sunnier, more open, friendly, and outgoing personality. You're a party waiting to happen. You love romance, in capital letters, and you love being in the throes of amour. What other human condition makes it possible to have serenades under your window, dancing until three in the morning, and Christmas every day of the year?

Although your inclinations are toward romance with all its sparkle, you realize that stability has its values, and in fact, a committed relationship is very important to you. You like to be chased, but your wish is to be caught by the most thrilling person on earth and to share a magical romance for the rest of your life. You see yourselves as a pair like the Duke and Duchess of Windsor, royal, elegant, and in it for the long-term.

Your Leo-Leo lover is a handful. He or she loves to have fun yet will do nothing to become the object of ridicule. A scavenger hunt with everybody wearing bizarre hats and costumes isn't quite right unless it's magically elegant. Instead, go out to fancy places where you can both dress in chic attire and sip champagne, the official drink of Leos everywhere.

This mate is happiest when loved and admired, for then he or she feels free to live up to your best expectations. The charm, sunny goodwill, and warm, loving spirit focuses on you like a balmy laser beam of energy. You spend hours in bed making love, for Leo-Leo likes to be known as a great lover and puts all of his or her considerable stamina into maintaining that image, which let's face it, is far more truth than illusion. Just relax. Who wouldn't enjoy being at the epicenter of all that focused Leo love for hours, and perhaps for decades.

Venus in Leo with Mars in Virgo

You appreciate the idea of the grand romantic gesture, but you're so careful and detail-oriented that you feel much more secure with something smaller and more subtle. You can spend happy hours planning the details of a treat for a loved one—a surprise party, a special gift, or even a valentine—which are all perfectly designed to please that special someone. At your best, you're generous and considerate, bending over backwards to do a good deed. At your worst, you can be arrogant and critical, feeling that nobody is ever as good as you are yourself.

You're ambitious and responsible, and because you're so achievement oriented, the chances are good that you advance to your desired position of importance and respect. You definitely believe in romance, but you also realize that a longstanding commitment is more important than glitter. Along the way you've kissed your share of frogs, because until you find someone worthy of that seal of approval, you keep on interviewing.

Your Leo-Virgo lover has high standards that must be met

by everyone who matters. These standards include loyalty, integrity, and careful attention to everything. Your attitude about work and your life must reflect a willingness to shoulder responsibility, just as any purchase you make must reflect good quality and fine workmanship.

In bed, these standards include sensuality and good taste. This individual knows how to please a lover, and puts much effort into doing so without attempting anything deemed ridiculous or gauche. You should follow the same guidelines. Knowing the exact pleasure points to stimulate and taking the time and care necessary to do so is essential—after all it's no more than this mate is doing for you.

If you want a relationship with this proud, picky individual, take some time to notice his or her behavior, likes and dislikes. You have a much better chance of interesting this partner if you mirror his or her choices. Mere flattery isn't enough—it has to be accurate, tasteful, and completely sincere. The cleverest gadget, tickets for an award-winning play, or a hand packed picnic—try beautiful health food—delivered to your paramour's office at lunchtime are good opening gambits. In return, you'll find a mate who is faithful, impressively successful, and someone you can always count upon in every area of life.

Venus in Leo with Mars in Libra

You're warm and friendly and so charming that you'd be hard pressed to find someone who doesn't adore you right from the start.

Socializing with engaging companions is more than just mere fun for you—it's what you live for. Although you like many people, you do prefer charming, well-off people who are outgoing and popular like yourself.

You're not particularly interested in a single intense relationship, nor do you enjoy very emotional scenes or interactions, for you prefer to keep things light, congenial, and friendly. Compromise is important, you know, and sometimes you back down about getting your way—or at least change your mind—to make a partner happy, and that spirit enables you to get along congenially with most people. Often your hesitation before acting saves the day, although it can be exasperating to you as well as to others.

You believe in love and want a commitment, but you don't want anything messy or sloppy. You want to enjoy one of those beautiful love stories about people who never shared a cross word in half a century of togetherness.

Your Leo-Libra lover is as much fun as a frothy milk shake. Nowhere can you find a more sparkly, good-natured companion. On a date, at a party, or even on a break by the water cooler, no one is more adept at social interaction. Standing around chatting with this lively, sociable individual is almost as much fun as going roller skating in the park. The only problem with Leo-Libra is embarking on a passionate affair. Intense passion isn't really in his or her makeup. This is not someone who enjoys a weeping spell while watching a tearjerker, or who wants to participate in impassioned quarrels and reaffirming reconciliations. Better to keep things on an even keel of good times and congenial interactions.

In bed, the sex is sweet and happy, and the scene is set with scented candles and a beautiful environment. Hugs and kisses and physical satisfaction are simply a matter of a nice time that is produced by good sexual manners.

Of course, the two people must care about each other or they shouldn't be engaging in such intimacy. But on considering all the modern talk about the earth moving and passion to end all passion, your lover furrows a brow and prefers to move along to a less messy topic. It's not that he or she dislikes commitment or demands freedom, or even falls prey to boredom, but rather this is a mate who just likes things peaceful and happily uncomplicated.

If you too see romantic drama as a bit silly, you're in good company. For when Leo-Libra meets a compatible someone, he or she is more than willing to build a life together, all for one and one for all, with the two of you enjoying yourselves in pleasant social interaction forevermore.

Venus in Leo with Mars in Scorpio

You're an intense, very determined person, and nothing stops you from getting what you want. Because you're so magnetic, it's easy for you to attract other people, despite the fact that there's some degree of smoldering hostility beneath your very attractive surface. Friction seems normal to you, and in the right situation can be quite useful. Friends who have those easy-peasy relationships seem a bit dull to you.

You're friendly and exciting, and everyone you meet senses that you can be a wonderfully loyal friend as well as a devastating enemy. It's not that you dislike many people, or even that you fly off the handle easily. On the contrary, you wait to express anger, visibly seething before you verbalize your feelings, and to a real friend you're eternally loyal and devoted.

Because you're so willful and determined, it would be impossible for a potential lover to maintain a posture of disinterest. You simply wear down any resistance until your desires are met. Of course, you're so magnetic and sexy that very few people indeed would fail to respond to your intense appeal.

Perhaps you've been a serial monogamist for a while, because in your heart you know you want the one soulmate who completes your destiny, but sometimes relationships crash and burn, and after many difficult scenes people part company. This is very painful for you because you hate to let go of anyone or anything. You keep looking however, and when it feels right, you say I do.

If you're interested in a Leo-Scorpio lover, you must be prepared to give in much of the time. This stubborn individual is used to winning all the time and just waits you out instead of considering a compromise. Besides, compromise implies that there is more than one valid choice in any matter, and this passionately decisive person knows that there is just one side to any story—his or her own.

If you're first meeting, it doesn't hurt to be on the same side—of anything. Being sexy and sparkling are also essential.

If you're alluring, super successful and equally sexy, not to mention a little bit ungettable, then you're all the more interesting. This mate wants to be adored, and agreed with, but a little friction doesn't hurt, and you have to be a partner worth working for.

Leo-Scorpio is generous, giving, and loyal. He or she is very interested in seeing that you have a good time and feel cherished. This mate adores sex and consumes a partner in a blaze of passionate, molten desire. Just remember that this is a very jealous and possessive combination, so plan on being devotedly exclusive. This individual is the one calling the shots, and that emphatically restricts you from fooling around, including innocent conversational flirting. You're with Leo-Scorpio, which means you belong to this person, and he or she belongs to you.

Venus in Leo with Mars in Sagittarius

You're very motivated by your ideals of justice, honesty, and loyalty. You love to go out and enjoy a freewheeling good time, mixing with as many interesting people as you can find.

Although you do consider your sexuality a normal part of your easygoing life, you don't really want to settle down in any one relationship because despite your easily sustained feelings of loyalty for your partners, you never want to feel confined by anyone.

You like to work in groups, doing things for the good of the world, and nobody throws a better fundraiser than you do. Your friends are fun and popular people, very successful, or impressive in some way, as long as they're not stuffy or stuck-up. You may know many top athletes, and you enjoy athletics yourself. That includes outdoor sex and romantic interludes.

You believe in love and want someone to hold in your heart, but your feet don't always agree. You sometimes decide to leave a relationship because it just doesn't feel like you any more.

Your Leo-Sagittarius lover is a real pal. Always lively and active, he or she is a terrific companion for anything fun and physical. For this mate, sex is another (slightly more fun) way to express physical exuberance. Being free to consort with anyone is important, and fidelity is rarely an issue as far as he or she is concerned— unless it has some moral connotations to it. Isn't monogamy a bit outdated? Such a casual attitude about sex can be disturbing to the more emotional among us, but Leo-Sagittarius is always exciting and so much fun in bed. If you want to perpetuate the relationship, you need to expend some effort, subtly of course, so he or she doesn't quite catch on.

Plan a safari. Or a celebrity tennis match (your mate may be competing). Have a Texas-style barbecue on your ranch. Leo-Sagittarius likes the great outdoors, and the bigger the better.

It may be quite a challenge to get this individual to settle down with a home and family, even though you love each other madly and always will, for Leo-Sagittarius likes the freedom to come and go and to hang out with whoever is new, glittery, and exciting. Tender visions of happily ever after that lurk in your heart have to be introduced slowly, in a way that makes togetherness sound more enticing than freedom.

Your best bet is to be a similarly freedom loving soul who wants nothing more than to have a good time and to see the world with few strings attached. Once Leo-Sagittarius recognizes the compatriot gleam in your eye, you're sought out more and more often. After all, who can resist a really fun pal who can throw a football as well as he or she can kiss.

Venus in Leo with Mars in Capricorn

You're so ambitious and status-oriented that you probably end up romancing people you meet in connection with your career. This way you can multi-task and combine the messy and time consuming dating rituals with work-related social events, making it a win-win.

Money and tangible evidence of success are your yardstick when judging others, and although some may consider you a snob, you acknowledge that your standards are high where others are concerned, but they're no higher than you apply to yourself. You'd certainly never consider a permanent relationship with someone who couldn't impress you and quite a few other people. Not really of the Henry Higgins mentality, you believe that it's just as easy to fall in love with a rich person as a poor one, and you intend to do the former. Your mate has to be someone, and if he or she is also famous, so much the better.

You may be a renowned party giver, particularly if it's a business or charity event. You always have the savvy, taste, and energy to make any social gathering sparkle with excitement. This social finesse helps you attract the right people, whether for pleasure or business. Ultimately you want a partner in life, someone who shares your values, interests, and who knows what's important. Then you can live the 18-Karat life you always envisioned.

If you're interested in securing the affections of a Leo-Capricorn, check your pedigree, for this individual is not the charming prince who marries the showgirl, unless she's Marilyn Monroe, and maybe not even then. If you have something substantial to offer, proceed. Go to a testimonial dinner for someone in high financial circles. If you can't manage that, tickets to a seminar on managing your stock portfolio would be a good second choice. Dress elegantly and create a mystique that implies you're deluxe far beyond his or her dreams, and you may successfully engineer a turn of the tables. Once this individual is pursuing you, it's easier. For this is a hardworking person, and matters of the heart are taken seriously only after your credentials have passed muster.

In bed, you're expected to make a great effort to please this sexually authoritarian partner. You're there to pay court until the level of devotion is equal. Then your lover spares no effort in satisfying you, for being rejected as a callous bedmate is just unthinkable. He or she may even relax a bit and share sunny loyalty and a wry sense of humor with you. Once you're a couple, you have a mate you can count on never to stray and who always has a substantial life style to share.

Venus in Leo with Mars in Aquarius

You're a rebel with a cause, and in fact you may be involved in quite a few worthwhile organizations. Because you're fair and so interested in honesty and justice, you may have quite a reputation as a liberal battler for justice and truth.

Even though you refuse to do anything in a conventional way, you acknowledge the importance of relationships and the need to compromise. Of course that seldom means that you enjoy being at the mercy of the give and take necessary to survive interpersonal dynamics, but you've probably learned how to deal with it because relationships are a major theme in your life.

How do you maintain your individuality without having to give up the relationship you want? How do you maintain your own identity while being able to mesh effectively into a group whose concerns are your own? You've been working on these issues for years. What you've learned is that it all comes down to finding the right partner. Being with someone who naturally sees life as you do and with whom you generally agree cuts through all the negotiations in less well-suited matches. That's your goal—to find your complement in life, and then side by side you can enjoy each other and work to make the world a better place.

Your Leo-Aquarius lover is a real friend. There isn't a more outgoing, genuinely interested person in the Zodiac. Any friendship you forge with this guy or gal lives forever. Unfortunately friend and lover hardly mean the same thing to most of us, but they are nearly synonymous to Leo-Aquarius. Start as good buddies, and even if you marry, be prepared to stay that way. Just because you're married doesn't mean that you stop being pals, not in this individual's estimation, and in a way it's sort of sweet, because friendships are easier to maintain than romances much of the time.

It's easy to generate this mate's interest in you. Just flash a warm smile and suddenly you're standing in a cozy corner of your group, and while the others debate the possibilities of success for whatever project they're attempting (movie stars for peace, a celebrity tennis match to raise money for orphans, and so on), you're exploring mutually appealing ideas and philosophies. After that, it's off to somewhere else, with plenty of time in between for personal athletics. For even though Leo-Aquarius doesn't focus on sex as often as some other Zodiacal combinations, your lover is willing to devote his or her full energy to it when the occasion arises.

Venus in Leo with Mars in Pisces

One of the big issues you must face is how to be as self-centered as you'd like when it feels wrong to act that way. You'd love to be the center of attention, but what usually happens is that you attract important or famous people who then expect you to pay attention to them. You may well be acting as the confidant to a number of minor (or major) celebrities who feel that the only payback owed you is to allow you to bask in their reflected glory.

You're a concerned, loyal friend and gladly devote hours of your time seeing to the needs of those you care for. You're very romantic and love to lie about, daydreaming of beautiful scenes with warm, loving people, set in magical places. You'd be the ideal honeymoon planner, in fact. When you're in love, you devote yourself totally to your mate, setting a beautiful mood of mutual adoration and joy. Your goal is to find the one person who can share your life in an equal way so that both of you feel cherished and are held warmly in each other's hearts. That's your definition of true love and it's also your goal in life. You realize that having that sort of permanent connection with another person is more important than anything else.

Your Leo-Pisces lover is a beautiful dreamer. Impractical and unambitious, he or she adores the more expensive things life has to offer but has little real drive to go out and get them. Something troubling you? This mate is a devoted nurturer and listener and will gladly provide tea and sympathy. Just remember to return the favor. This is one person who has acres of people clamoring for attention, and it's up to you to offer the same generous levels of affection being lavished on you. It's only fair.

In bed, plan on doing most of the work, for this mate feels quite natural as a sex object, and although he or she is committed to your happiness in this arena, swinging from a chandelier may require more athletics than Leo-Pisces can devote. Calm and cozy sex in which you provide the gymnastics and he or she concentrates on wrapping you in tenderness is how you balance things in bed. Ask for what you want, and this mate will certainly try to meet your desires.

Planning a trip? Leo-Pisces loves to be in the sun by the sea, so invite him or her along to the shore. Pick up some chips, a stray jug of wine, and pack the backgammon set. As the sun begins to set, you can tickle each other's fancies with made-up tales of magic and mystery featuring two shipwrecked lovers. Love affairs that combine sensitivity with frivolous fun are so grand.

Venus in Virgo-Mars Combinations

Venus in Virgo with Mars in Aries

You have some difficulty getting along with others, whether in the context of work or romance, and often the problem is that you're not particularly relationship oriented because you'd rather do as you choose than make allowances for the choices of those around you. As you see it, there are too many people who could interfere in your life if you let them.

Despite all the aggravation you feel from human interaction, you genuinely enjoy helping people. You go far out of your way to do a favor, and your feelings are as honest and genuine as your actions, something you find annoying when other people don't offer the same consideration. To the few people who matter to you and who live up to your standards, you're a devoted friend who can always be counted on for a favor.

Where love is concerned, you may see yourself as a loner, for the reasons we already mentioned. You're all right with having casual interludes if the perfect mate doesn't come along, but you don't really stop to consider that you often choose not to look for that perfect person because life is simpler alone. That doesn't mean that being with someone is impossible—of course not. If you decide you want to give your heart, share your life and your bed permanently, you can do so. It's all up to you.

Your Virgo-Aries lover is a rugged individualist. Always busy and on the go, he or she may often seem too preoccupied to have a real love affair. This mate might be content with a friends with benefits scenario, and although one-night stands are repugnant to him or her, they might also be a better alternative to loneliness.

What this individual really wants is a relationship with a tasteful, understanding partner who fulfills every need—when he or she wants it—and to be free to concentrate elsewhere when the mood strikes. This is no tender romantic dreamer, and the thought of Plato's idea of two souls meeting to be joined into one perfect entity is not a pretty picture to Virgo-Aries. Being half of something like that would feel more like a loss of individuality than a gain of a soulmate.

So be prepared to keep it loose. The last thing your lover wants is to be smothered or confined in any way. However, that's not to say that Virgo-Aries objects to having a good time. Despite being hard to pin down where commitment is concerned, this is a hot and sensual lover who enjoys sex and will want to please you in many ways. In fact, you may become so addicted to this mate's bedroom techniques that you agree to that friends with benefits offer.

To move it out of the bedroom and into the dating scene, tour the factory where sports cars are manufactured; elegance of design in machinery particularly appeals to this mate. Just remember that the things that capture your lover's fancy for a moment aren't necessarily items he or she might like to own. For example, an unusual Swiss clock with visible gears might be fascinating, but a single look is probably enough; buy a sleek digital model if you're gifting. Be considerate, tasteful, interested, and retain your own involvements and your own independence, for more than anything, Virgo-Aries wants a mate with whom he or she can feel simpatico.

Venus in Virgo with Mars in Taurus

You're a practical, down-to-earth individual who likes to be careful, thorough, and painstaking about everything you do. You have excellent taste, and because you're so picky, you may spend hours shopping to find just the right one of each item you buy. Determined and stubborn, you like your own way of getting things done. Others may try to interfere and offer suggestions; this never bothers you because it's so easy to shrug and ignore them as you continue with your own strategies.

A relationship is very important to you. You want to have a stable lifestyle, and you need a partner who shares your level of taste and high standards. When you find such a person, you have no trouble making a commitment. You do tend to be extremely constant, and you dislike going through breakups, but sometimes you just have to steel your nerve if you've managed a liaison with someone you've discovered is the wrong person. As you see it, compatibility is essential, or else you'd end up arguing over the drapes, the china, and who gets which side of the bed.

Your goal is to go slowly and not get bogged down, and sometimes that means you pre-reject someone who could be good for you because initially it seems you're wrong for each other. To you that's easier than a tearful breakup at the end. You want it to work perfectly from the start and all the way to death.

Your Virgo-Taurus lover may be picky about which soap to use, but there's no denying this mate's earthy sensuality. In fact, it can almost be hard to understand how somebody who is so finicky about everything else can enjoy sex so much. Of course you won't be making love on the kitchen table or the bathroom floor, but those who consider that level of discomfort as exciting are just out of touch.

Buying a present for this guy or gal can be quite a challenge. After you spend hours pondering the one thing your lover might like that he or she doesn't already have, then you must spend additional hours in the most luxe boutique looking for one that will meet this mate's standards. Of course, if you succeed, you'll be amply thanked.

Go out to dinner. Virgo-Taurus loves beautiful, delicious food that is perfectly prepared. If you can cook, prepare something at home, for this mate appreciates quality as well as effort expended and gives you points for trying. Once you're a pair, things are set. You have devotion, pampering, presents, and tender loving care for the rest of your life. And you have a mate who knows just how to scratch your back or to tickle your toes, not to mention your every erogenous zone from A to Z.

Venus in Virgo with Mars in Gemini

This is a highly intellectual combination, and you may use as an excuse to stay single the fact that you can't find anyone clever enough to interest you permanently. In fact, you may actually prefer to be single and unencumbered by the demands of other people. You have a tenacious mental outlook, and you think of yourself as an orderly, responsible individual. However well you outline the steps of a project, you don't always have the will to follow through, although the desire may be there. When this happens, you feel grouchy and self-critical, and the last thing in the world you want to do is to be around other people. This translates into relationship issues, for you're kind hearted and want to be there for a mate, but when you lose interest in the person and are faced with his or her disappointment or heartbreak, you feel guilty.

Often it's less stressful to stay at home with a book. You love to read, study, and learn, and you may be a minor expert on more than one subject. You're a super debater, and heaven help anyone who asks you for a list of his flaws. You're no more critical of others than you are of yourself, however, and your complete lack of malice can go a long way toward making up for your candor.

If you do decide you want a mate, you can easily find one. You enjoy exercise and can meet someone out in the world, although on some days you feel like a shy librarian. In fact, you're kind and can be a giving partner if you learn to tolerate other people's quirks.

Your Virgo-Gemini lover is not particularly emotional, as you no doubt discovered early on in the relationship. There is no desire to deal with heavy emotional scenes, nor the energy to perpetuate them. People who interact in an intense angst-ridden way are a curiosity better avoided. This individual loves to argue. He or she can create a debate better than any politician, and as long as you like to indulge in mental gymnastics, you enjoy each other's minds. In fact, attending a debate is a great way to break the ice. Anything intellectual is a good bet for a date.

As for things physical, this mate seems rather cool, as though reading a romance novel is satisfaction aplenty, and no actual lovemaking is necessary. There is hope, however, for he or she is sensual, and enjoys touching, once that mental itch slows down. Offer a massage as a prelude to sex. It provides some relaxation that can segue into something a little steamier.

Venus in Virgo with Mars in Cancer

You're a very sensitive person who often focuses on a loved one rather than yourself, and you're famous for your perfect gifts. You have a warm, well-run home, no matter your gender, and you have a talent for hosting wonderful parties. You love to help others, and seldom does a day pass without a request from friends or family for help and advice on major or minor calamities. Because you're able to combine the best of sensitive emotionalism with a finely honed analytical ability, it's easy for you to draw others out, let them share their feelings openly, and help them work through any problems they may be having.

You enjoy the company of sensitive, well-mannered people, for displays of angry words and thoughtless behavior are very disturbing to you. You'd rather keep your feelings on an even keel, because having to express negative emotions can be very upsetting. Even when you know you're entitled to be angry about something, it's much more natural for you just to hold those feelings in, although doing so can sometimes make you feel rather ill.

You seek a calm and happy relationship with a trustworthy mate who is as loving and nurturing as you are. You feel that your values are positive and want someone who feels as you do, so you can combine forces to build a happy home and family. You can envision this mate even before you meet, the tender moments of snuggling and laughter you'll share, the sense of camaraderie right from the start, and a sort of knowing that you belong together. It's called finding the perfect soulmate, and it's your overriding goal.

Your Virgo-Cancer lover is a staunch family person, a good friend to all, and the most willing dispenser of TLC you're likely to encounter anywhere. Before you've even mentioned what you'd like for dinner—or your birthday—there he or she is, gliding in smoothly with exactly the dish—or the hand-knit sweater—you'd been wanting.

In bed, your lover knows just how to please you, and surely the skilled and cherished courtesans of other eras shared this combination. Taking care of your sexual needs is just another way to show love, and he or she never even considers for a moment whether you're doing your part to return the favor.

Unselfish and considerate, this lovely person is appreciated by all, for where else can we find someone so totally willing to focus completely on another person? In fact, someone so special can make the rest of us (even though we may be genuinely wonderful ourselves) feel like clods by comparison.

How do you interest this mate on first meeting? Just be yourself—your good qualities are clearly evident to this insightful mate. Sitting around quietly having a good talk about your interests and ambitions is a nice way to break the ice. Follow that with a pleasant dinner at a really nice restaurant. Soon you're on the way to a close relationship with someone who never takes you for granted and who is capable of making you feel like the most important person in the world.

Venus in Virgo with Mars in Leo

With this combination, you prefer to do things your own way, without the interference of others, yet you care very much for their admiration and approval. You're very conscious of the impression you make on others, and you sometimes get very nervous about their opinion of you. Usually, however, most people have far less strenuous standards than you do, and you find yourself worried for nothing. Most of the people you know do like you, and you probably have the reputation of being reliable, honest, and forthright.

You realize that you might come off as a tad inflexible in relationships, and you're considering working on that, although you'd prefer to spend time with mates who are flexible enough to allow you to do as you choose and sometimes to follow your lead, rather than debating another perspective. If you've been single a very long time, you may have discovered how difficult it is to find those congenially yielding individuals, for most people want at the least to have compromise and few just say, "Yes dear, whatever you want." The key to this situation is to examine your absolute certainty in your own ability to do things in the best possible way. Once you realize that it's more about happiness and less about values such as *best*, it becomes easier to coexist.

Despite his or her helpfulness and generosity, your Virgo-Leo lover can sometimes seem insufferably arrogant and smug. It can be very hard to get along with someone who feels that being right supersedes being human. Because this individual is so concerned with an image—an image you might rightly have pointed out that nobody else is even aware of—he or she may be hesitant about dealing with feelings, preferring to remain somewhat closed off.

Virgo-Leo needs a partner who can see beneath an unintentionally gruff exterior to the genuinely kind person there. Of course, if you need someone to do that for you, you both may be in trouble. Perhaps the best way to understand this mate's true feelings is through sex. Such a generously loving nature is easy to spot when you see how tenderly he or she attends to your every need sexually. Just don't point this out in those terms or you'll evoke more embarrassment than joy.

Virgo-Leo has excellent taste and the highest of standards, so if you're planning a dinner date, be sure the restaurant is excellent, and if you're buying a gift, the quality must be superb. When you've established a relationship with this demanding individual, you have someone who truly loves you, who's forever supportive and totally on your side, even if he or she occasionally acts as though you're the dumbest jerk on the planet.

Venus in Virgo with Mars in Virgo

You may have gone for years wondering why your various partners have considered you so sexy. If you've finally realized that this happens all the time, you've probably decided that your sexy image is the result of some peculiarity in the people you date, rather than a quality truly a part of yourself, for the truth is, you don't think of yourself as sexy. You're picky and cautious, and it's so hard for you to meet anyone whom you think is good enough for you that you may find yourself quite lonely. It's not that you look down on others so much as that you have high standards, and, in fact, you may not even be good enough for yourself. It's quite the dilemma.

You never take action without considering the consequences, for you like to be careful about everything you do. A master of details, you're excellent at completing any number of complicated tasks, and you never fail to notice even the tiniest flaw, which comes in handy when you tire of a romantic partner, for then you can easily move on. A responsible and considerate person, you would find life in a world without good manners and breeding unthinkable. It's probably your innate sense of courtesy that softens your austere, exacting nature, and prevents you from hurting the feelings of those who come under your critical scrutiny.

You admit that you believe in love, but also that it's difficult for you to find someone with whom you can settle down. You want a partner of whom you can approve on many levels, but that is challenging to find. If you can temper your natural criticism with love, and focus on the sweetness between you, it's easier to see a future with an all too human, totally normal, but less than perfect mate.

Your Virgo-Virgo lover may well be the most efficient, best organized person you know, but because of hidden insecurity, you must provide support and encouragement. A flow of reliable positive feelings from you helps him or her immeasurably to relax that nagging little inner voice.

Virgo-Virgo loves sex and touching, although his or her approach may be more sensual than emotional. This lover pays attention to all the little details of lovemaking for which more impulsive, more exuberant types have no time or patience. And it won't take this master of details long at all to discover precisely what turns you on.

No one ever desired to please a lover more than Virgo-Virgo. Whether it's buying you the perfect gift that you always wanted, or giving you a back rub after a long, hard day because it's so obvious that you need it, no effort is spared to make you feel good. And that kind of service may well be worth a narrowed glance when you're wearing your unsightly but snuggly old robe.

Venus in Virgo with Mars in Libra

You really want to coexist with others harmoniously, but somehow now and then you find yourself in the middle of these arguments about efficiency and good taste. During the squabble you feel awful and find yourself wishing you could flee to a life as a solitary artist, creating masterpieces in solemn harmony, but that doesn't last long, for you know how much you need to be around other people.

Because you're so careful and cautious, you like to explore all your options thoroughly before you take decisive action. In fact, your expectations of perfection may be holding you back. You have great expectations where romance is concerned. Those hours spent fantasizing about your perfect mate have led you to what you consider is a workable blueprint for precisely the qualities your true love should have. If only you had a factory where you could build Miss or Mr. Right. Instead, you wait, knowing that soon this paragon of a paramour will arrive and then you'll share a relationship combining the best of harmony and fulfillment. You'll each be the other's ideal, and never will there be a moment when either of you feels doubt, criticism, or concern.

Depending on how long you've been perfecting this fantasy and comparing it with reality, you may have gleaned the tiniest inkling that human interaction falls rather short of your own spectacular expectations. The phrase *snap out of it* comes to mind. The sooner you decide to explore the truly beautiful possibilities of reality, the sooner you can make yourself happy, so look at reality with a smile as it does contain quite a bit of the magic you seek.

Your Virgo-Libra lover is a nice person who has the best possible intentions despite the way that relationships often crash and burn. Certainly this mate desires to exist in an atmosphere of harmony in which everyone is happy and all needs are joyfully met. This is never more obvious than in bed, where charm, dedication to pleasing you, and lots of tender caresses are the rule.

Go ahead and invite Virgo-Libra to dinner. Look for soft music, elegant surroundings, and simple but perfect food, perhaps a café near the local museum. This mate adores art and probably has a museum membership.

Keep your feelings balanced and this mate will feel comfortable with you. Strong displays of excessive emotion are never well received. If you feel an argument is imminent, simply and calmly point out that your feelings are being hurt, and furthermore that you hope he or she can just give a moment to consider your side of the matter. Your lover will kindly retrench and rethink in no time.

Venus in Virgo with Mars in Scorpio

This is an intense combination, and because of your serene self-assurance, you're easily able to exert a considerable influence over the people you encounter. You seem cool and magnetic, like an unobtainable prize that is eminently desirable to all. You may have heard that there's something in your glance, or the way that you hold your head, making you every bit as formidable as you seem.

All of this might be quite amusing to you, yet you know that you possess a kind of determination that's not easily swayed. You're so poised that you glide through life—and the dating scene—easily able to accomplish your goals and gain admirers. Inscrutable, you have one of the great poker faces of all time, making you very much a catch. And a little scary!

You seek a partnership of equals and want to be with someone with whom you instantly can connect and trust. Your instincts are strong and vital, and you know in your gut what works for you. That can mean that although you're often asked on dates, you prefer to remain aloof until that thunderbolt strikes and the soulmate of your dreams appears. Quality over quantity is always your motto.

Your Virgo-Scorpio lover may seem like a chilly character indeed, but you probably sense the passion lurking below the surface. Every action is imbued with an intensity that's lacking in other people. And when he or she focuses that beam of energy on you, it's as if you're being revealed, all the way to your soul. This is one person who easily can have flings, but doesn't really want them. Flirting seems silly to this serious mate, although he or she has no lack of charm.

This is a dignified person who always lives up to his or her beliefs, and to this mate the object of romance is love and commitment. Even though a grand passion doesn't come along daily, this mate is willing to wait for the one and only soulmate who instantly and always is perfect. Although this individual can be critical and exacting about choosing that person, his or her automatic pilot is strong and accurate, allowing no wrong choices.

The best way to deal with someone like this is to be cool yourself. Adopt the attitude that sex can wait until deep feelings are established, and take your time to become acquainted. It's not necessary to try to impress this mate, for action is never as important as genuine feelings and communication below the surface. Be yourself. Instead of dining out, a relaxed good meal at home feels much more comfortable and intimate. It's all about what passes between your eyes.

When you both decide that this is it, and you glide into the bedroom, you find that your every desire—and more—is met as you both melt into each other wordlessly, beginning a lifetime of joyous partnership.

Venus in Virgo with Mars in Sagittarius

You may be a kindhearted, idealistic, and even friendly soul, but you're not always all about relationships. You keep things cordial, interesting, and casual, always maintaining your freedom and happy to return to your home alone. You recognize that from the moment a relationship begins, you feel a bit hemmed in by your mate's ideas and routines. Perhaps you had a sense early on that you liked the idea of remaining single, and if so close friendships fulfill your need for companionship in a way that feels comfortable to you.

Friends who love you may be determined to fix you up or to discuss your single status, but you chuckle and change the subject. As long as you're content, no problem. If you do decide you want to be in a romance, there's nothing holding you back, once you learn that loving someone makes it worth it to compromise a little and to be more flexible. If so, your kindly nature and natural helpfulness are much appreciated.

Your Virgo-Sagittarius lover is restless and fidgety, often refusing to be tied down, even if you're making almost no demands, but this always seems to be an issue. In fact, the closer you get to each other, the more aggravated this mate may act, as the fear of being pigeonholed is projected onto you. The whole idea of love makes this individual a bit nervous, so if you can enjoy yourselves in a friendly way, so much the better. If you've managed to share a philosophy or a good cause, you might just be on the way to a more substantial friendship. Just don't push for more too quickly, and you'll be happier in the long run. In fact, if you're considering a serious involvement, it might be wise just to sit down and ask what your lover's ideas are on the subject of long-term relationships.

In bed, Virgo-Sagittarius is cheerful and sensual, but it seems as though you're in the middle of a one-night stand, no matter how many times you've been together. The best approach might just be playful, cheerful, and no pressure. If you enjoy each other in bed and out, there's no reason why you can't keep things going along happily for quite a while. And once your lover relaxes and discovers you have no desire to entrap, he or she may start moving closer and closer to you.

Venus in Virgo with Mars in Capricorn

You're ambitious, practical, and careful, and you're so

busy establishing yourself in a career that generates the type of financial success and security you want that you may not have the time for romance. That's not a huge worry to you, however, for although you consider dating a waste of time and resources better applied elsewhere, you strongly believe in marriage. Early on you created your game plan: wait until you're well established in your career with a sizeable income, money in the bank, and property of your own, and then meet and marry someone substantial and reliable who shares your values and who wants to have a proper family.

Luckily for you, matchmakers are currently having a renaissance, and you think they're a great idea. They pre-screen and find someone who has the assets you desire. Then all you have to do is meet and test the chemistry. Of course many people regard falling in love as a really important and memorable event in their lives rather than a mere prelude to the creation of a dynasty, but you're not immune to tender feelings, you just don't want them spilling out on a constant basis.

Your Virgo-Capricorn lover is down-to-earth and practical. It's not that dinners by candlelight are wasted on him or her, but they may be beside the point. It's almost impossible for you to set out on a quest to win this mate's heart and hand.

If this person sees you as a prospect, he or she will happily take the lead, but don't expect a tender romance complete with intimate emotional conversation, inane laughter, and whispered endearments. Advance to one of the Pisces chapters for that.

Instead, you share earthy sex that is satisfying and sensual, and all the back rubs time allows. And although this individual may be lacking in romantic inclinations, a natural, unembarrassed approach to sex can be a refreshing and exciting change for people more used to partners who require an appalling level of exotic eroticism to generate any passion at all. The Virgo-Capricorn sex drive is as dependable and lasting as you might desire. You'll have a solid, committed relationship which endures reliably, and a happy family. Having someone you can count on for years to come—both in bed and out—provides a warm, secure feeling that lasts far beyond the silliness of initial romance.

Venus in Virgo with Mars in Aquarius

This is a very independent combination. Not only are you sure that your way is the only right way to do anything, but you're also so determined to be unique that even if you like a suggestion, you often reject it. You're innovative, efficient, and perhaps quite the dynamo at work, and you're also rather generous and unselfish, doing good deeds for those in need and the world in general.

You love helping people, and although you're fairly picky, you willingly befriend many who do not share your values or standards, just because they need you. Friendship matters to you, and you tend to focus on happy, enduring friendships rather than a committed relationship with one individual. Even if you think you do want romance, you somehow choose to remain aloof and untethered unless you make the effort to immerse yourself in a relationship. Should you decide mating is better than being alone at night, seek a best friend you admire and with whom you can share interests as well as a life.

Your Virgo-Aquarius lover is not an easy person to know. Unemotional, private, and seemingly uninterested in any relationship, this mate acts as though you're acquaintances, or at best casual friends. Emotions and emotional behavior are a source of extreme discomfort to this stoic character. To build a connection, try working together on a project or meaningful cause. Being totally involved with something of that sort will develop the relationship through a sense of camaraderie.

Seduction is difficult, for this is one individual who easily could enter a monastery without complaint. You might try a little subterfuge—by pointing out how healthy sex is both for the body and the mind, releasing tensions and stresses in a pleasant, painless, efficient way. Show your partner the many books written about the benefits of sex, and then embark on a program designed to demonstrate your theories. Just remember not to do anything that could be interpreted as confining, limiting, or possessive, or you'll lose a lover and a good buddy at the same time.

Venus in Virgo with Mars in Pisces

Relationships are a big issue in your life, and you've probably learned that offering love, support, and kindness is a happier alternative to being critical. Although you're particular and detail oriented, you're also rather emotional and quite sensitive, and you don't enjoy hurting anyone else. It feels more natural to reach out, offer loving attention, and to soothe away any hurt.

You seem to seesaw between focusing all your considerable attention on those in need and fleeing the scene for a bit of solitude so you can recharge your batteries. You know that you're good at taking care of other people, but wisely realize that an unbalanced relationship in which one person is the flower and the other the gardener is healthy for neither.

It's very difficult for you to end a relationship, for you don't like hurting anyone or being that assertive, so sometimes you hold back, not starting what you know you won't want to finish.

You want to find a mate who can give as good as he or she gets, and that's a positive goal. The key is, of course, finding the person you'd never want to leave and who'd never leave you in the lurch.

Your Virgo-Pisces lover is always thinking about you and worrying about your problems to the extent that you may feel greedy just by comparison. You can share whatever's on your mind, and he or she is interested, concerned, sympathetic, and ever ready to focus understanding eyes on you. Your lover happily listens for hours to your dreams, fantasies, and ambitions. He or she sees that you're eating your favorite foods, rubs your back willingly, and soothes you to sleep with a fanciful bedtime story if you're unselfconscious enough to accept one.

Sex is always tender, giving, and gentle—an emotional

mingling of body, mind, and soul. Your lover wants to please and satisfy you, even if he or she isn't immediately in the mood for sex. Before you begin to feel like a selfish slob, deliberately turn the tables. You make the dinner, get the tickets to a show, and surprise him or her with the choice. Later, draw a hot bubble bath and scrub your mate's back after a long soak in the fragrant water. It's be such a novelty for this mate to be on the receiving end, that he or she expends redoubled efforts to nurture and please you.

Venus in Libra-Mars Combinations

Venus in Libra with Mars in Aries

You're very aware of the necessity for harmonious relationships, and have plenty of energy to devote to your own. Although you're well aware of the frequent need for compromise when two people are intimately involved, you never feel you must lose sight of, or give up, your own individuality. In your world, it's all about a balancing act in which you get what you want but attempt not to step on anyone else's toes. Some days this is easier than others. You're certainly able to act swiftly and decisively without a second thought, and you try to be considerate when you can, although you're not usually willing to put yourself second to anyone else.

In your mind, you're part of a team—of two—and you want your mate to be a fully involved partner in that team. To you, a relationship is about sharing like interests, fulfilling compatible needs, and making yourself happy while pleasing your loved one as well. The key is clearly to find that sort of perfect partner who likes what you like and sees the world as you do. You can be friendly to anyone, but you won't make a commitment to anyone you think won't be just right for you.

Your Libra-Aries lover combines the best of charm and excitement. A genuinely friendly, outgoing person who loves to socialize and have fun, he or she can be a terrific asset at parties when a touch of enlivening is needed without a loss of decorum. The grand romantic gesture never had a greater champion. Remember how the "Great Gatsby" was hopelessly in love with his Daisy, and by giving party after party, hoped to attract her back to him? Libra-Aries is fully capable of living a life totally devoted to love and filled with larger-than-life gestures.

If you want to be the darling of this lively lover, make him or her the central part of your well-developed social whirl. Attend glitzy parties, meet your lover's variety of jazzy friends, smother each other with flowers, share marvelous treats, and indulge in grand affection. Appreciate being swept into bed with swift and calculated elegance, and although this mate never loses sight of his or her own desires for an instant, neither will Libra-Aries forget to indulge you in yours. For no lover is better able to sweep you off your feet without making you lose your balance.

Venus in Libra with Mars in Taurus

You're the indolent type, and pampered may be your favorite word. You could teach us all a thing or two about living the good life. You like being surrounded by the most luxurious, most beautiful things and people, and dealing with luxury items in some respect may be your business.

You're a great entertainer, and people who enjoy your deluxe style of feting won't soon forget the splendid treatment they received in your home. There's no such thing as a simple get-together as far as you're concerned; a grand buffet for a thousand, a costume ball, and a twelve-course sit-down dinner are more your style.

You prefer to remain calm and peaceful at all times, and although people sometimes seem to be taking advantage of your good nature, you find it difficult to speak up and set them straight. Actually they think your calm exterior is a sign of approval. You'd really rather not be forced to express angry feelings, for doing so is almost an impossibility for you—plus it's just so vulgar—shudder. When you do feel that an explosion is due, you usually just retreat from the relationship and the person causing you the problem rather than confront such a sensitive issue.

You seek a peaceful, happy, and tasteful partnership, and you're willing to make a lifetime commitment to the person who brings grace and pleasure into your life. Being companionable is key, as is the chemistry that brings you together. Then you can envision a happy lifetime together, which is what you really want to build.

Your Libra-Taurus lover is one of the most generous

people you're likely to meet. A bountiful expression of affection feels normal to this extravagantly romantic partner. An invitation to a simple dinner for two at home turns into a lavish spread prepared by a four-star chef while you loll fireside and listen to a violinist.

Libra-Taurus wants a partner who knows how to live well without exerting too much effort. Enough energy is expended during the hectic social season without having to go jogging or horseback riding during the day. Far better to use that extra energy in bed, indulging in lazy lovemaking sessions designed to give in-depth attention to every erogenous zone you both might have previously only suspected you possessed. Some people feel that approach worked better in times less hectic than these modern days, but to this mate a quickie is a dirty word. If you're willing to unplug the clock and devote yourself to romance, you've found a home and a warm heart to be your match.

Venus in Libra with Mars in Gemini

This is a highly mental combination. You prefer to keep things light, intellectual, and unemotional, and in fact, you may be the only one ever to woo a prospective mate in a book club. Because you have such a delightfully sparkling intellect and a natural ease with your own sexuality, a less than traditional method of courtship may work very well for you.

You love to be around people in social situations, communicating and exchanging ideas. Although others may not realize it, expressing yourself by sharing your thoughts is one of the chief ways in which you like to be close with someone you love. It's called pillow talk, after all, and to you it's the ultimate in intimacy. In fact, you may prefer the conversation to the physical.

You definitely want a relationship, but may find it difficult to be tied down, which to you could sometimes feel rather smothering. The sort of people who're so close that they seem to be living out of each other's pockets bewilder you totally. How can they breathe like that? Other people may call you noncommittal and unable to stick to your course, but you prefer to think of yourself as creatively unstructured, at least by anyone else.

Of course you do want love, but on your own terms, just as does everyone else. In your case it must be with a mate who remains interesting, perhaps someone who enjoys change enough to keep you guessing, and someone who can let you flirt a little at parties without calling it cheating.

Your Libra-Gemini lover is friendly and funny but cool and unimpassioned. This individual may be totally content with an affair of the mind, in which the two of you share your intimate thoughts without ever getting physical. One of those online romances or pen-pal situations could be ideal. That's because this mental mate lives mostly in the mind, and it's the intellectual things that seem most real to Libra-Gemini. So if you're seeking a passionate liaison in which the two of you are totally wrapped up in each other's bodies, souls, and minds, with constant touching, steamy sex, and a little possessiveness thrown in to keep things lively, advance to the Scorpio chapter. The two Air signs, Libra and Gemini, wouldn't think of burdening anyone with such a heavy style of relating.

Libra-Gemini prefers to indulge in lively chatter with a group of intellectuals, share clever flirting while nibbling through a fancy buffet, whisper in your ear during an art film, and if your hands brush while you're dipping into the popcorn, a wink may pass between you, but no sexual sparks are expected to fly. If you're seeking a clever, courteous person who has many social contacts, is never dull-witted or slow on the uptake, who keeps your interaction lively without any of the pressures of traditional romance, and who adores you but never smothers, this could be your dream mate. If you think about it, many married couples stop talking after the first flush departs. With this mate, you could be together into your dotages and still looking forward to what each other has to say. That's romance.

Venus in Libra with Mars in Cancer

You're romantic, tender, and gentle, and you live for the

moment when you can settle down with that special someone for a life of eternal, satisfying bliss. Because you're so other-person oriented, you're caring and solicitous with just about everyone you know. Even total strangers can sometimes be the lucky recipients of your ministrations. No matter whom you're with, you feel obliged to attend to the other person's needs or feelings, and in general to provide better care than anyone's mother ever did. Naturally this can be exhausting!

In fact, it can be exhausting for your significant other as well, for many people think that anyone so nice must have an ulterior motive. The fact that you spent an entire day cooking a favorite homemade delicacy for a virtual stranger can sometimes cause that individual to run in panic—fearing that you're setting some sort of emotional trap. You're not, of course you're not, but it's good to learn that other people sometimes just don't understand that anyone can be as nice as you are with no strings attached. Once you learn to go a little more slowly and to refrain from sharing your whole basket of goodies immediately, you attract the very partner you deserve—a soulmate who adores and appreciates you for those wonderful qualities.

In your mind, nothing less is acceptable. You want to be bonded permanently with the mate who completes your destiny, and on whom you can lavish all the love in your heart, and who will return the favor. It's the perfect ideal of love, but to you it simply feels like love the way it should be—and you're right.

Your Libra-Cancer lover is determined to make you the center of his or her world. No geisha ever did a better job pampering an emperor than this intuitive individual does for you. This lover just naturally knows what you like and is delighted to please you. Special presents for ordinary occasions, your favorite meals, and TLC on all fronts can be deliciously habit forming. Just try to be as considerate in return. Although it's hard to be the aggressor with this assertively nice individual, your mate would love to be the one receiving the flowers or being indulged with the breakfast in bed.

Romantic and sensitive, this sweetie loves being wrapped up in your arms as you take turns whispering sonnets (or rock lyrics) in each other's ear. Although the sex might not be wildly acrobatic, old fashioned coupling that fosters greater intimacy might be even more fulfilling, for more than anything else, this considerate mate wants to please you, for he or she derives pleasure from yours. Libra-Cancer is serious about love the way some people are serious about their careers. Forget casual flings! This mate wants a relationship with one special partner whom he or she can love and pamper into delirious eternity, and whoever rejected the idea of having your own personal geisha?

Venus in Libra with Mars in Leo

This is a proud, almost royal combination, and what you lack in emotional depth, you make up for with dignity and social awareness. You don't have to make an effort to get people to like you, for your naturally sexy sparkle and personal magnetism draw admirers to you.

You love to be around others, especially if you're the center of attention—not that you would behave like a show-off or do something as outrageous as dancing on a cocktail table wearing a lampshade on your head. You always radiate a dignified warmth, and maintaining your high standards of acceptable behavior is very important. You're just naturally adept in social situations.

Tasteful, you're uncomfortable with slushy displays of emotion from others. Such behavior is completely unacceptable, for you regard a lack of dignity as embarrassing and totally unsuitable. Loyal, you want a dependable, loving relationship with one person. You don't fall in love quickly or impetuously, and once in love, you stay that way. You absolutely refuse to indulge in tawdry affairs that will ultimately be meaningless despite their easy availability.

You want to be in a committed partnership with someone you love and admire, someone who is worthy of your affection and trust, and who other people see as a mate they wish was theirs.

Your Libra-Leo sweetie is loving, loyal, and determined to maintain high standards, making sure that you know what sort of behavior is acceptable and what is not. Your actions must never reflect badly on either of you. You might meet this socially solid individual at a yacht christening, a benefit performance, or a diplomatic soiree. Introduce yourself politely and make discreet conversation. Your assertiveness will be considered a sign of your good taste.

After you're well acquainted, it's okay to invite him or her home for a cocktail, provided that home is tastefully splendid and you have suitable makings for a private cocktail party. You won't earn points with the expectation of guzzling beer from a bottle while sitting uneasily on orange crates. If that's your situation, it's better to find a little boîte or to accompany this mate to his or her home, where you'll be entertained in tasteful elegance.

Your lover may even make the first pass, as long as it's obviously welcome. Libra-Leo is a very thoughtful, giving lover. And making love in a style to rival that of even the most exalted movie idols is no more than routine. Did you want your grapes peeled?

Venus in Libra with Mars in Virgo

Whether you're an artist, a craftsperson, a clothing designer, or an everyday individual, you like good design, and being surrounded by well-made, beautiful objects is very important to you. To every task you approach, you bring a careful attention to detail and a desire for form within function. Your taste is so excellent and so exacting that your friends may cringe when it's time to buy you a present.

You're a thoughtful and helpful lover. You just naturally help those you care about, and you're more than glad to do it. The tense perfectionism you bring to your work is mellowed somewhat in your dealings with people. That's because you desire good relationships, in which harmony and balance are prime components. You enjoy fun, as long as everyone is behaving tastefully, but you're a responsible person who must deal with obligations before allowing yourself to frolic.

You want to be in a peaceful relationship that isn't too terribly complicated. You're willing to go the extra mile for a lover, but you'd prefer not to be with someone who brings too much drama into the interaction. There should be a sense of peaceful commitment in which you each look out for the other and provide support and tenderness on a regular basis.

Your Libra-Virgo lover embodies the best of conservative virtues. Traditional in the best sense of the word, this individual works hard to maintain a world of balance and good taste. Charming and refined, he or she is always dependable, supportive, and a pleasure to have around.

If you're just beginning the relationship, take it slowly. Why should anyone trust instant intimacy, or people who blab every personal detail they can summon to relative strangers? Likewise, your mate does not respect those free souls who awaken each morning in a different bed.

Libra-Virgo wants a solid mate with whom he or she can build a secure relationship. It's permissible to spend plenty of time on the effort—good things take time to create. Get to know each other by sharing pleasant outings When you've established that the two of you are a couple, it's time enough to head for the bedroom. Then you discover that Libra-Virgo is as careful at making love as with everything else. You didn't just end up together by chance, did you? And your deepest sexual needs are just as worthy of his or her attention as is your favorite dessert. This is one situation where the phrase practice makes perfect really pays off.

Venus in Libra with Mars in Libra

You're a real team player; being with other people is just the way you like to live, and you consider those lone-wolf types a little strange. You're sociable and charismatic, always friendly and well mannered. You're blessed with much personal magnetism, and your charming, sparkling personality makes you both a sought-after partner and party guest. Totally at home in any social situation, you'd make a fine judge or diplomat because you're so able to maintain harmonious interaction among many different people.

A master of compromise, you realize that relationships require a willingness to engage in give-and-take, and this ability often puts you in a position of leadership. And because you feel that getting along happily with the people in your life is more important than simply getting your own way, you bend over backward to keep your relationships going smoothly.

Indecisiveness is one of your flaws. When you take any action, you feel compelled to consider both sides of every issue, and you may waver from choice to possibility while all your friends are biting their nails. In fact, you may be so busy weighing possibilities that the chance to act evaporates.

Thus you'd do well with a decisive partner, although you also don't like the idea of being steamrollered. You need someone who clarifies things for you and points out the way you'd want to take all along.

Your Libra-Libra lover is as pleasant a person as you might wish to encounter. Always thoughtful and considerate, he or she would never commit the slightest faux-pas, let alone thoughtlessly hurt your feelings. This isn't because this is a very sensitive mate, but rather one with excellent manners. Unemotional, unpossessive, and untemperamental, this individual is the antithesis of the word intense, and if you're used to a more impassioned style of relating, you may wonder if you actually have a relationship because your partner seems to be so emotionally uninvolved.

A cool mental approach to human interaction is just this mate's style of relating, and once you become used to this, you feel secure about his or her affections. For if you've received a commitment from this careful soul, you can be sure that his or her affections are genuine, and will remain constant. You'll have a mate who's always careful with your feelings and who tries to understand your needs and fulfill them.

In bed, this mate is sweet and loving, and endeavors to create an air of beauty and romance. The setting is lovely, soft music plays, and together you can recreate scenes from the great love stories throughout literature. It's not just about passion, but about the beauty of merging on all levels.

Venus in Libra with Mars in Scorpio

You desire a lovely relationship, and you have all the passionate intensity in the world to actualize it. Although you seem (and are) calm, affable, and easy-going, you persist forever until you get what you want. In fact, you can be a bit of a puzzle to others, who expect you to give in much more easily because you're so friendly and charming.

You refuse to engage in quarrels or arguments, preferring instead to manipulate others to your point of view. You're a master of persuasion, and so subtle and incisive is your brand of mental mastery that people rarely know they've been dallied with. They just feel that it's somehow much more pleasant to go along with your ideas because you have a way of making them sound so much more appealing, and since you keep interjecting them again and again, they eventually come to believe that the thought is mutual.

In relationships, you require a balance of good taste, social interaction, and passionate intensity. You want to give yourself over to a timeless love, and you will—as long as you don't have to give up good taste. You need to be devoted to, and count absolutely on, your partner.

Your Libra-Scorpio lover is very interested in you, and sometimes the trouble is that you feel he or she may be able to read your mind. While that may be more than delightful in bed, in other situations most of us prefer to keep a few things to ourselves. And, in fact, your mate may be a lot more private than he or she expects you to want to be. But your lover so clearly wishes to make things nice for you, it's hard to complain.

This is one partner who's never detached where your relationship is concerned. Building a closeness that can always be expanded upon is a main motivation. This lover reacts in such a viscerally intense way to everything, even he or she thinks a little mellowing might be in order. However placid Libra-Scorpio might like to appear, being uninvolved is simply not in his or her makeup.

Libra-Scorpio loves to entertain you at home. Having a nice place where you can retreat with your friends for cozy evenings is important to this mate, and he or she loves to make meals for intimate tête-à-têtes.

After the last toast is drunk, you're propelled, with a gentle yet insistent hand, toward the bedroom. There you discover a lush style of lovemaking that's designed to open you both up to the deeper, more intimate secrets that lovers can share. You easily can see how this mode of lovemaking could be addictive—and it's meant to be—for a lifetime.

Venus in Libra with Mars in Sagittarius

You're a very idealistic individual, and seeing that others get a fair shake may be a full-time job for you. You're interested in making the world a better place and may try to actualize your ideals on your own personal level. Relationships are very important to you, but you may be more comfortable with many casual but very pleasant friendships instead of one primary romance. On the other hand, you may be intimately involved with one person who shares your ideals and who works with you to actualize them.

You very much enjoy outdoor activities, and to you romance is sweetest when you're strolling hand-in-hand outdoors in nature beside someone who appeals to you. To you a mellow relationship in which you enjoy each other's company, share common goals and ideals, and treat each other with kindness, is the way to live. That's the sort of commitment you could easily make.

Your Libra-Sagittarius lover can be hard to pin down. Not only does this individual resist making a decision, but also he or she hates to be tied down by the wrong partner. Often a free spirit, this mate loves to roam the world, having fun talking with people and discussing interesting notions. No matter how charming your lover seems, and how certain you are that he or she adores you, just try to give your mate orders and watch him or her fade permanently from view.

Likewise, jealousy is not an emotion you should express. Possessiveness is something this individual refuses to tolerate, first because it's tacky, and second because it can be so confining. Keeping things light and pleasant is always preferable, and you can be certain that no affair (or even marriage) will be characterized by the type of closeness that could be considered even remotely limiting.

To express your interest in this mate, offer an invitation to an event that's intellectually stimulating and located in pretty surroundings. Just because this mate may be gorgeous, and have a dynamite body, don't assume that hopping into bed is uppermost on his or her mind. When the time is right, you may have to be the aggressor, for this mate likes to talk and may need some encouragement to get physical. Once you focus his or her energies on a little physical communication, you may discover that you share a lot more than a mere philosophical orientation.

Venus in Libra with Mars in Capricorn

You're an ambitious person, a hard worker, and a disciplined leader who never loses track of your basic humanity. Although relationships are sometimes problematical for you, you're determined to make every effort to have a good marriage and a comforting family life. Practical and conservative, you like order and responsibility in others, yet you never lose sight of your basic idealism and fairness. You enjoy beauty and require pretty surroundings, but you're not likely to be any sort of collector unless it's art or something else that will appreciate in value.

You naturally attract prominent friends, and judging people according to their social status maybe one of your chief flaws. You don't readily appreciate people who lack polish, and you have no real desire to change this about yourself. When you marry, you seek a partner of status equal to or greater than your own and who enhances your life.

You're not the sort to marry your secretary, unless this person is exiled royalty and extraordinarily gorgeous. As in everything else, a relationship is another way in which you're building something of substance. You want a long-lasting partnership with somebody you esteem and admire.

Your Libra-Capricorn lover is as proper as your great-grandmother. This mate never appears in public sporting an outlandish Halloween costume, nor is he or she likely to want to fool around in the backseat of a car. A hidden sensor resides inside this individual's head, continually passing judgment on what's acceptable behavior. So if you're interested in advancing a beginning relationship, don't plan on an invitation to an orgy or even to a group hot tub party.

A family dinner (especially if your family has a pedigree) is a great way to break the ice. This individual appreciates tradition, and enjoys a chance to know you better, combined with the opportunity to give your background the once over. It's wiser after that to let your partner take the lead, for this mate feels more comfortable at the head of the group, and even determined wooing on your part won't generate an interest where there is none.

Libra-Capricorn is seeking a spouse, and dating is really more of a prelude than an end in itself. Once you're a pair, your mate will find a luxury abode in a safe neighborhood, where your children can attend good schools. If this seems like an excess of effort to put into a mere engagement, think how careful and considerate he or she will be of your needs once you're married.

Venus in Libra with Mars in Aquarius

This combination is more intellectual than emotional. You love to think and to communicate your ideas, and because of your innate graciousness, you have a way of making even the most outrageous concepts seem acceptable. That's because you recognize that innovation and originality are much better accepted when you don't step on people's toes.

You work well in groups and enjoy belonging to many different organizations, situations in which it's quite natural to meet people for romance or friendship.

Although you believe in marriage as a worthwhile ideal, often during your life it feels more comfortable to you to have many friendships rather than a single romantic involvement. You don't feel compelled to marry early, and in fact may wait until quite late in your life to tie the knot. Once you meet someone you feel shares your concerns and outlooks, you're able to make a commitment and settle down. You need a partnership of equals that functions on all the necessary levels, physical, spiritual, and intellectual.

Your Libra-Aquarius lover demands a free rein. Forget passionate outbursts, jealous fits, or even helpful suggestions, and if any of these are typical of the way you like to relate, you'll be home alone before you can say oops. If you like to have things free and easy, with each person guaranteed the liberty to come and go according to his own desires, you've met the right partner.

This person loves parties with a purpose, and if you spot an attractive individual with terrific bone structure wittily offering an appealingly outrageous proposal to a group of people at a cocktail party to raise money for a good cause, go on over. Libra-Aquarius wants to get to know you. This mate loves the opportunity to add someone to his or her collection of friends.

When you're a pair, you spend hours discussing the virtues of a variety of ideas, ideologies, and philosophies. This is this mate's way of developing intimacy. After many hours of talk and cocktails in his or her well-appointed home, you may be ready to scream, but make a discrete pass instead. Sometimes Libra-Aquarius forgets about sex altogether. Put a copy of "Physical" by Olivia Newton-John on the stereo to give a hint! Eventually he or she will lean down and bite you on the ankle, in what must be the most original-yet oddly tasteful-opening move in history.

Venus in Libra with Mars in Pisces

You're the nicest person in the world, and unfortunately sometimes people tend to take advantage of you. You rarely enjoy being assertive enough to put them in their place, which can be quite frustrating. Having congenial relationships is very important to you. You'd far rather withdraw from a problem then slug it out, even though you may feel that this attitude limits the intimacy you can develop with others.

You enjoy very much socializing with friends. Your friendly, sympathetic manner makes you a sought-after guest, as well as the receptacle for many confidences to which you prefer not to be privy. When you develop friendships with people who're light and cheerful, and who do not need a Wailing Wall, you feel much happier.

Because you're so nice and congenial, it's sometimes difficult for you to reveal yourself to others—you find it easier to play the role they choose to assign to you, which means that unfortunately they are not getting the benefit of knowing the real, complete you. Keep in mind that this makes it much more difficult for people to consider your feelings or your real needs—how can they if you refuse to reveal them? Likewise, slipping away from a conflict or resisting in an underhanded manner may reduce momentary aggravation, but it does nothing to curb repeat offenses.

Ironically, you're the perfect person to have a truly happy relationship, but your selflessness sometimes gets in the way. Once you look after your own needs a little bit more assertively, it's easy for you to find the true love you want and deserve.

Your Libra-Pisces lover requires a good deal of attention from you. Because this individual is determined to go along with whatever you plan, it's important for you to make an effort to discern his or her real opinions, needs, feelings, and preferences. It's always worthwhile to peel away the glossy veneer to get at the real person underneath, especially if it's someone you care for.

Because your mate may lack self-confidence, be assertive

enough for two. Demonstrate that expressing true feelings is not only acceptable, but a positive step indeed that you welcome.

In bed, it's wise for you to take the lead, and also to encourage him or her when natural hesitation and insecurities surface. As you spend more and more time developing a healthy and happy level of intimacy, it becomes easier for each of you to express your needs and desires. All Libra-Pisces needs is a little encouragement and a lot of TLC, which will be returned in abundance. With some effort on your part, you'll have found a truly gentle human being who can be your best friend, confidant, cheerleader, and soulmate all rolled up into one.

Venus in Scorpio-Mars Combinations

Venus in Scorpio with Mars in Aries

This is such a hot combination that when you walk outside in the rain, the drops of water sizzle on your skin. Seriously, you have a kind of fiery, passionate intensity that's hard to mask. You want to be involved with a partner at a very deep level, and you have the intuitive sensitivity to discern your true mate and the impulsiveness of action to make the relationship a reality almost instantaneously.

You allow no interference from anybody. You know what interests you, as well as the way you like to operate, and you feel right only when you alone set your course. That does not mean, however, that you grant a partner the same grace. Along with being determined and possessive, you must be the first in line, with those you care about following in your wake. This could prove a mighty annoyance to a great many individuals, but fortunately you deign to interact with so few people that you're dominating only to those who really matter. As for the rest of the world—who cares?

This single minded approach to life carries over to everything you do. It's all or nothing for you, whether you're involved in a love affair, an athletic competition, or a project at work. Sometimes your intensity of emotional involvement bothers even you, and you make yourself feel smothered, then retreat, leaving your partner bewildered. The give and take of love may be difficult for you, but you more than make up for it with the degree of passion and complete affection you bestow on a lover.

Your Scorpio-Aries lover runs hot and cold, but is never lukewarm. Sometimes you're totally enveloped by this magnetic presence, leaving not an instant's worth of time or space for you to entertain even a thought in which your partner is not central. Then you're left alone for days at a time without even a phone call, wondering if you'll ever see this mate again.

If you protest, your lover is quick to insist that feelings haven't changed but that he or she needs to be free. Demand the same courtesy and you haven't a chance in the world. Although loyal, generous, friendly, and helpful in many, many ways, Scorpio-Aries can be very selfish and very self-centered in his or her treatment of a mate, and only when your love style demands such magnetic intensity is a liaison with this firecracker worth it.

In bed, Scorpio-Aries can be wickedly delightful. Not only can this demon intuit your deepest fantasies, he or she hasn't an ounce of inhibition about actually trying them all. If you're susceptible to this brand of chemistry—and who wouldn't be—this lover will habitually sweep you up in a crescendo of passion that can make you hear Ravel's Bolero even when the stereo's broken. No wonder this magnetic individual can get away with so much—with Scorpio-Aries, it's easy to see how one can be "by love possessed."

Venus in Scorpio with Mars in Taurus

You're an extreme person, although your implacable exterior may hide this fact from all but a very few intimates. You go your own route, and no one can make you even consider wavering. When you want something, you really want it, and owning that which you desire is of utmost importance. Unfortunately, this attitude also extends to your mate, and although it may be flattering to be wanted so much, most people balk at being thought of as a possession. Of course, in all fairness, you also tolerate much jealousy from a mate, but then you have a lot of ability to tolerate.

You may hesitate to express your feelings, particularly anger or love, and particularly in words, because often you feel that you're on the line, and this is very uncomfortable for you. If you become angry, you often repress it until it builds inside you into a mighty force that just has to erupt in a big way, usually far out of proportion to the event that triggered it.

Nobody combines sexuality and sensuality as well as you do. Your libido—and the week-long lovemaking marathons you engage in as a matter of course—may have made you a legend among past lovers. You feel that sex is something really worth devoting plenty of time and all your considerable energy, and since you're not physically active in a lot of other ways, there's nothing to stop you short of your partner's exhaustion.

Your Scorpio-Taurus lover likes to lick, bite, kiss, touch, stroke, and demonstrate every other verb associated with sex. This mate tucks you into bed and proceeds to take over your body as though it were a new toy that belongs only to him or her. Have a wish or a suggestion? Fine, as long as your partner didn't have something else in mind first. At least where sex is concerned, this fixed individual is more willing to receive suggestions—not that there is much he or she hasn't tried, except the quickie.

Scorpio-Taurus knows that relationships are important, and thus the value of compromise is obvious, so much so that your partner is more than willing for you to do so. Obviously, if you're a strongly independent, freedom-loving individual, this may be hard for you to swallow, but then so will be the rest of this mate's jealousy and possessiveness. On the other hand, if you're calm and cool and very self-assured, and you like to laze around and be consumed by a partner's total involvement with you, if you can enjoy being fed treats in front of the fire while someone decorates your body with whipped cream, which then will lovingly be licked off for hours, then you might feel right at home.

It's quite obvious to focus on sex when considering this person as a mate, but the fact is that there's way more than sex involved. This individual is capable of true devotion over decades and decades, and could provide you with hot, fantastic sex for the rest of your life. That's in addition to devotion, a secure family life, and plenty of money. This is a partner who's hard to beat if stability and a long-term relationship are what you seek.

Venus in Scorpio with Mars in Gemini

You want to have a single, passionately intense relationship with one individual, but it's really hard for you to sit still long enough to allow one to develop. This ants-in-the pants tendency is as frustrating to you as it is to everyone else. It's not that you're fickle so much as that you get physically itchy with too much continuity. And you do tend to like to try on new partners. It's easy for you to become quickly enamored with someone you've just met, and your tendency is to want to rush into bed with this person whether for actual sex or a lot of laughter and giggling. You like the idea of early intimacy, intimacy on-the-fly, or something that just passes for intimacy, when really it's just a little bit of fun. Friends may tease you about this love-the-one-you're-with philosophy.

Eventually you'll certainly want to have a close, caring relationship with a multifaceted partner who can make you feel eternally interested. And as long as that person permits you the freedom to be on your own enough to stave off the specter of boredom, you're be faithful. You just like to keep things lively whether on your own, or with a mate. That's why you're a playful and cheerful lover.

You enjoy many levels of interaction, including conversation, and you're more willing than most of the Scorpio combinations to share your feelings verbally. Your intuition is strong, and if a mate is struggling to share something important, you sometimes can verbalize it for him or her.

Your Scorpio-Gemini lover is a strange combination of heavy and light, as if someone were trying to play a Hungarian Rhapsody on a piccolo. Inside this mate is all that serious, single-minded passion that desires only closeness and depth, yet he or she seems able at the same time to flit from acquaintance to acquaintance, partaking only of cocktail party banter and keeping this true nature secret from all.

The best way to interest Scorpio-Gemini is by being truly fascinating—the sort of person who has two careers, an anecdote filled family, ten or twenty hobbies, and a lot of experience with life. Then you'll always have a new facet of yourself to reveal.

Being a bit of a chameleon in bed is good as well. For although your lover may not want to stray, he or she doesn't mind at all the idea that you're several people all rolled up into one. In return, you get a mate who can be both passionately emotional and sparklingly intellectual. And that's a rare bird, indeed.

Venus in Scorpio with Mars in Cancer

You're incredibly emotional, but you may sometimes go for weeks without revealing your feelings to a single soul. It's easy for you to intuit everyone else's emotions, but somehow you try your best to keep your own under wraps. And considering the fact that almost everything you do is based on your feelings, that's no small task. You're a super friend who just naturally knows how to mother everybody you meet. Because you're so sensitive to others, people usually trust you with their deepest confidences and come to you when they need some understanding and TLC. You may often wish that you felt free to be as unguarded with the people who reveal themselves to you, but more often than not, the help is one-sided.

You're a devoted family person, and anyone who has inspired your love will retain it forever, unless he or she injures you so deeply that the bad feelings you refuse to air cause you to harbor a permanent grudge. And although you may have one relative or two about whom you feel this way, it's more likely that you feel very close to your family.

You desire a deep, close relationship with a partner you can count on totally. Casual flings are anathema to you, and you may be one of the few people left nowadays who remains a virgin until marriage.

Your ability to form such close ties is enviable, unless you become involved with someone who needs looser reins. Then you're both in trouble, for you're more than able to love in a way that some people would feel is smothering. At some point your children, in particular, may rebel strongly against this smothering mothering, but they of course will still love you.

Your Scorpio-Cancer lover may retreat to a closet for days

to brood over some slight that you weren't even aware of having made. If you ask what's wrong, the answer is invariably "Nothing." Perhaps it's the snarl in reply that gives him or her away. So you need to remember that this is one person who responds well to the kid glove treatment.

When your lover is happy, nobody is nicer, and you know that this mate will be devotedly on your side forever. This individual bends over backwards to please you, whether in the kitchen or the bedroom, and he or she is an expert at knowing what will do the trick. Tender and gentle, passionate and intense, your mate's style of loving combines all the subtle emotional nuances that mark a really sensitive partner. He or she delights in serving you breakfast in bed, hugs and cuddles through the night, and knows how to make you feel more cherished than you ever thought you had a right to feel. When you consider how special this could be during the course of an affair, it seems worthwhile, but imagine decades of this sort of devotion, and you have a good sense of what it's like to spend your life with Scorpio-Cancer.

Venus in Scorpio with Mars in Leo

You're proud, independent, and insist on having the upper hand in any situation. Whether at work or in relationships, you must be the boss. Often you attract partners to challenge your authority, and then the sparks really fly; but even with a mellower mate, lots of friction is a normal way for you to relate. Lovers' quarrels followed by passionate reconciliations may well be part of your everyday routine, and if you could manage a calmer liaison, you would probably consider it deadly dull. Intense interaction is the only kind you want.

You're a very loyal friend who'll fight to the death for any cause or person you love. You take yourself and everyone else very seriously, and heaven help the individual who decides you need a little teasing. Being made the brunt of anyone else's joke is your least favorite thing—you can do a slow burn for ages until you finally blow, which is an awesome sight to behold.

Financial security is important to you, not just for

sustenance but because you want to be able to have the kind of lifestyle that includes expensive vacations, lavish parties, and deluxe presents for those you love. Because it's so hard for you to express your emotions, you may rely on expensive presents to do it for you.

You have a good heart, and a lifetime of devotion to offer to the right mate. It's your goal to find that perfect soulmate and settle down forever together.

Your Scorpio-Leo lover is quite a handful. Somehow this individual radiates an aggravating arrogance that manages to be sexy as well as annoying. And not only does this mate note the effect on you, but also he or she takes it for granted that you're wildly attracted in return—why should you be any different from everyone else? It might be enough to turn you off entirely, if he or she weren't so genuinely nice. Under the surface is a real friend. Scorpio-Leo will go all out to help you realize your goals, dreams, and potentials.

Not big on sweet nothings, Scorpio-Leo isn't likely to spend hours whispering in your ear. That doesn't mean he or she won't bite it, however. This mate loves sex, and likes to make a production out of a seduction. It was probably someone with this combination who invented those adult motels with faux fur covered waterbeds, mirrored ceilings, whirlpool baths for two, and closed-circuit adult-only television. Chances are you'll be entertained at home where your lover can maintain control. The music will be hot, the bed warm, and your reception far from cool. And after you witness all the trouble aimed at providing you with a really spectacular night, you'll understand why your lover feels everybody ought to be crazy about him or her—and you'll probably agree.

Venus in Scorpio with Mars in Virgo

This can be a very healing combination. Even if you don't work in medicine, you have the ability to help people feel better when they're ill. Often the way you choose to show your affection is by helping out and doing favors.

Serious and intense, you would have to study frivolity for

years at an accredited institution before you could acquire the knack for having meaningless fun. It's not that you're antisocial, although any Gemini friends you have may think so; it's just that to you life and love are very serious matters, and you prefer depth to quantity. It's impossible for you to stand around drinking martinis and chatting aimlessly when you know there is so much you could be doing.

You can be incredibly critical, and if someone really makes you mad, you know just what to say to devastate him or her. When young, you may have been known for your teasing remarks that could produce tears in your innocent victims, but with adulthood you probably do your best not to use your sensitivity to hurt others.

You understand the importance of kindness, and it's your goal to find a soulmate and share a healing and happy life together. You want to be with someone you can love in a devoted way and have that devotion returned in kind.

Your Scorpio-Virgo lover has a million things to do that are really crucial, and tends to be totally immersed in work until it's done satisfactorily. Then this individual is more than willing to focus that laser beam energy on you. This is one person capable of doing everything that pleases you from A to Z, from mild pleasure to quivering ecstasy, from fantasy to reality, and if this sounds like a catalog, that is exactly how he or she goes about it.

Hard-working, even in bed, Scorpio-Virgo takes an amazing facility for details and turns it onto you to turn you on. Making you feel good gives him or her the most pleasure, so this mate orchestrates spectacular sex, and even slow to excite partners end up completely satisfied.

This is not to say that such expertise is a result of having had many experiences with many partners. Scorpio-Virgo can be almost prudish about sex unless it's a result of love. Sexual merging represents a very special kind of communication, and he or she sneers of those people who engage in sex the way they play tennis. So if a Scorpio-Virgo has been making your nights sizzle, you can probably consider that as strong a declaration of love as a valentine pinned nightly to your pillow.

Venus in Scorpio with Mars in Libra

With this combination you often find yourself in relationships that feature intimate, one-to-one combat. You may feel that you're willing to compromise when necessary, but that you somehow manage to end up with partners who just like to fight. You really do want a close relationship that allows you and your mate to express yourselves totally, but you often just can't figure out how to get what you want. Sometimes you (or your partner) are too competitive, and even a friendly game of ping-pong can be a battle to the death. A relaxed sense of balance may be what you need to strive to maintain.

People are very attracted to you, and you may find yourself habitually with many more invitations than you can accept. As much as you enjoy being affable and charming, your ease in social situations may trap you in interactions that you consider far too shallow for your taste. You really want a few friends and just one mate who can understand your true self and with whom you can relate in a serious way. Since you often keep your inner feelings hidden, most of the people you know would probably be surprised if you shared this information.

Your Scorpio-Libra lover always wants to be together, even when some time spent apart would be far better for your relationship. If you want a permanent liaison with this well-meaning individual, take some responsibility for your relationship and demand some time apart so that tensions can disperse. I'm not advocating separate bedrooms, just an occasional solitary afternoon a week.

You need to make sure that you both can feel your individual needs are being met—and Scorpio-Libra is liable to feel that those needs should merge, which is often impossible.

Sex is a great way to put that competitive energy to positive use. Scorpio-Libra is very willing to experiment with new ideas in bed. And although this mate is probably better at responding to your advances, he or she is happy to follow your suggestions. Seeing that each of you has different (but equally important and equally enjoyable) preferences in bed may make this individual better able to recognize the validity of compromise in every day life. And that is what he or she wanted to achieve all along.

Venus in Scorpio with Mars in Scorpio

If you were to tell your closest friends that you have far too much sex appeal for your own good, they probably wouldn't understand. By now they've noticed that you always have someone attractive in hot pursuit, but it's hard for others to recognize the fact that you don't often want to be caught by the people who respond to your magnetic, sexy presence. Just because the most gorgeous person around takes a fancy to you, doesn't mean that you'll return the favor—no matter how skilled he or she is at seduction. Fending off advances is a tedious business, but you refuse to be swayed from your true course.

Love is an all or nothing proposition, and the words casual and sex do not belong in the same sentence as far as you're concerned. So you may be providing quite a comedy for your less magnetic friends to watch as you retreat from the ever-present sexual advances of a parade of admirers. You do not fall in love every other Thursday as your Libra-Gemini friends do. In fact, you may fall in love only once in a lifetime, but to you, that's the right number of times.

You can look into someone's eyes and know instantly—even before the first hello—that this is the mate of your soul, and from that moment on, every fiber of your being is involved in capturing his or her love forever, but your quiet, casual manner will not give your feelings away for some time, even to the one you love.

Your goal is always the one and only true love, and that is a daunting task. But when you find what you truly seek you can create the kind of partnership that others envy. You want to have a love for the ages, and in your mind nothing less will do.

Determined, stubborn, and intense are extreme words for

everyone else but may be quite mild where your Scorpio-Scorpio lover is concerned. This individual absolutely always prevails, so why not just go with the flow? If you're a similar person, there may be some mighty battles of will between the two of you. In order to live together without seething constantly and engaging in fisticuffs occasionally, it's important for both of you to maintain your own independence. If you make it clear that you're doing what you must, just as he or she does, chances are your mate will understand.

Of course, this understanding does not extend to other partners. Scorpio-Scorpio is very possessive and very jealous, and if you want to play the field, do not dally here, for this individual's rage is frightening. On the other hand, he or she is more than willing to make and keep a commitment forever, so despite ample opportunities, it would be quite rare for this mate to be unfaithful. The Scorpio devotion is as legendary as its passion.

When you're propelled wordlessly to the bedroom, you learn what all the fuss is about. Scorpio-Scorpio wants to consume you in an absolute inferno of passion in which you both melt, are joined together into one quivering entity, and are reborn as new individuals. Never again will you be able to look into each other's eyes without the recognition of what you shared. And that's why forever is the only time frame this mate knows.

Venus in Scorpio with Mars in Sagittarius

You're a passionate idealist. You're very involved in a number of causes in which you believe, for example animal-rights, And to you, right-minded people are the only ones you're willing to tolerate. You don't care for people who shrug and say *well, whatever* when something important is at stake.

You can experience people very intensely in a short time, and often require time outdoors alone to recoup from social interactions. When you love someone, you're very possessive, wanting always to know his or her whereabouts, yet you absolutely refuse to allow a partner the same rights, and you realize that this is very unreasonable. But you must maintain your freedom at all costs, even if breaking off a relationship is the only solution.

You may feel that you're unlucky at love, because you have trouble building a lasting relationship that provides the intense kind of interaction you crave. What may really be happening is that you feel smothered by the kind of partner who's able to relate as intensely as you crave, so you press for greater closeness with someone who's better at freedom than intimacy. Such challenges help you define your own romantic requirements in specific terms.

Obviously it's a question of balance. You need to find someone who can relate at the level that feels comfortable to you and yet who doesn't hem you in. With the right mate you can create a relationship that is highly rewarding and long-lasting.

Your Scorpio-Sagittarius lover needs to be possessive without being possessed. Once you're as close as you both want, even without a confrontation, your partner is able to relax. And when you insist that you have things to do on your own, just as your mate does, he or she won't feel threatened or smothered. The people who most fear entrapment are sometimes the ones with the tightest grips, and often the best way to get somebody to come closer is to let go. This is an important lesson for Scorpio-Sagittarius to learn.

Once he or she learns to relax with you, you share rousing philosophical discussions as you lie on the grass under the stars. That gives this mate the perfect opportunity to discover the true you as a prelude to sharing other, more intimate things. Your partner enjoys making love outdoors, and may prefer sex in any number of crazy places, as well as sex at home in bed. Experimental, innovative, and uninhibited, Scorpio-Sagittarius is willing to try anything once. The key is for you to make him or her see that once is not enough.

Venus in Scorpio with Mars in Capricorn

This is a highly-charged, powerful combination. You're quite used to telling other people what to do—and to getting your own way. Success may be the most important thing in your life, and if it is, you can be sure that you'll have it. Although you do have intense feelings, you may channel them into achieving your goals rather than into romance. An expert at concealing your true feelings, you may be perceived as quite unemotional. Serious and hard-working, you have no regard for frivolity and shallow fun. Everything must mean something to you for it to matter; you don't waste your time on things that don't.

If the casual observer assumed that to you love was unimportant and you didn't believe in marriage, that person would be very, very wrong. You want a relationship with a partner you can count on to help you in life, to share your goals and their achievement, and to fill your sexual needs. You love sex, as long as you can always be on top, but the obsession with sex that's part of our contemporary culture strikes you as jaded and foolish. As in every other area of life, you have serious objectives. You want a marriage that is a true partnership, and in reality that is a very important and worthwhile goal.

Your Scorpio-Capricorn lover is not big on expressing sentiment verbally, or sharing cute little gestures of affection, but that does not imply a lack of tender feelings. The fact that this individual is spending time with you at all means a greater degree of involvement for him or her than an engagement ring means to someone else. In fact, if you want to know where you stand, ask for a declaration of intentions. That's something that this mate will understand, and he or she is more than willing to tell you where you figure in future plans. Scorpio-Capricorn may have your entire future mapped out for decades—step-by-step, with precise detail—and you're rarely consulted. If you think this mate may mellow with marriage and loosen up, you're just fooling yourself, so if you prefer not to take orders, say "I don't," not "I do," because he or she doesn't intend to stop giving them.

In bed, your lover may be as bossy as everywhere else. You receive directions about where to put your head and your feet, but this doesn't mean that your partner is selfish. He or she can tune in very clearly to your sexual messages, and, being proud of a successful performance, makes a real effort to see that you both are completely satisfied. As long as you're willing to dance to your mate's tune, you'll have an extremely nice, well-heeled life.

Venus in Scorpio with Mars in Aquarius

With this combination, you might be quite a loner unless you feel able to align your own energies with friends with whom you share deep personal commitments. Only when you feel a sense of simpatico with another person do you let down your shield. Otherwise you prefer to remain guarded because you don't wish to allow anyone to have a chance to interfere with your plans. Self-determination is all to you.

Relationships often feel oppressively complicated to you. Social interaction can feel stressful, although you're truly capable of devotion, and can love with your complete heart.

The idea of a permanent relationship makes you nervous, because you don't want anybody to restrict you. When you connect with people who respect this about you, they usually feel that you're too possessive and bossy for them. And casual dating is a bore.

Obviously a bit of work is needed. Finding a balance between intimate commitment and personal freedom is the key. Then when you're with the right person, whom you trust and adore, it becomes easy to give your heart and share your life.

Your Scorpio-Aquarius lover needs somebody who can scoff at traditional values without feeling threatened. This individual absolutely refuses to follow the usual patterns of social behavior, particularly in love. He or she may invite you away for a weekend half an hour after you've met, then ignore you for a month. It's hard for this mate to get into the routine of romance.

Scorpio-Aquarius is quite shy about expressing feelings, and in fact, feels very uncomfortable with personal, very intense passion, unless it's being channeled toward a good cause. When he or she is faced with passion for a single individual instead of a group cause, panic sometimes ensues. Until this uneasiness is conquered, this mate may prefer to experiment with group sex in those adult clubs that cater to couples who swing. Even if you only go with each other, and never touch another person, your mate feels that it's less threatening in a group atmosphere. Ultimately Scorpio-Aquarius can be a totally loyal, committed mate. All that's needed is for him or her to feel that the two of you form a group that's useful, meaningful, and good.

Venus in Scorpio with Mars in Pisces

This can be either a very manipulative combination or a very healing, unselfish one, depending on how you use it. You're a terrific psychologist, and not only can you easily see people's motivations, but also you can pick up on the feelings that cause them, as if by osmosis.

Because of your extreme sensitivity to all sorts of vibrations, you sometimes prefer to stay at home in the security of an atmosphere you can control. That doesn't mean that you're acting like a hermit however, because you love to entertain your close friends at home. Although you don't make a big deal about being a host or hostess, you have the ability to make people feel really at home when they visit you. Your sensitivity to their emotional needs makes you able to help others feel their best. Your devotion to a mate is just as touching, and you're greatly in demand as a partner.

You find this is very comforting, for all you really desire is to be wrapped in the arms of the one perfect soulmate who completes your destiny. You believe in true love, and you want to share it, to spend your entire life in mutual devotion and tender affection with the right person.

Your Scorpio-Pisces lover is so healing that many people just naturally take advantage of him or her without meaning to. This individual finds it hard to be assertive or to yell "Hey! I've been listening to your problems for hours! Why don't we change the subject? Or better yet, why don't you pay some attention to me?" And, if you never suspect there's a problem, and how you stop taking advantage? Sometimes it requires a decision to be aggressively considerate.

Scorpio-Pisces loves to hole up at home with you to cuddle, exchange ideas, and listen to music. This mate adores being treated to a champagne bubble bath for two, or for you to cater dinner from a great takeout place. You get the idea-put some effort into turning the tables instead of always being on the receiving end.

A vacation from doing unselfish good deeds can be so refreshing that your lover might suggest a weekend alone in bed where you both can take your time exploring each other's bodies and each other's fantasies. And nobody is more able (or more willing) than Scorpio-Pisces to discern and act out the fantasies you didn't even know you had. Not only do you get to know each other better, but you discover more about yourselves as well. And that, after all, is one of the purposes of love.

Venus in Sagittarius-Mars Combinations

Venus in Sagittarius with Mars in Aries

High-flying and fancy-free is your MO, and honesty, integrity, and independence your credo. You're one of those naturally twitchy people—sitting still for an hour is a major trial and sitting still for someone else's routine is an impossibility. When in school, you probably were often in trouble for being so restless and disruptive, and you felt that the teachers were narrow minded, rather than justifiably annoyed. Maintaining the integrity of your own self expression is the most important thing in the world to you, and you'd much rather get in hot water than compromise yourself. Doing things your own way, for your own reasons, is more important to you than getting along with others.

You're not particularly emotional or relationship oriented, which is not to say you're unfriendly, for nothing is farther from the truth. You love to meet new people, and you're often the life of the party. The guy wearing a lampshade or the girl dancing on the cocktail table might very well be you, for you're always more interested in the activity of the moment then in the impression you might be making on others.

While other people might bemoan dating as horrendous, you find it highly enjoyable. You love hooking up with new people and I mean that literally. You like having a collection of lovers on the spur of the moment and you don't mind letting go when it's time to move on. You're hard to harness and very hard to rope in. Does that mean there's no chance at all for you to have a permanent relationship? Of course not. If you want it, someone will want you. You just have to want it.

Your Sagittarius-Aries lover is rarely interested in forever. This is one of the Venus-Mars combinations that experiences the most difficulty in settling down, and the fact is that not everybody wants permanence. Sagittarius-Aries might have a hard time with even tomorrow. So if you want happily ever after, consider moving along to the Cancer-Taurus chapter before you get too invested. If you want action, excitement, and fun, read on. Nobody knows how to have a better time than this expansive individual. No idea is too bizarre, no convention too forbidding, and no adventure worth missing. "Let's do it now!" says your lover, and you both may be on a freighter bound for Africa before you remember you don't speak Swahili.

In bed, Sagittarius-Aries may not be sensitive or tender, but he or she surely is exciting and fun—if you get to the bed, that is, for you may find yourself making love impetuously under the bleachers during the game, in the grass beside the highway, or in the backyard when it's (you hope) too dark for the neighbors to see. Now is the most vital time of all to him or her, so if you can enjoy an affair of colorful, carefree abandon, this is absolutely the best person for you to date.

Venus in Sagittarius with Mars in Taurus

You have a streak of idealism that won't quit, and you're a tireless doer of good works. When a new idea inspires you, you dig right in, determined to give your all. You love the outdoors, and you probably have a really spectacular garden, even if it just resides on the windowsill.

Sometimes you're at odds with yourself over your conflicting desires. One of these is the urge to be free of anything that could tie you down versus the desire to acquire a great many possessions. What probably happens is that you buy on impulse and then, feeling overwhelmed by all the things surrounding you, give the things you buy away.

Another conflict is in romance. You alternate between the desire to remain unattached and the need to settle down. In a relationship, you can sometimes feel possessive and then be disgusted with yourself for being so narrow-minded. These swings can be confusing to your partners as well as yourself.

What may happen is that you find yourself dating people who are very hard to pin down; this way your internal conflict is expressed externally through the significant others in your life. The key is in finding a balance, finding the person who is exciting yet who wants a stable life. That way you can share good times without feeling smothered by each other and always remain compatible.

Your Sagittarius-Taurus lover needs a solid mate who has a flexible approach to love. You should seem reliable yet not limiting, a free spirit who nevertheless has two feet firmly on the ground. This partner combines a fiery idealism within an earthy appreciation for the good life, which can mean lots of fun evenings lying on a blanket under the stars, picnicking on delicacies, and discussing the future of the planet in a leisurely way. Walk hand-in-hand to the park, stop for hot dogs, fly kites, stop for ice cream, and end the afternoon being carousel cowpokes.

Sagittarius-Taurus isn't particularly emotional, and this mate finds it difficult to deal with emotional outbursts from you. Long intimate discussions are not his or her style. Instead, your lover prefers to get intellectual. Or physical.

In bed, your partner loves to be spontaneous and sensual. His or her suede covered bed may sit in a room with a jungle motif that inspires fantasies, as you make love in a slow, relaxed way. He or she is interested in something new that you propose, but in general Sagittarius-Taurus likes to go at a slow, determined pace. And if that means a night of covering each other with designs from a wash-off body paint kit as a tickly lark, why not just get out your brushes and brush off your giggle?

Venus in Sagittarius with Mars in Gemini

This is one of those ants-in-the-pants combinations. The longest you can stay still happily is about the length of time it takes to soft boil an egg. After that you get restless, and boredom sets in along with a touch of wanderlust. You're a terrific communicator, and you never feel so alive as when you're having a rousing ideological conversation. You're friendly, outgoing, and interested in the whole world. You want to meet and explore ideas with as many people as possible, which can be a wonderfully enlivening experience, but necessarily shortens the amount of time you can devote to any one individual, and reduces the depths of your interactions in general.

That's no problem for you, however, for you may prefer to skim along the surface of life, taking in as wide a spectrum of experience as possible, and leaving the depth to others. The way you see it, there's far too much out there to experience to allow yourself to become bogged down in any one thing or with any one person.

You're uncomfortable with emotions. They feel heavy and draining to you, and you don't like to have other people weigh you down with theirs. You much prefer ideas, and when you're dealing with your own feelings, it just seems natural to intellectualize them.

You seldom focus on romantic issues or romantic problems. That's because as you see it, those problems belong to other people. In general you're content with your choices and with your life, and you don't have a driving desire to settle down. There's too much fun to be had.

Your Sagittarius-Gemini lover is not unaware of the need for give and take in relationships. He or she is just unwilling to feel confined, and a steady relationship is a major source of confinement to this individual. This is one of those combinations that strenuously resists the idea of making a commitment to love.

You could try seduction, if it's a beginning relationship, but enjoying a fun fling could be all that results. To this mate, talking and exchanging ideas is as exciting as making love, and with someone so mental, an exchange of ideas often represents a greater degree of intimacy than physical contact. So you might attempt a version of seduction that involves more conversation and less lovemaking.

Sagittarius-Gemini loves to travel, so you could become traveling companions. Driving cross-country or through Europe is super fun, as is a long bike ride or even a stroll through an unexplored local neighborhood. And as long as you're a spontaneous, free-spirited individual yourself, with loads of ideas and a gregarious nature, you're in good company. What could be more fun than a lively companion who is never slow, dull, or pokey, whose wit is as sparkly as his or her eyes, and who wants to see and improve the world? It may not be a traditional relationship, and it definitely isn't a traditional marriage, but it certainly is a very fun time.

Venus in Sagittarius with Mars in Cancer

When it comes to romance, you waver between wanting real intimacy and total freedom. You want to be a playboy (or girl) and also have a close family, which is usually pretty difficult to accomplish. Often it may be that you attract partners who reflect one but not both sides of your nature. Thus one relationship may be with a loving individual who requires a level of closeness that makes you feel entrapped, and the next with someone who only wants a fling, leaving you yearning and calling for a deeper commitment. Until you come to terms with these two diverse characteristics within yourself, it will not be easy to find the mate you seek. Ultimately though you have a good heart and a kind nature, and that's easy for other people to spot. Once you're ready to settle down with someone, those qualities attract to you a person with a similar outlook.

You can envision yourself with just the right person, and then you sense that everything will be all right. You know that it's possible to have closeness that doesn't smother, and that's the sort of relationship you want to build. You sense that it begins by finding someone with whom you have non-stop fun, lots of laughs, and the occasional deep conversation.

Your Sagittarius-Cancer lover is an exciting free spirit who is a sensitive human being as well, and is willing to deal with your feelings as well as your ideas. A Sagittarius-Cancer probably invented the picnic, and packing one and inviting him or her to the park, the beach, or on a fishing trip, is a good first move. Anything that brings home along to the outside—or the outside back home—is great. If you're invested in any idealistic programs that help the underprivileged lead happier lives, share the involvement, if he or she is not already at the forefront of the cause. This is something you can happily work on together.

In bed, Sagittarius-Cancer wants to see that you're having as much fun as he or she is, and is very good at intuiting your needs and fantasies, as well as very willing to let you voice your desires. So go ahead and take the initiative, speak up, and don't feel shy. Sex is nothing to be ashamed of; it's one of the best ways to communicate, have fun, and cuddle up all at once. And when you discover that your physical needs are as compatible as your philosophies, you may have met your match.

Venus in Sagittarius with Mars in Leo

Proud, idealistic, and honest, you must be free to go your own way, preferably with a bunch of loyal followers in your wake. The chief source of your personal satisfaction is the work you do for worthy causes. Generating positive energy and working for the betterment of the world makes you feel good about yourself and optimistic about humanity.

You're a real people person. You adore being in the middle of a crowd of people, talking, laughing, and having a good time. Whether you're giving the party or going to the party, you're in your element. You enjoy dating and spending time with a variety of partners, yet you seek that one perfect person to complete your life.

It's not as though you're desperate when all alone, but you do prefer to be with other people. You can be quite content as a single person, for there are many diversions to keep you happy and busy. You're perfectly willing to take your time in finding a mate, and if love doesn't strike immediately you're still content. When love does hit, you're happy to go with the flow.

Your Sagittarius-Leo lover is not particularly romantic or emotional, although he or she is aces when it comes to having a good time. If you're feeling weepy or depressed, this is probably not the shoulder to cry on, but if you want to go dancing or horseback riding, pick up the phone and make that call.

This mate is quite content to be the pursued rather than the pursuer, despite the fact that being at the forefront is enjoyable. That's because receiving your attention is so flattering. This individual is not a confirmed single, but will always be a little self-centered when it comes to the give and take of marriage. Sagittarius-Leo must be self-determining at all times, and when he or she is a little too pushy about your comings and goings, a suggestion that such an autocratic attitude is a teensy unfair restores your independence to you. This mate's gregarious, friendly manner and good-natured, loving ways go a long way toward softening your annoyance at a bit of aloofness.

In bed, it seems as though you're the honored guests at a party for only two. To this mate, this is the best time you can have together, two sexy animals mutually enraptured by the magic created by the mingling of your bodies.

Your lover has much pride invested in the fact that he or she can satisfy a partner, and all the energy in the world to devote to your needs, So if you're not getting one-hundred percent satisfaction, speak up and make a gentle suggestion about how he or she could drive you even wilder. A word to the wise—well phrased, of course—is all you need.

Venus in Sagittarius with Mars in Virgo

You're honest, forthright, careful, concerned, and friendly, but when it comes to romance, you'd often rather be left alone. It's much easier for you to be an interested, helpful friend than a partner in a one-on-one situation. That's not because you're so critical that you can't find anyone to please you, although you do sometimes use your overdeveloped critical faculties as an excuse to avoid getting into relationships in the first place. You like your freedom and the autonomy to come and go as you please, and you sense that a relationship could tie you down to an unreasonable extent.

You're very invested in the work that you do, and the charities that you support. You put much energy into making the world a better place, and that is so fulfilling that sometimes it feels that your need for a relationship just evaporates.

If you do decide that you want romance, you need only put some effort into finding it. You do well to connect with someone who starts out as a friend and then turns into something more. As you grow closer with someone, your dependence and emotional connection increases and you feel comfortable thinking of that person in your life day after day.

Your Sagittarius-Virgo lover can go on for hours into so much detail about what's wrong with the world, that it's easy for you to feel that he or she is ignoring you totally. And sometimes the way in which your lover pays attention to you is by detailing ways you might be happier, more efficient, etc., which is hardly very romantic.

It can be very frustrating to someone who just wants to live in the here and now for half an instant and cuddle up together, oblivious to the rest of the world. That's difficult for Sagittarius-Virgo because this mate seems always to have the whole world on his or her mind. Not terribly emotional or even very adept at dealing with the emotions of others, this mate often prefers to retreat into a well-developed intellectual process when feelings are exposed, which can make a sensitive suitor feel downright ignored. If you want tangible proof of your lover's degree of affection for you, observe the way he or she is always willing to pitch in and help you out.

In bed, you recognize the same concentrated effort, because he or she wants to be certain that you're satisfied and are having a good time. Where sex is concerned, your mate is much less picky and critical, or at least this ability to be discerning is turned toward paying sensitive attention to every special inch of you that can be stimulated. All you must do is reveal your likes and dislikes, which feels very rewarding with a truly interested partner, and that is Sagittarius-Virgo's best skill of all.

Venus in Sagittarius with Mars in Libra

You're a real group person. You love to go out with your many friends, to socialize and have a good time. You probably have acquaintances from all walks of life, and knowing so many people enriches your life immeasurably. It's important for you to find someone who shares your ideals and goals, for then the two of you can combine forces to present a unified front in working to better the world, or at least your immediate surroundings. When you're alone, you don't feel quite right, as if part of you is somehow missing, and even though you need to be free to live your own life, having someone to share it is essential.

You prefer to keep things light and carefree in your interactions with others, and heavy emotional scenes are draining and embarrassing to you, so you attempt to avoid people who are insistent on burdening you constantly with their innermost feelings. Whispering shared confidences is all very well, but your idea of romance is more friendly and social than deeply intimate emotionally.

Your Sagittarius-Libra lover really knows how to have a good time. Parties galore, art gallery openings, cocktail party benefits—he or she is prominent on all the guest lists, and popular with all the hostesses because your lover adds a certain friendly sparkle to every gathering. An interest in everyone and everything is apparent from the instant you meet. And it's a terrific feeling to have all that sparkle turned on you.

If you're interested in focusing that diffuse, friendly energy into a committed relationship, it must be obvious that you're his or her other half, the one person who is able to share an alliance that makes you both more able to exercise your true independence as well as makes you a stronger force in accomplishing your goals. Of course, the only way to reveal this is for it to be true, and then you both recognize the inevitable instantly.

In bed, Sagittarius-Libra is more interested in having a good time than in burning up the sheets. You chat, tell friendly stories, laugh as you share nice music, good wine, and delicious kisses. This mate may not be very sexually aggressive, so if you feel like taking the lead, so much the better. All you have to remember is how fair he or she is, so a system of "you scratch my back (tickle my toes, etc.), I'll scratch yours" is easily instituted. Just make sure that you're not so busy going out to parties every night that you forget to stay home altogether.

Venus in Sagittarius with Mars in Scorpio

Most of the time you seem cheerful and easy-going, despite the intensity beneath the surface that is so often masked. When you do become angry, you usually disappear for a while, resurfacing only after you've cooled off. If a confrontation is necessary, you can embarrass yourself with the intensity of your own reactions, so you try to avoid revealing this part of your nature.

In love, you can alternate between being a free spirit who would never for the world try to possess another person, and being a jealous lover. Usually you manage to laugh at your own possessive tendencies, thereby curbing them. You do demand absolute loyalty from a partner, for you consider honesty and loyalty in love a prime example of an individual's integrity, which is a key factor in assessing that person's character.

Sometimes you can be rather ambivalent about commitment. The question is: are you the one who seeks freedom or are you attracting partners who run away? Usually it's a little bit of both. You do want to feel that you can have a stable relationship because you don't like the sensation of having to scramble to seek companionship. You're just a bit conflicted about giving up your full self, heart and soul, to another person.

Your Sagittarius-Scorpio lover has a friendly personality coupled with a magnetic appeal. If you do manage to win this mate's heart, you can be sure it comes with steadfast affection and an honorable level of fidelity. Even if you see your mate chatting with someone else, deep inside you know it's just casual, and that this person values integrity enough never to cheat.

In bed, Sagittarius-Scorpio likes to combine friendly exuberance with passionate intensity. This is a very adventurous combination, so if you're interested in acting out fantasies, and re-creating the Kama Sutra, or in trying something that always struck you as faintly naughty, go ahead and suggest it.

This is one partner who takes a very liberated attitude that anything giving two consenting adults pleasure should be tried and expanded upon. You may find yourself acting out fantasies that you never even had the nerve to dream up—not without some very imaginative, very able help, that is.

Venus in Sagittarius with Mars in Sagittarius

Being idealistic never stopped anyone from being a playboy (or playgirl); at least it never stopped you. All those worthy causes you espouse give you a great opportunity to flit around the world, meeting and greeting any number of fascinating strangers, and that's just the way you like it.

Absolutely nothing can tie you down for long, and despite the fact that people find you wonderfully sexy, you're often not looking for a permanent mate, at least not for a long, long time. And although you may be willing to have a number of casual, friendly affairs, you never deceive anyone into thinking that you're available for more until you absolutely are. Being honest is something on which you pride yourself deeply, and you'd never consider deception on any level or for any reason.

You like sex as much as the next person, but you may feel that far too much attention is being paid to sex in today's culture. You're not adverse to having a sexually-based interaction, but you would never build a relationship on mere physical attraction. People who continue relationships with mates with whom they share nothing more than sexual compatibility bewilder you. If lovers are going to settle down, philosophical, ideological compatibility is the essential thing, as you see it.

Your Sagittarius-Sagittarius lover always seems to be just catching a breath between planes, no matter how long he or she has been on the ground. This individual wants to see the world, and to meet every possible person on the face of the earth.

There's so much to see and so many ideas to explore and to share, that there isn't enough time in the day. Life is exciting, communication is exciting, and being alive is so terrific, because each one of us really has the ability to contribute according to his ideals.

No wonder this exuberant, lively, idealistic individual has captured your fancy. Honorable and irrepressible, no one beats this mate at combining intellectual idealism with the unstoppable ability to mingle with people and create an unfettered atmosphere of fun and good times.

In bed, this mate likes to be your pal, sharing a few physical comforts without the sense of competition. It's as if you're two cowpokes, settled in by the fire to have a comforting drink and to share a quiet moment under the stars to set off the rigors of the day. Kick off your spurs, partner, and end the day right.

Venus in Sagittarius with Mars in Capricorn

You're friendly and gregarious up to a point, but you don't like to waste too much time in meaningless socializing. People who know that you feel this way are amazed when they see you having a grand time in any number of benefit parties; little do they realize that you're "working" the crowd, circulating and making connections, and gaining support for your organization.

You want to settle down in a good marriage with a partner who doesn't interfere in your life and is an asset to you in business and social situations. Your mate must be intellectually interesting as well as practical, reliable, and hard-working, just as you yourself are. Combining forces, you form an unstoppable team. In your view it's not really about the emotions that bind you, but the commitments and other hardheaded realities that draw two people together to stand side-by-side and build a life. Does that mean that to you life is all seriousness, no pleasure? Hardly. You feel that being with the right person opens you up and makes you more receptive to the joys life has to offer.

Your Sagittarius-Capricorn lover is fun without being frivolous. Education is taken seriously, because a broadly experienced mind has practical uses. Gain this mate's attention by sharing the workload in a worthy organization; he or she is glad to devote time to those after-hours work sessions, during which you can explore your mutual goals and philosophies. Once you become a compatriot, your lover is more than willing to share the limelight as well.

And when you invite this individual home to see your collection of pre-Columbian artifacts (or whatever), he or she is receptive to relaxing with an after dinner drink in front of the fire, as you both unwind from a long day's grind. Offer a backrub if you're in doubt about the progress of your seduction. Your lover often drives so hard that body aches plague him or her at the end of the day.

In bed, Sagittarius-Capricorn correctly feels that sex is a great way to unwind. This mate puts the same driving need to succeed into a sexual performance as any other, because he or she does want to please you, but there is no sense of competition or urgency of time. So relax and enjoy yourself until the next battle to conquer makes its presence known.

Venus in Sagittarius with Mars in Aquarius

This is a real humanitarian position, but it doesn't make you very interested in having a permanent relationship with a single individual. Instead of you often prefer to keep suitors at arm's length while you pursue goals that allow you to work within groups for the betterment of the world at large. Your idealistic concerns are certainly genuine, but what is also operative is a need to remain totally free and unencumbered.

You want to determine your own actions at all costs, and the idea of anyone having any say-so about your behavior is untenable. In school and as a child at home, you may have gotten involved in any number of battles with the authority figures in your life. Not only do you need to be free but you often like to rebel just for the sake of being different, which is a hard position in which to succeed as a child.

As an adult, you still demand this level of freedom and self-determination. Obviously this creates problems within relationships because they are supposed to be partnerships with equal input. That for you is problematic. It may be that you're more content to have casual friendships rather than intimate partnership. If you do you want a partnership, compromise is needed on your part.

Your Sagittarius-Aquarius lover is a bit scary. The thought of a white picket fence is immeasurably frightening, and so this individual may be determined to remain single forever, or at least until he or she feels secure that no degree of personal independence will be challenged. The nesting instinct takes a secondary place by far to a need to assert individuality, so if you're interested in more than a casual friendship with this slippery eel of a lover, you have your work cut out for you. Even the world's greatest lover, with a gorgeous face and body, a shipping magnate's bank account, and a seduction routine that never quits, could take years to make a chink in his or her armor. This mate wants to be with someone he or she likes (mad passion is a kind of foreign emotion) and to feel a sense of ideological camaraderie.

So if you share this need to make the world a better place for us all, you have a shot. Take your time in getting to know each other. Long rambling walks are a great opener—nothing much need happen but a lively exchange of ideas. Developing a warm friendship is the first step toward a romance.

Sagittarius-Aquarius is not particularly anxious to get to bed, nor is he or she reluctant either, but the first move had better come from you, for this is one of those combinations that refuse to melt at the whiff of chemistry. Once you do manage an affair, you discover that your lover can be as warm, receptive, innovative, and yes sexy, as anybody else. And it may be as much a surprise to him or her as it is to you.

Venus in Sagittarius with Mars in Pisces

This is one of the most unprejudiced, least selfish combinations in the Zodiac. You can see the good in almost everybody, and you're genuinely interested in broadening your knowledge of the world and the people in it. You want to make the world a better place.

You're an interested conversationalist and a supportive friend who can be helpful and emotionally sensitive to all you meet. The problem with this approach is as long as you're focusing all your energies on the other person, it's hard to get your own needs met. Rather than assert yourself, you sometimes choose to focus more on friendship within your group of intimates rather than on a single relationship. This way you don't feel hurt and if someone is overstepping, you can just retreat to your home. This avoidance of a relationship plays into your need for freedom, but it isn't very emotionally rewarding.

It's up to you to take yourself in hand, and to take a chance on love, if love is what you seek. Remember that a relationship involves two people, and both people should be made happy and fulfilled. Sometimes it's just a matter of speaking up and saying "Hey, this is what I need." Once you do that, you get the love that you need and feel happy with your partner.

Your Sagittarius-Pisces lover often seems to be off somewhere in a dream world, far beyond your reach. Why not just take the initiative and say, "Let's be really selfish for a while, go somewhere together, and do nothing but concentrate on each other. It would mean a lot to me." A plea like that ought to get some results, and as long as you're willing to be the aggressor in the relationship, you have a better chance of achieving one.

The same goes for sex. You should be the one to make the pass, although your lover is usually willing to play ball. Just remind him or her that we all need to take some time out to concentrate on our own personal, physical needs, and offer to get things going by a healthy exchange of foot massages, back rubs, or sexy fantasies. Organized, admittedly selfish time is just what this mate needs to put you in touch with each other and yourselves as well.

Venus in Capricorn-Mars Combinations

Venus in Capricorn with Mars in Aries

You know what you want at virtually every moment of the day, and you make no apologies when you get it. You're strong, determined, and assertive, and when you find attractive people, you have no problem letting them know. Sometimes you're interested in a one-night stand, because relationships are really a whole lot of trouble, as you've communicated to pretty much every partner you've ever had. You're conflicted much of the time because you feel that you should want a permanent commitment, you do want a permanent commitment, but how do you get a permanent commitment? It's difficult. And the reason why is because other people don't always do what you say, and you find that unacceptable. When it comes to flexibility, you may be unable to manage that except perhaps in bed, if your limbs are willing. Your ego however seldom is.

It may be quite obvious to all your exes that working on this flexibility issue is something that might benefit you. The only problem is it's not so obvious to you. You don't see getting along with other people as your number one priority, although you're absolutely willing for them to get along with you.

Action is usually preferable to emotion in your opinion, and the people with whom you share intimate moments may be few and far between as a result. Admitting your own normal human frailty is much harder for you than for the rest of us, so often you choose to maintain a controlled and impenetrable exterior. Being absolutely free from the control of anybody else is essential to you, and often is the reason why you refuse to yield your inner self for even a lover's scrutiny. Obviously you must learn to take a risk now and then, and because you recover so easily and move on so readily it might not be so difficult to share some emotional intimacy. You just have to decide it's what you want to do.

Your Capricorn-Aries lover is often the victim of a raging

inner war. The totally conflicting urges of controlled austerity and insouciant flamboyance battle within for control. Should he be hasty, should she be prudent—who knows? That's the problem. And, of course, this mate often sits at home in a chair, twitching with impatience while cautiously planning out the next step, when in fact the natural choice might be just to act without thinking. What can you do to help? Go outside and insist on having some fun. Drag your mate along when you go running, or demand to play football. Anything physical is a great release and will bring out your lover's sunniest nature.

When first courting, you need to make your interest known, if your partner hasn't already stepped up. Smile, be playful, but make sure you have something serious to back up your offer, unless you're seeking something quick and casual, which may not be impossible, but isn't what this mate truly desires. Gifts should be something creative and unusual, a trip to an interesting location, even if it's just an amusement park. Capricorn-Aries likes speed and often resists admitting it.

And, among things physical is everyone's number one favorite—sex. Capricorn-Aries loves sex and can prove to be a really exciting lover, combining sensuality with unpredictable speed and flamboyance. All you must do is buy a new how-to sex manual, suggest mastering it chapter by chapter, and your energetic mate will have something fun that's a challenge as well, which is the essence of the successful mingling of the difficult to combine Capricorn-Aries nature.

Venus in Capricorn with Mars in Taurus

Remember Silas Marner, gleefully seated before his mounting pile of gold? I bet he had this combination, although he did refuse to spend the money on even his own comfort, which is one mistake you won't be making. Being comfortable and well taken care of is one of the prime reasons you work so hard, although your idea of comfort is a bit austere compared to others with planets in Taurus.

You simply like to be aware of the difference between comfort and opulence. Being surrounded by an excess of worldly possessions strikes you as a breach of taste of the worst sort, so you tame your acquisitive nature by applying the strictest standards of quality to anything you buy.

Practical, hard-working and serious, you're goal-oriented in the extreme. You can always be counted upon to maintain your course of action and achieve your goals. One such goal is to have a good marriage with a stable partner on whom you can count. Being in a partnership is important to you because it doubles your effectiveness and it gives you someone who understands you, understands the way you think, and shares your goals. Two heads are better than one, and that's how you see it where relationships are concerned—it's a partnership of like-minded individuals who're working towards the same end, in this case a secure family life, a high-value home, and financial security. This doesn't mean that romance is unimportant, for to you of course it's important. You're very sensual, you love sex, and you want to please your mate. Mutual satisfaction is very important, because it produces happiness, and therefore guarantees continuity—which is your ultimate goal.

Your Capricorn-Taurus lover wants a traditional lifestyle. Remember that white picket fence that people with planets in Gemini and Sagittarius avoid so studiously? Capricorn-Taurus invented it. Marriage, home, family, tax deductions: this mate wants the whole thing. You know those television marriage brokers? That's not just reality TV—that's a cottage industry designed for people with this placement.

Are you marriage material? That's the question this individual asks, even before the first date. Plan to meet in a good restaurant, for consuming quality food is important to this mate, although he or she does not want to pay for atmosphere. But frolicking on a miniature golf course or holding hands on the beach just doesn't get things down to business soon enough for this individual's practical tastes. As romantic as the date may seem, it is still, after all, an interview.

Once you've shown that you have enough positive attributes (and yes, money) to maintain this mate's interest, it's up to you to interweave charm with interesting conversation. Hiring a private chef to cook for you at home is a nice way to impress him or her. Offer sweet, quality gifts, such as a cashmere throw that you can both snuggle under, when the time feels right.

It's amazing that anybody so serious can have such a relaxed, natural attitude about sex, but this mate does. Capricorn-Taurus is terrific in bed—sensual, stress-free, determined that you both should have maximum satisfaction without seeming to work at it. Perhaps it's because sex is this mate's primary leisure activity, but this sweetie just seems to radiate an earthy sensuality. And in case your interview leads to a lasting relationship, it's nice to know that you can depend upon your lover to keep you physically satisfied through the years, and to keep the picket fence painted as well.

Venus in Capricorn with Mars in Gemini

You find it difficult to balance impulsiveness with caution, and often what happens is that you simply alternate between the two modes, never feeling quite at ease with either form of behavior, and bewildering yourself in the process. You know that normal people mate and they settle down, and you know that you're normal, but you don't feel that settled. In fact, you like focusing on work as long as the work doesn't tie you down too badly either. You might say that you have traditional values but itchy feet. You like flexibility and you like to keep yourself on the move.

Sometimes you wonder if you really are a relationship person, although you do seem social and you can be devastatingly funny. It's just that sometimes you wonder if there is a genuine motivation to mate buried there somewhere deep in your heart. The more potential partners come on to you, the more you're determined to flee. It feels as though they're trying to chain you down and you know that isn't true, yet it does feel true.

Obviously there are some life lessons at work here, and the key for you is to decide just how much you want to enjoy the company of one specific person. The right individual enriches your life and doesn't hold you back, and that is the person you need to find. Then as long as you're allowed to express yourself, you're content within a warm and cozy relationship.

Your Capricorn-Gemini lover can be a great deal of fun for the short run. This mate tells marvelously funny stories and shares a sense of humor outrageous enough to prompt a chuckle from just about everybody. When it comes to more intimate moments, Capricorn-Gemini is often at a loss. This individual finds dealing with emotions rather vexing, and he or she would much rather pretend emotions didn't exist at all so everyone can stop feeling awkward.

The key to turning great party banter into an ongoing relationship is making it fun, while seeming like a solid person with your own agenda, someone who's too busy and successful to try to entrap this mate with any sort of noose. If you have interesting contacts, bring him or her along to meet them. It's a party that's also a networking opportunity. Offer cute gifts, such as an electronic reading device or a case for one. If you treat each day like your first meeting, your mate could stick around.

In bed, he or she enjoys regaling you with funny stories, an occasional raw limerick, and tricks that tickle more than just your funny bone. And as long as you're open and receptive without demanding that you define the relationship, your lover is happy to keep seeing you. If you're someone who doesn't make too many demands, and someone with whom your serious free spirit feels really at home, then there's no reason why this individual shouldn't make a permanent commitment and, in so doing, discover that it's just what he or she needed all along.

Venus in Capricorn with Mars in Cancer

Relationships have always played an important part in your life—often they provide the forum, and the mirror, in which your deepest self is reflected and developed. You recognize the need for compromise that exists in any intimate situation, but often feel as though you're the one who always gives in. You just want people you love to be happy. Attracting partners who are a lot tougher than yourself also diminishes your win-lose ratio.

Nurture is an important theme to you; often you're giving while wanting to be uninvolved emotionally, and sometimes you wish you could be more emotionally intimate, but something within you won't let go. On good days, you're a caring friend or lover who attracts people who accept your tender ministrations without returning them in kind. On bad days you withdraw your love, retreat to a closet, and mope in solitude while making self-deprecating jokes. Of course, the truth is that you feel much more comfortable being the giver in any situation, because you then retain the power.

There's no question that you want to love and be loved, but you also want to have a partner who can advance you socially and nurture you physically. Sometimes you feel this is impossible to find, but you're wrong. The right person is out there—you just have to find him or her.

Your Capricorn-Cancer lover wants a traditional home, marriage, and family life. Children are the hope for the future, and most of this individual's adult motivations revolve around creating a substantial base for your children's future. This mate reminisces about his or her childhood, and looks forward to being a grandparent with the kind of relish that is usually reserved for a dream vacation. First date or thirtieth, Capricorn-Cancer hates to go out and waste money when a far superior dinner—and time—can be had at home. Sharing the chores in the kitchen, cooking and cleaning up together, and relaxing in front of the fire or the television are his or her idea of the most sparkling kind of evening's entertainment, and suggesting a nightclub will not produce an about face.

In bed, your partner loves to touch, hug, kiss, and cuddle, after you both warm up from an initially awkward period of hesitation. Sex is something that we have a right to—and it's entertainment that's good and dependable and—best of all—free—so this mate's willing to make you feel as satisfied as you might like. If you're courting—or being courted by—a Capricorn-Cancer, be prepared for the worse. Buy a down comforter, two matching nightcaps, subscribe to TV Guide, and get ready to snuggle together for a lifetime of winters. Nothing less will do.

Venus in Capricorn with Mars in Leo

You're so determined to be a leader and to uphold your own standards that you can be quite difficult and quite arrogant at times. It's difficult to be a leader if all your followers have become alienated, and learning this early helps you in life. When it comes to friends and a mate, you want nothing but the best. Money and a high position impress you far more than other, more subtle, but equally valuable assets. Having an elevated status and being somebody of recognized importance that everybody can look up to and admire, are two of your major goals, for yourself and for the person you marry.

Emotions of all sorts can be rather off-putting, and you would be much more comfortable if you didn't have to deal with your own feelings—at least not in front of anybody else, and you'd rather not be confronted with a mate's deepest emotions either. You're one of those "on camera" people always aware of your image and very determined always to maintain a dignified front. This is an effective strategy in a public setting, particularly if you're running for political office, but it doesn't always work in your favor where romance is concerned. A mate wants to get to know you, and seeing your frailties can often be endearing rather than alienating. It's up to you to decide how much of a risk you're willing to take in order to generate some much-needed intimacy.

Your Capricorn-Leo lover isn't likely ever to let you take the lead, not even in bed. This individual is determinedly convinced that he or she—and only he or she—can chart the course of your future or make the right selection for tonight's movie. It can be exasperating, particularly if you have a healthy ego yourself, and would like to take your turn being the boss. Although your ambitious lover resists those intimate moments where you gaze into each other's eyes, revealing your innermost souls to each other, Capricorn-Leo definitely plans to be married. Marriage is part of the normal course of life, something that everyone must do to be solid, substantial, and a grown-up member of society.

This individual wants a mate whom everyone else admires, who contributes income and status to the partnership, and with whom he or she can create the kind of enviable home everyone desires. Substantial and solid gold are his or her values, and if you share that view, you have a good chance of landing a permanent mate. Once married, this mate goes all out to see that you and your children have everything you need. Being the kind of husband or wife who can be relied upon is part of a good self image, so you never have to doubt your partner's loyalty or question his or her fidelity. When this mate says "I do," he or she is committed to you totally and forever.

It's obvious by now that mutual interest must be initial, for unless you're extremely rich or persuasive, this mate isn't easily swayed. You can amp up the situation with interesting connections, good stories about life, and thoughtful, clever gifts. Something antique and priceless (or antique and difficult to price) is an excellent token of esteem.

In bed, this mate wants you to be happy, for it's a matter of pride that being good in bed is part of his or her résumé. Part of this talent will be handled by the swankiest of surroundings—who couldn't feel aroused in silk sheets, cashmere blankets, and the softest of down pillows. The rest will be provided by hard work, careful attention to detail, and stamina that could become legendary—at least to you.

Venus in Capricorn with Mars in Virgo

You're so practical that you may think of relationships as contracts of the you-scratch-my-back-I'll-scratch-yours variety. In fact, it was probably someone with this combination who devised the first prenuptial agreement. Because you're so prudent and cautious, you probably wait until you're really ready to commit and marry, and if that means well into middle-age, so be it.

As capable as you are of being a steady, devoted mate, it may take much effort on your part to get to the place where you can commit. That's because you find dating and mating rather frivolous pursuits that don't engage you—figuratively and literally. Thus you may find yourself alone quite a bit of the time, and you're not terribly unhappy in that regard because you're so busy with hard work and hobbies that you find interesting, such as building a little room onto your house, or a part-time business. You're not the frolicsome sort.

Obviously the first step in moving toward a happy, committed partnership, is to realize that dating isn't frivolous. Until they invent a do-it-yourself kit for building a mate, dating is the only way to go about it. So get out there in the social stream and have some fun. In meeting and greeting all sorts of people, you're likely to connect with that one perfect person who ultimately becomes the ideal, practical, and adoring mate that you seek. And by that time, you might learn that the heart and soul of romance speaks very strongly to you. An unenthusiastic dater, you can be the perpetually devoted mate anyone would cherish for a lifetime. That's your true goal.

Your Capricorn-Virgo lover has many requirements in choosing a mate, and chances are, if you're having any sort of relationship at all, that you meet some of them already, for this is one person who isn't likely to spend time casually. The one-night stand is something he or she wouldn't consider in a million years.

This individual seeks a partner who is financially stable, emotionally cool and collected, someone with an established career, who can be relied upon to display good taste and to exhibit proper behavior. And proper behavior includes not going to or giving lavish parties or squandering the family cash. This is an exceptionally modest financial combination, and even if this person is a billionaire, he or she parts with cash only when absolutely necessary.

During courtship you'll not be treated to four course meals at five-star restaurants, nor will you be whisked away to Paris for glitzy weekends. A single perfect rose (on a very special occasion) is more along the lines this mate prefers. Flashy dinners and diamonds are as vulgar as they are expensive, and a couple could better use that money on major appliances when they set up housekeeping. The fact that your lover doesn't want to spend money doesn't mean that he or she won't appreciate an expensive token of affection from you, as long as it's something of genuine value, something made of gold or something whose value will appreciate, such as major stocks—and those things make excellent gifts for this mate. Likewise, when courting, the efforts that you put forth to impress this mate do not go unnoticed. He or she does in fact appreciate kindly gestures and sweet sentiments. Of course once you're married, sweet is probably better than expensive, for this mate constantly keeps a careful eye on the purse strings, and if your choices run towards the extravagant, you might be better off with a different partner, in order to avoid confrontations over money.

In bed, Capricorn-Virgo has a natural, earthy ease. What's all the fuss about, really, when bodies melting together in good, honest passion is such a normal, natural thing? People who require liquor, drugs, or pornography to get turned on bewilder him or her totally, for if it's that much work, why bother? Isn't it easier just to take your time, go slowly, and touch each other a lot until you discover all the special places that need attention? When you're this calm and practical, even sex can be managed with aplomb.

Venus in Capricorn with Mars in Libra

You're quite competitive, particularly in relationships, and often you find yourself involved in power struggles with romantic partners. As much as you understand the need to compromise with other people, in relationships you often want to be the boss and the unquestioned leader, but unfortunately you sometimes attract partners who value the relationship less than you do, and who make it impossible for you not to give in.

This problem does decrease as you concentrate more on the human issues and less on the logistics of any situation, but that isn't always the natural thing for you to do. You feel that when you meet the ideal partner who shares your views totally, you can then establish a perfect, smoothly flowing relationship that fills both of your needs perfectly. Of course, human interactions often require more work and less idealistic expectations as we create what we want, rather than happen upon it, which at some level you realize. You're willing to work to make your relationship a happy one and that is one of your very good traits.

Your Capricorn-Libra lover sometimes seems uncomfortable with emotion. It's not that he or she doesn't care about you, but opening up to someone else is difficult, as is hearing your most intimate thoughts. Such personal revelations, even with a marriage partner, are embarrassingly sloppy. Better to keep things at a cool, more superficial level, even with a most beloved mate. Good taste and good manners are important issues to Capricorn-Libra, so don't plan on meeting him or her in your oldest jeans or at the last minute. This individual expects you to put as much effort into your relationship as he or she does, and that includes tasteful gifts on appropriate occasions, reciprocating on invitations, and pleasant evenings at quality restaurants, even if the price tag is a bit more than moderate.

The key is being willing to go slowly, so that enough time passes for a level of comfort to be generated. You can't hurry intimacy with this partner. It must feel right before you confess all your deep secrets and feelings. Something as simple as finding a restaurant with a dance floor can be the turning point in the relationship. As you glide around to romantic music, it seems easy to melt into each other's arms, opening a chink in your mutual armor, and making it all right to share on more intimate levels.

In bed, your lover is an expert at concentrating on you and meeting your needs, while being sure that he or she is satisfied as well. All that's needed in such a situation is a bit of work and a bit of concentration, and both partners should have a good time. After all, it's just another example of good manners in action.

Venus in Capricorn with Mars in Scorpio

With this combination, power is your motivating force, in relationships and outside them as well. You really want to gain power over others, and you're determined that no one will ever have any control over you. You can be subtle, but more often you're just determined to have your way, an immovable stone wall that yields to no one. You radiate an air of self-confidence, and an aura of power such that other people yield to you almost automatically, often leaving you amused by your own prowess. Svengali probably had this combination, and he definitely knew how to get his own way.

You want a mate who always defers to you, but whom you can always respect, which is sometimes hard to get. When you do find such a mate, your loyalty never waivers for an instant, and your complete, unspoken devotion and deep commitment are among the steadiest in the Zodiac. You're like one of those animals who mates for life, whether the mate survives or not! And you learn much along the way, realizing that your need for power is a lot of work, and that having a partner who can pull half the load, and whom you can trust, makes a huge difference in your happiness—and your blood pressure.

Your Capricorn-Scorpio lover has a smoldering quality below the surface that can either be very sexy or a little frightening, depending on the context. You might imagine that if ever this mate lost his or her cool, it wouldn't be unthinkable to tie you to the bed for hours of sex that just borders on the edge of abuse. This almost never happens without consent, however, but sex with this magnetic, passionate person always has that intense quality of conquest and surrender that some people find really exciting. Of course, if you're Gemini, nothing could be farther from your ideals than being consumed by someone else's icy fire. At other times, a brief tiff may be followed by days of the most devastatingly cutting, sarcastic remarks, designed not merely to bruise but actually to wound. A really serious fight may be marked by a furious blow up after several days of stony silence. In any case, this is not a bland individual, although the surface may be disarmingly calm.

If you've just met and are thinking wow, this might be fun for a very steamy weekend, but no way could you handle all the drama, it might be better to fantasize about this mate but move along before you're entangled. If you sense this is the soulmate without whom your destiny is incomplete, express your interest, but seem just a little ungettable. This person likes to take the lead in the chase, so you must be the alluring fly, ready to be enticed into Capricorn-Scorpio's web. Once involved, special gifts are much appreciated, but they should be truly special. Collectables from people or subjects of interest are a good choice, even if they're as macabre as the chains that a magician failed to escape, leading to his death.

Capricorn-Scorpio is interested in a serious, permanent, intense relationship. Forget casual interactions, and know that this individual may refuse even to attend a party more than once a year. Better to stay at home with a mate, and occasionally with a few very close friends, for a quiet evening of good food and serious talk. Anything more frivolous is a waste of time. So before you let yourself become carried away on a wave of passion, be sure that this is the lifestyle you want as well. Once Capricorn-Scorpio decides on you, there's very little room for maneuvering, so exercise your rights early, or be prepared to settle down in his or her ménage forevermore.

Venus in Capricorn with Mars in Sagittarius

You have big dreams, and you're always at the head of those dreams. You do have many ideals you'd like to realize, but you never lose sight of the practical, hard-edge nature of reality, and that helps you a great deal in the reformulation of your goals. You don't think of yourself as a completely serious person, because you're playful, humorous, and a good deal of fun, but it never seems that you're completely focused on finding a partner and settling down. You enjoy the company of other people, there's no question about that, and you believe in a serious partnership, but sometimes you just want to get away from it all, and that can cause current relationships to fizzle. It's rather baffling.

The truth is there are two sides to your nature, the one

side that wants a truly adult, happy and ongoing partnership. And then there's the other side—that doesn't. At some point, you realize that it's really all up to you. If you make the decision that you're ready to settle down, a partner comes along, and although you can be somewhat critical, you use your instincts and know that this is the mate for you. And as long as you have a person who combines your qualities of seriousness and fun, you're happy with each other for years to come.

Your Capricorn-Sagittarius lover often seems to be involved in issues of such overriding importance that concentrating on you seems irrelevant by comparison. It's hard for this mate to focus on a single other human being, and being in love doesn't make it any easier. In a relationship, this individual demands a hard-to-find combination of total reliability and undemanding freedom. In the best relationships, total commitment is understood, yet neither party infringes even slightly on the freedom of the other. "I love you, do what you want," is his or her motto, and it can be pretty exhilarating for the right partner.

Capricorn-Sagittarius really wants to own land and to have a home with sizable acreage. Being the lord of the manner, or a cowboy with a giant ranch, is a real dream. If this is the sort of reality that also appeals to you, you could happily work together to build your dynasty. Adventuresome, outdoorsy dates are much appreciated, as are nice little presents that can be rather quirky. To woo this person, you must be attractive and interesting, someone who can stroll around and enjoy life actively on foot.

Sexually, your lover is both earthy and filled with a fiery exuberance that can be brought out very quickly. It may be quite a surprise when you discover that this serious individual has the most fun in bed of anybody you know. Sex is just too pleasurable to take seriously, and as long as they keep making sleeping bags that zip together, this is the one person who plans to take advantage of both technology and Mother Nature.

Venus in Capricorn with Mars in Capricorn

You're ambitious, hard-working, serious, practical, and very materialistic. That's not to say that you love things, just that you're aware of the value of money and of the importance of material goods. You've known since you were a very small child about the kind of success you wanted to achieve, and you let nothing stop you from attaining your goals, because nothing is more important to you.

Working hard is your primary source of pleasure, and people who spend their weekend swinging idly in a hammock inspire not your envy, but your disgust. When it comes to choosing a mate, you can be sure that no Cinderella will capture your heart. You're far more interested in acquiring a Prince (or Princess) Charming. "It's just as easy to fall in love with a rich person as a poor one," may be your motto, and even if it isn't, it's just too hard for you to respect someone who doesn't have his or her act together sufficiently to have acquired some cash and some social clout.

It's not as though you don't believe in love and commitment, for you surely do. You think that going through life with a partner makes good sense, because it gives additional resources and more hands to do the work. And you believe in love as well. You just don't always have the time to devote to acquiring it. You might be signing up for one of those matchmaker services at this very second, for it's a great deal easier to shop when someone else does the legwork. Once you do settle down, you're content to remain with that partner for the rest of your life. As time passes, you look back on happy memories, and take pride in all that you built together working side-by-side.

Your Capricorn-Capricorn lover is such a workaholic that you may feel it's unfair that he or she is so sexy. After all, with less sex appeal, maybe everybody would leave this individual alone to pursue a dreary routine. But this mate manages to radiate an earthy kind of appeal and has such a sidesplitting way of making droll jokes that it's hard not to find him or her appealing, although Capricorn-Capricorn remains oblivious to it all.

Steady and secure is the life this mate desires, and although courtship is attended to only halfheartedly (and with a wallet to match), marriage requires the serious determination to work hard and succeed that he or she brings to the other areas of life. Capricorn-Capricorn may feel that nothing even remotely meaningful happens before middle-age, when one is settled down with marriage and family, which is not exactly an attitude that generates flamboyant romantic interludes, and in fact, he or she is seldom interested in flamboyance or, sadly romance.

So if you find this person appealing, it may be up to you to take the lead and put a little bit of fire in your budding romance. Capricorn-Capricorn doesn't mind being wooed, and, in fact, finds it rather flattering, as long as you don't make endless calls during the workday. Respect work times and understand that sometimes practical goals must be put ahead of fun and games.

Likewise, practical gifts are always appreciated. A briefcase, a gadget case or a gadget, or anything that helps this mate get ahead in life, is the perfect gift to offer.

In bed, your lover is willing to work as hard as everywhere else. Seeing that you're satisfied is more than a pleasure—it's a duty, and this individual always lives up to every responsibility. Where sex is concerned, he or she wants to take time, go slowly, and get it right, which may be the best thing about that workaholic, Boy Scout attitude.

Venus in Capricorn with Mars in Aquarius

Your goal is to combine the old and reliable with the new and innovative in order to create a present that's more satisfying and a future that's even better. A very socially forward individual, you're concerned with the greater good and may well be a politician on some level. Dealing with individuals and with smaller structures—like the couple—is much more difficult. It's just hard for you to get intimate. Broad, sweeping strokes are so much more comfortable for you to paint. The kinds of relationships that feature quiet, tender moments of shared intimate talk, accompanied by enraptured eye gazing and impassioned handholding seem to elude you, and if you had such an interaction, you might be too embarrassed to deal with it at all.

You prefer to be around people who share your ideological point of view. Feeling a sense of mutual commitment is the way you identify those who matter to you on the deepest level. It's not that you're unaware of emotional and sexual attraction, or that you're immune to them; you just have other priorities where relationships are concerned.

You enjoy socializing on a certain level, but often you're very busy, and your own priorities take precedence. When you do find a partner who's the right person for you, you're steady and faithful to that person. It's just a question of making it a priority on your part to mate and marry.

Your Capricorn-Aquarius lover is ambitious, hard-working, and distant, which is both admirable and aggravating. It's natural for you to feel that you want your lover's total, undivided attention sometimes—without having to become a cause, that is. Just because this mate doesn't have the patience to listen to the ins and outs of your day in detail doesn't mean you're not loved, but that's hard to accept when you need some TLC, and he or she doesn't seem to be there for you. Speak up and voice your complaints. A plea to your partner's inner fairness regulator won't go unheeded. In fact, you may have won this person's heart by working together side-by-side on mutually important causes. A simple date is never going to be enough; you have to make it matter. Likewise when buying gifts, it's a bit of a conundrum. This person does like beautiful luxury items, but resists owning too many things. Gadgets and devices that help with daily life are good choices, as is a star that you can name yourself, or a donation to a good cause.

Although not a particularly marriage minded combination, finding the right other half will go a long way towards helping this individual to want to settle down. You must truly be partners who share your hopes and goals, and who can make the world a better place together.

In bed, your mate is willing to try most anything you might suggest. Initially he or she may feel a little self-conscious and awkward about trying something new. "Is it dignified?" He or she wonders, and then mischievous little inner voice answers, "Who cares? There's nobody here watching, silly, so loosen up." And then your lover feels free to give you something you've been wanting all day—his or her undivided attention.

Venus in Capricorn with Mars in Pisces

You combine practicality and serious good sense with the understanding that feelings are always involved, and that we must all follow our instincts rather than just doing what makes sense logically.

You don't think of yourself as romantic in the sort of silly way that involves romance novels or other fictional plots, but you do romanticize marriage and true love rather strongly. You believe in the family unit and you revere your very own family, feeling that you would not be the person you are today without them. What you want as an adult is to build a family of your own, one where all the members love and support each other and provide an enduring foundation for happiness and emotional security.

When you're mated with the right partner, you feel able to express your best self. You love looking after and taking care of other people, particularly those with whom you're intimately involved. Although you see yourself as more of a caretaker than someone who receives care, it's your ideal to be in a relationship where each person gives and receives equally.

You're quite sensitive, or you can be, and you can intuit other people's feelings and needs. Sometimes you don't understand why those around you can't return the favor. You don't like the sense that you're being taken advantage of, and you try never to let that happen.

Your Capricorn-Pisces lover is very sensitive and can be rather sentimental. He or she loves to reminisce about the good times you've had, and even to sit with a scrapbook of pictures of all the activities you've shared. This is someone with excellent values, a partner you can count on to care for you and be there for you all the days of your life. It's not even terribly hard to generate some interest from this person, as long as you're not completely frivolous, or tasteless and sloppy. You may meet while volunteering at an animal shelter, or another place that does good for those in need.

This mate does tend to worry about money, and he or she likes to save more than to spend, so don't expect to be wooed extravagantly, or to be taken to tony night spots for overpriced meals. Certainly if you're willing to foot the bill, your lover won't mind at all going along with you to enjoy something that he or she might not want to pay for.

Likewise, a sentimental gift is much appreciated, and if it's rather pricey, that's all right too. Just don't expect your partner to go out on a shopping spree that benefits you. He or she just doesn't enjoy that sort of thing.

In bed, your needs are absolutely important to this mate, and although he or she is probably not the sort to sweep you off your feet and toss you into bed, that does not preclude long pleasurable evenings of slow, tender lovemaking. Speak up and reveal your heart's desires. This is one mate who's willing to try pretty much anything in bed, so you don't have to be shy.

Venus in Aquarius-Mars Combinations

Venus in Aquarius with Mars in Aries

You're determined to go your own way, and anybody who attempts to dictate to you is rapidly axed from your life. Your own self-expression is far more important to you than anything or anyone, and if your relationships must suffer because of it, too bad. Since your attitude toward relationships—and all human interaction—is so mental and action oriented, you never find yourself in the emotional traps that many people experience. In fact, often you may hurt the feelings of the people who are closest to you without meaning to or being aware of what you've done. You're just a great deal hardier than most of us.

Settling down is the last thing on your mind. The words are often enough to disgust you. There is a world out there with so many people to meet, confront, and experience that you can't see why anyone ever considers being tied to just one partner. You'd love to live in a commune that's totally unstructured, with everybody swapping partners freely. In fact, you may experiment with alternate lifestyles throughout much of your life.

If, by chance, you have other, more sentimental elements in your horoscope and decide you want to settle down, you still seek a large measure of freedom and independence. Maybe you travel for work, or do something else that pulls you away from the routine of partnership. The ideal for you is a best friend who is also a mate, someone who's similar and who gets you.

Your Aquarius-Aries lover may have told you right out that marriage was out of the question, and you probably should believe it, because when you're heartbrokenly protesting, "I thought you loved me," he or she will be disgusted by your emotional outbursts and remind you that you were forewarned.

Love has nothing to do with it; this individual might love you to the death, but he or she just can't always stay. A totally open relationship in which there are no demands placed on each other and in which you see each other on the spur of the moment as the fancy strikes you is often preferable. Group sex is also a terrific way to spend an evening. The point is never to get bogged down.

In bed, Aquarius-Aries likes to be outrageous. There is nothing you could suggest that is too shocking—except 30 years of the missionary position with the same quilt and the same partner. One of the really terrific things about an affair with this dynamo is the uninhibited approach to sex that you both can take. If you have a secret fantasy, now is the time to act it out; Aquarius-Aries will come up with embellishments that even you hadn't thought about. Exciting, unconventional, wild, and untamable, this is one partner that you'll remember with a chuckle of amusement forever.

Venus in Aquarius with Mars in Taurus

You're a real party person. You love to be friendly and social, and to go out with a gang of people for a good time and a good meal. Often you host large gatherings of unusual people, for you love to have friends come to your home for festivities.

You're also the most determined, most stubborn individual on the planet, and you absolutely always do things your own way. Because you have such persistence, other people just have to give in—or grow very old while waiting for you to change your mind.

Relationships are a bit difficult for you for a number of reasons. Firstly, you must be allowed to have your own way, and that extends to telling your partners what to do as well. You alternate between being ho-hum about a relationship, and saying do whatever you want, and being incredibly possessive and clinging, and that is confusing to everyone you date. The problem is you're a bit ambivalent. You like everything secure, steady, and predictable, but you're never quite sure if you want to settle down with one specific person. It's complicated.

Secondly it doesn't feel all that abnormal to engage in quarrels and to share some friction with a romantic partner. You don't quite get how people exist in perfect harmony, although you would like that very much, and you sense that the way to do that is for your mate to do exactly what you say. Your mate may have other ideas, however.

Obviously once some thought goes into the situation, and you consider your life and your options, this problem can be solved. If you really want to be with somebody, you can do it. It's just a matter of you offering your mate the sort of respect that you would like to have offered to you.

Your Aquarius-Taurus lover wants a close relationship that expresses the principle of "one for all, all for one," but that's not always easy to create. Often a congenial, friendly, solid manner masks frustrations lingering below the surface that he or she is loathe to voice. Eventually there are periodic eruptions that shatter your perfect love affair temporarily.

There's a good deal of confusion going on here about how to combine a mental, idealistic nature with the desire for material security. This mate wants to dig out toward uninvolved freedom, and dig in toward traditional commitment, and if you think that's confusing for you to deal with, imagine how he or she feels.

In bed, Aquarius-Taurus likes to take plenty of time. Your lover may like some of the new sex toys, or may even have an electric vibrating bed. In any case, he or she seeks always to bring innovation to the bedroom. And as you both learn, the bedroom is absolutely the best place to take advantage of the friction between you.

Venus in Aquarius with Mars in Gemini

Remember how Woody Alan says that his brain is his second favorite organ? Well, your brain is easily your first choice. You're a real thinker, and to you action follows naturally from thought. In fact, talking about your ideas may be just as good as acting on them.

You demand the same intellectual approach to life from

your close companions, or you get bored quite easily and prefer to move on to be with someone more like yourself. People who are much more emotional or more practical than you are find communication with you awkward because of your level of abstraction. You find them dull and ponderous in return.

You rarely communicate emotionally or seek a stable relationship with a single partner. Just lying together cuddling and saying nothing doesn't create the connection for you that verbal exchange does. And finding a partner with whom you can work to establish a home and a life with material security is also not high on your priority list. Thus it's important for you to make friends with a group of people like yourself. And as long as you do have a number of friends, you may not feel compelled to marry at all.

If other aspects of your horoscope indicate a greater sensitivity, obviously this may be untrue. If you do in fact seek a one-on-one relationship with the love of your life, all you need to do to get it is to be willing to concentrate on the other person—at least some of the time. And that means giving time and attention to expressed emotions, and sensitivity to emotions which remain unexpressed.

Your Aquarius-Gemini lover lives the life of the mind. Since this mate never bothers to check and see if reality matches his or her ideas, there's no problem about the inevitable discrepancies. You debate and argue, and if you challenge this individual's ideas, it could result in a sense of outrage similar to what you might expect if you'd insulted someone's mother. With an individual so glib, it sometimes seems perfectly natural to agree with whatever your mate is purporting.

A broad social base feels quite natural to this mate, and knowing many people casually—as long as they're intelligent people—is preferable to a few intimate acquaintances. Your lover is not really interested in a permanent relationship because concentrating on emotions just isn't something he or she can manage. Even where sex is concerned it's often quite possible that Aquarius-Gemini would rather talk about it than do it, so if sex is very important to you, you must learn to be an excellent seducer. Or you could move this relationship into the realm of friendship, and in that way it could last a very long time. Aquarius-Gemini would usually rather have a friend, anyway, and he or she is so free from jealousy and possessiveness that nothing prevents it. As long as you're interested in a lively exchange of ideas and communication that really sparkles with intelligence and wit, you're set.

Venus in Aquarius with Mars in Cancer

You're a natural humanitarian, and you're always on the lookout for someone who needs your help, guidance, or spare change. When you can do a good deed, it makes you feel very good about yourself, and you feel that if everyone would behave that way the world would be a better place. Sometimes you attract lovers who need your help, and although this feels like a project, to you it feels natural, and even worthwhile.

Where relationships are concerned, you walk a bit of a tightrope. You know that you need your space, and you don't like to be strangled emotionally, but you understand the need for an emotional dimension in life and within relationships, and you want other people to be sensitive to your feelings and your motivations. You just don't want them smothering you. It may feel more natural to you to spend your time doing good deeds, volunteering for charities, helping people and animals, and not doing anything personally on a one-to-one basis. Sometimes you don't mind that solitary lifestyle, particularly if you're very busy with your good deeds, but other days you have a sense of loneliness and the desire for someone to comfort and protect you.

The key is obvious—you need to find a person with whom you're compatible. Then when you have someone who shares your mindset and agrees with what you think is important, you have mutual interests and things to do together. You also find that the perfect person won't smother you but is there providing a comforting aura, even if just from the background.

Your Aquarius-Cancer lover can sparkle with fun when

feeling cheerful, and can predict global gloom and doom when distressed. These mood swings disappear as suddenly as they appear, although some gentle prodding from you about whether or not you've caused hurt feelings might help to clear the air.

You come home from a long day at work and what do you find? Your generous partner has filled the house (again) with an odd assortment of humanity, all of them needing attention and (usually) dinner. Straight cats and dogs of the human species as well as the animal kingdom just naturally wend their way to the door and are taken in. The extended family concept was pioneered by people with this combination, so relax and make friends with the interlopers. Your mate won't run out of love or attention before it's your turn, so don't worry.

If you've just connected, and you're seeking the best way to woo this person, it's obvious—show your kindhearted side. If you have tales to share of your volunteer efforts, pet shelters you've aided or other such good deeds—that sparks a flame in this mate's heart. Gifts of technology are much appreciated, and even more appreciated is a donation to this person's favorite charity.

In bed, Aquarius-Cancer likes to be innovative and traditional at the same time. That may mean purchasing a water bed and covering it with an antique quilt or it may mean reading up on the latest how-to sex book while you cozily lie together and laugh at all the fuss everyone is making over something so simple.

Venus in Aquarius with Mars in Leo

Defining yourself and establishing your place within the larger social order are two of the major themes in your life. Relationships are one forum in which you seek to accomplish this, and although you recognize the need for compromise, you often refuse to do so. You rarely have an emotional stake in any one relationship, so often you change partners and begin again.

You're a very social person, and you adore group activities

where you usually prefer to be at the very center of the action. You desire a great deal of attention, and you love praise, but needing too much of both of these things can alienate those around you, so try to be a bit more mellow.

Where personal relationships are concerned, dealing with emotions feels rather difficult to you. You feel embarrassed and even intimidated by people who make a show of their inner feelings. You keep yours under wraps, and you'd prefer they do the same. In an intimate relationship, this is clearly impossible, so be prepared to open up a little bit, and to embrace a mate who does the same.

Your Aquarius-Leo lover is incredibly generous. This is the type of person who gives you the proverbial shirt off his or her back. This individual is loving and supportive and can make you feel that he or she is really on your team. That doesn't mean that you're invited to spend hours divulging an inner monologue about your feelings, hopes, and desires. This mate just likes you, even without intimate details, and that's all that's necessary.

This is a really stubborn individual. No one can take the lead because he or she simply remains on course. Often this perseverance becomes bossiness where a mate is concerned. Not only does your lover expect to run his or her life, but this individual may want to run yours as well. It's ironic that the people who brook the least interference from others are also the ones most likely to inflict this trait on their loved ones.

You get along best if you don't feel threatened by this order giving, and firmly but pleasantly accept "suggestions" only when they are truly welcome.

In bed, your lover's just as bossy, although the intention to please you is genuine, as long as you follow his or her rules. You might appeal to your mate's sense of fairness with a joking "Hey! You never let me be the guy!" (no matter what your sex) and he or she might laugh enough to let you take the lead.

Venus in Aquarius with Mars in Virgo

You're a real humanitarian, and also a real loner, which

can be a difficult combination to integrate successfully. You meet so many people you're certain could benefit from your clever mind and advanced methodology, and often you can truly be of service to them. And other times you get into trouble because you're so sure that you're right, and that your way is the best, and you try to ram your solutions down other people's throats. That results in some angry words followed by alienation all around. Often you're right about what you're suggesting, but concentrating on the mechanics of the situation instead of the human elements can be a little off-putting to people who want to feel better rather than accomplish more.

Obviously this approach to life can complicate a relationship. Most people desire a partnership of equals, not a mentor-underling situation. As sympathetic as you can be, you never really empathize because being in other people's shoes always cramps your toes. It's this inability to understand emotionally how another individual feels that keeps many of your human interactions intellectual. To you this almost feels comfortable, because your tendency is to confuse your feelings with your thoughts.

A little work at discerning the difference between a feeling—which has no logical basis, and a thought—which does have logic behind it—can make a huge difference where a personal relationship is concerned. It allows you to give value to a mate's feelings, and usually that is what's desired.

Your Aquarius-Virgo lover always has the perfect solution, and if you allow it, together you may re-create My Fair Lady. While many suggestions for your self-improvement campaign may be excellent, some people resent being looked at as the raw material for sculpting, so you may want to point out that surely there was something about you that your lover actually liked when first you met. This word to the wise may halt the chipping at your personality for a bit.

The obvious ploy for attention when just meeting is to come to this person with a problem, and to crow with praise at the offered solution. Alternately, a discussion about problems and solutions in which you both have a similar approach can lead to a strong initial bond based upon mutual respect.

Nobody is more clever and inventive, or truly a genius at making innovative ideas workable. It's people like Aquarius-Virgo, with head in the clouds and feet firmly on the ground, who pioneer the innovations that our society really needs. In bed, this individual likes to be both outrageous and thorough. If anybody can come up with new positions for sex, or new sex toys, it's this combination, although often he or she likes to develop slightly different favorite tricks and work them into a routine that can be repeated. And the good news is that the bedroom is one place where your mate is very willing to listen to your ideas and suggestions. What a relief to see the very human side of the Professor Henry Higgins you love.

Venus in Aquarius with Mars in Libra

Human rights is a big issue to you, and you go far out of your way to see that everyone gets a fair deal. Other people are very important to you, both as a group and as individuals. You really need to find your niche, because belonging to the team is the way you function best. You're social, friendly, and lively, and you love to interact with people and to communicate with them. Your conversation sparkles with a natural charm.

Although you do love people, you often refuse to communicate on an emotional level, preferring to keep things intellectual because feelings strike you as messy and a bit embarrassing. This does not mean that you forgo relationships, but rather that you often get into and out of a number of attachments without ever really feeling a deep emotional bond based on the sharing of each other's most intimate selves.

If you've decided that there's one special person with whom you want to share the rest of your life, this is something on which you'll need to work. You have to learn that taking a risk, sharing those unspeakable feelings, and listening to someone else's tender sentiments is all worthwhile. You'll always be the sort of person who enjoys interacting within a group, but once you realize that a group of only two has its benefits, the rules can change within that framework.

Your Aquarius-Libra lover is a true social butterfly. This individual loves to party and to get to know all sorts of people. You won't spend many cozy evenings at home alone, for your lover would much rather be out and around other people. This is not a traditionally romantic combination. He or she is not likely to camp on your doorstep writing sonnets through the night, strewing violets at your feet, or gazing love-struck into your eyes. The way this mate sees it is that you're each half of a twosome, and together you form a cog in the larger wheel of society, and it is that urge that propels him or her toward the altar, not the music of violins or the magic of your kisses.

This attitude seems a little cold, but it can work in your favor when you're first meeting. As you connect on a positive intellectual level, with a few good laughs, and the sense that socially you mesh, you could be well on your way towards a permanent tie.

In bed, Aquarius-Libra could use some prodding. This mate is much more social than sexual so if you have the hots, it's your job to do the warming up. Coming up with something tastefully unconventional is your best bet, if you can manage to be that inventive.

If not, you might just take a bottle of champagne and a couple of books of erotic art to bed for the two of you to discuss the artistic pros and cons versus the possibly sexually exploitative nature of such work. Eventually, if you've steered the conversation in the right direction, all that talking might lead to some communication on a more intimate, physical level.

Venus in Aquarius with Mars in Scorpio

You're a devoted humanitarian, but you're sure to let only a very few individuals get close. Instead, you'd rather remain powerful and inviolate, for you really like maintaining that distance that enhances your power over others. And when you decide that those you know should do something, it's almost impossible for them to have their own way unless they remove themselves from you totally.

You sometimes feel conflicted where an intimate relationship is concerned. On one hand you like the idea of being—and remaining—friends with anyone you've ever dated. On the other hand you're very passionate and you love sex in a physical way. Physically, sex is just great. But then there's all that pillow talk, and while you're interested in other people and what they have to say, you don't want to reveal your innermost secrets, not to a lover, not to anyone. At least not for a very long time.

You believe in love that lasts forever, but to other people it feels that you're more interested in the act of love than the emotional content of love. You're the sort of person who enjoys the idea of friends with benefits, but to the friend involved the sex feels so passionate and intense, it's as though it should go further, and that's where the conflict begins. If this happens, you shrug and figure well, that's normal. It just doesn't seem unusual for relationships not to go smoothly, and if they did you'd probably consider your partner bland and boring. That's not to say that you indulge in many instantaneous blowups and happy reconciliations. Instead you're more likely to let hostile feeling simmer below the surface while everybody around you worries about an impending eruption.

Your Aquarius-Scorpio lover is far different from the way he or she appears. This friendly, congenial soul who exposes such a placid exterior is really a private, intense person. And if you're having any kind of close relationship at all, then know that you're really special. This individual can be an incredible force for good, and chances are he or she is involved in some very important global projects. More than most people, your mate has the ability (and the sheer force) to achieve his or her ideals. So be sure to join your partner's team. That doesn't mean he or she is on your team, unless you're a project to be rehabbed. Unfortunately this can be rather frustrating, because you'd rather be with somebody who sees you as perfect—at least at the beginning.

In bed, Aquarius-Scorpio always takes the lead, and if you're easily shocked, forget it. People with this combination are capable of the most outrageous sexual activity of all. Orgies are only a mild form of sexual self-expression, so let your imagination wander from there. And if you always desired a partner capable of outdoing the bluest blue movie, you've made the best possible selection.

Venus in Aquarius with Mars in Sagittarius

You're often so busy roaming the earth, experiencing new people, and sharing philosophies and ideals, that you never get to know anyone very well at all. For sheer numbers of acquaintances, no one outdoes you as long as depth of the interaction isn't a factor. Idealistic, honest, and honorable, you care far more about the course the world is taking than you do about your own narrow self-interests. It's impossible for you not to put personal considerations aside when faced with a choice involving larger issues.

You enjoy and require relationships, and the emphasis is always on the plural. Although your feelings of affection may remain constant, you still want to enlarge your sphere. Those who insist on becoming tied down to one mate are likely to get ulcers rather than happiness.

If someone you enjoy refuses to accept your liberal standards and open relationship requirements, it's far easier for you to smile and wave goodbye than to grit your teeth and compromise. There are many fish in the sea, and you want to taste them all.

Should you have other, decidedly more sentimental factors in your horoscope, you might opt for a committed relationship, but you'll always want to be surrounded by many friends. It's very easy for you to feel abiding affection that endures, but that doesn't mean you want to be smothered.

Your Aquarius-Sagittarius lover is about as big on long-term relationships as Morris the cat is on Dobermans. Why get involved with someone who's determined to eat you up? Commitment feels the same as confinement, and this mate doesn't want any of either. Be forewarned, you romantics seeking diamonds and forever. This guy or gal may be glad to remain your pal forever, but the chances for a trip down the aisle are slim. Better to have a good time with someone who shares important ideals. Feeling respect and admiration for another person is the basis for any relationship with this beautiful dreamer. Having ideas and concerns you can share creates the strongest bond between you, and if you do get a shot at something permanent, this is how it will come about.

Aquarius-Sagittarius believes in free love, group sex, and spur of the moment assignations in all manner of unusual situations, inappropriate locations, and with a diversity of partners. After all, sex is an interesting experience, and people who put rules around it are just too narrow-minded. So if you're open to new experiences, new people, and to broadening your world in many ways, this is your opportunity.

Venus in Aquarius with Mars in Capricorn

You're a determined leader, and you never let emotional considerations interfere with action. In fact, you're not terribly emotional, so you recognize that people's feelings often get in the way of achieving their goals. When faced with someone else's feelings, you're totally at a loss. Therefore you choose to abandon a relationship rather than to become embroiled in emotional chaos.

Although romance isn't your number one priority, you do believe in a close connection with a single partner. You just want that person to be a good friend, someone who will always have your back, and someone on whom you can count. You like being part of a social circle, although often that circle consists of people with whom you work. You understand the benefits of networking, and you choose your closest companions within that group of people. Thus you may find yourself married to a business partner, and every aspect of your life closely connected. To you, friends are the people who can help you get where you want to go, people with a like mentality, and a mate is the best friend of all.

Your pillow talk tends to revolve around practical matters that must be attended to, idealistic causes which you back relentlessly, and things that seem important to you, none of which are about emotions. To a sensitive mate, this can feel a bit like a slap in the face, as though you're stating a lack of interest in what matters to him or her, so consider this and reorient your thinking a bit so that you can pay due attention to someone you truly love.

Your Aquarius-Capricorn lover is hard to get close to. Either this individual is at work leading some charge toward a goal, or has that distant look in the eye, indicating a major plan in development. "Yoo hoooo! Remember me?" You can try it, but no guarantees about being heard. What does help is if you're similarly occupied much of the time with your own life and your own concerns. If you live for love and look for romance at every corner, you won't get the kind of attention you need to feel happy and beloved.

Although Aquarius-Capricorn may be willing to settle down with the right person (and I do mean someone who truly is a working partner), marriage and a relationship are not at the top of this mate's list—not usually. Other concerns are far too compelling. And since this individual seldom gets too intimately involved with anyone, no entreating tugs at the heart strings urge him or her to do otherwise.

Likewise, pure sex is almost never a motivation, not because it's against your lover's principles but because he or she sublimates sexual energy into work. With an available partner who's willing and interested, Aquarius-Capricorn is delighted to respond to the occasion by taking over completely. As in a working environment, he or she expects to be in the lead. And if you can enjoy being told exactly where to put your head, your feet, and what to do with everything in between, then surrender yourself for the night.

Venus in Aquarius with Mars in Aquarius

Your goal is to find the people who encourage you and who share your philosophies, for then you can be a selflessly hard-working member of the team, and much good for the world at large (or at least your own community) can be accomplished because of your efforts. If, on the other hand, you live surrounded by people who try to restrict you in any way, or to make you adhere to what they consider normal, conventional behavior, you go from one disruptive scene to the next, rebelling often just for the sake of proving yourself different. Therefore it's up to you to find your ideological kin, for more than almost everybody else, you need group interaction and group support. Without that you feel almost totally isolated and ineffectual.

Finding a harmonious network in which to mesh does more than connect you socially in a positive way. It can take the place of more intimate one-to-one committed relationships that other people need far more than you do.

Marriage may not be one of your major concerns, and you may regard it as an institution that has outlived its meaningfulness. The "serial monogamy" that much-married people engage in today may be a frequent source of ridicule in your circle, although you consider it preferable to staying with a dead relationship because of an ancient commitment.

Should you find yourself in the bewildering condition that most people describe as being "in love," you're a little bit baffled, but willing to see where it leads. If you can find a person who is the bestest of best friends, someone who feels just right in your daily life, and even in your arms, and you might surprise yourself and say "I do."

Sometimes you should take what a person says at face value. If you meet Aquarius-Aquarius and hear repeatedly that this person just isn't interested in commitment or—heaven forbid—marriage, then listen to what you've been told. You can be friends, if you're willing to be friends, and you might enjoy that relationship very, very much. Just don't be determined to turn it into something else. On the other hand, if you're enjoying the friendship, and Aquarius-Aquarius is clearly enjoying it too, your relationship can continue for a very long time, to the satisfaction of both of you. The truth is, it depends upon you, and what you actually want. If you're a super emotional person who needs to be allowed to weep on someone's shoulder, to laugh uncontrollably, and to express all manner of feelings much of the time, this mate might not be the perfect choice for you, because he or she just doesn't enjoy that sort of thing.

Your Aquarius-Aquarius lover is not a callous playboy (or playgirl); he or she just has other interests. While most of us prefer to concentrate the greater part of our energy on ourselves and our personal needs, your lover just naturally sublimates personal needs to those of the group by focusing on a larger framework.

This individual may live in a commune, engage in group sex freely (although not all that frequently, as this is one of those combinations that is often rather disinterested in sex), or if he or she does marry, you can be sure it will be in an open situation in which each partner retains the freedom to do as he or she wishes and with whom.

Venus in Aquarius with Mars in Pisces

You're a very friendly, very social person, with a sensitive side. You care so much about the people in your life, and you always want to be there for them. This kindly part of your nature is wonderful, and your friends adore the fact that you're there for them, happy to listen to their problems, and willing to offer advice. The question is can you do this full-time.

When seeking a mate, obviously the most important factor is friendship. You want to be with someone with whom you feel simpatico. You want to know that that individual is your sort of person, so you can look deep, deep inside him or her and see something that warms your heart and makes you smile. This is actually a good approach, for ultimately friendships can last, whereas hot and searing romantic attractions so often cool down.

You want to feel that if you bother to be in a one-to-one relationship, as opposed to just being friends with many people, which actually is quite comfortable for you, that this single relationship will succeed and last. You'd like to be one of those people who celebrates a fifty year anniversary, hand-in-hand, still in love, side-by-side with your very best friend.

Your Aquarius-Pisces lover is the sweetest person in the world. Nobody is kinder and more helpful, but sometimes it seems as though this kindness and helpfulness is channeled into virtually everybody you both know, making it hard to discern just how special a place you hold in this mate's heart.

Even something as simple as a weekend date can be hard to arrange, because of all the prior commitments with friends that he or she has agreed to keep. Want to go to a romantic restaurant? You can't because there's a painting party at a best pal's house. If it happens once, this isn't a problem; when it happens constantly, this is a problem.

Communication is the obvious key here. You need to be able to speak up and share your innermost feelings, and what's really important to you. This mate wants you to be happy. But on the other hand, he or she doesn't want to be overwhelmed with commands or to feel as though you're some sort of romantic slave driver.

In bed, your lover is often willing to follow your lead, and he or she is totally nonjudgmental, so be as unconventional as you like. Play dirty word scrabble or strip checkers atop your waterbed, buy some body paints and turn each other into works of art, or share a champagne bubble bath. Whatever you try, just have fun, as you both take a much needed retreat from the concerns of the world around you.

Venus in Pisces-Mars Combinations

Venus in Pisces with Mars in Aries

You have fantasies galore, and all the energy in the world to act them out. Although you're strong and independent, you're emotional and sensitive as well, so you usually find a way to satisfy yourself without hurting anybody else. A loyal champion of the underdog, you're a devoted friend and ally worth having. Although you like to be kind and giving, you refuse to allow others to take advantage of you, because you know you have the right to put yourself first—at least some of the time.

When you fall in love, it's with your whole soul, and you feel that nobody ever loved as you did. Whether or not this is true is irrelevant; epic proportions just feel natural to you. Meeting the love of your life, experiencing instant magic, and eloping all on the same weekend doesn't strike you as imprudent; it strikes you as the sort of grand romantic gesture that you were meant to make. Of course, the recognition that you don't always attract partners who're good for you comes eventually, and that is the day you hate to experience. Breaking up a relationship pains you deeply, even if you're the one who wants out, because you dread hurting anyone. If this is a regular pattern in your life, it may be that you're attracting weaker partners who don't challenge you in any way, but compromise between equals is something you must learn to value.

An early heartbreak can be a useful thing, however, because it teaches you to hold back a beat before you give your heart so that you can do so when you meet someone who is good for you rather than just sexy. Your goal is to be in a happy relationship and when you find someone you love and admire, you're willing to put aside any temporary urges to cheat so that you can focus on what really matters—devotion and great sex.

Your Pisces-Aries lover is sensitive, exciting, more fun than a party, and practically a vacation in human form. Prepare to be swept off your feet, feeling all the while that your wish is your lover's command, and this is just the sort of lover who can both discern your wishes and put them into action.

This sweet and sultry individual is impulsive, impractical, and almost totally irresistible. Ten minutes after the introductions have been made, you're gazing into each other's eyes, making plans for the next decade, and recalling the lifetimes you spent as lovers on other continents. "I always knew we were meant to be together," your partner whispers softly as the key turns smoothly in the lock of his or her door. So what if the bank account is empty and the apartment untidy? Your lover is splendid.

In bed, this mate wants to create magic. Intense passion combines with a matching depth of emotion, causing you to feel as though you're falling into a hypnotic dream of intoxication. Intuitive and ardent, your lover can sense and meet your moods and level of arousal, so that it feels that you're partners of the best sort, finding satisfaction together at the perfect moment. It's always urgent, but it's never too fast, and afterwards there is sweet pillow talk, sensual snuggling, and a level of tenderness that never fails to touch your heart.

Venus in Pisces with Mars in Taurus

You're dreamy and romantic, yet practical and earthy as well. You need a great deal of stability, both emotional and material, for it's easy for you to feel insecure. You want to turn a magical attraction into an enduring love affair that you can count on for both stability and continuing romantic fantasy, but that can seem difficult.

The people you attract who can provide the kind of fairytale romance you seek often are not interested in staying around for the long haul, and your tendency to be jealous and possessive is very hard for them to endure. Other more solid and substantial types strike you as far too bland and unromantic to sustain your interest.

The challenge for you is to find a love that is beautiful yet has a practical dimension as well, and with some experience you're able to do just that.

You can envision yourself as half of a long-married, deeply in love couple, sitting together on the porch holding hands, sipping lemonade, and watching grandchildren frolic in the yard. That's your goal, and it's a worthwhile one to pursue. You just need to find a partner who has your sense of romance, and the ability to be loving and faithful for the next fifty years.

Your Pisces-Taurus lover is whimsical and sensual, which is a great combination if you enjoy lying around trading fantasies and back rubs. Staying home and doing just that is this individual's favorite type of evening. Playing house—whether or not you're married—is such a kick. What's better than the cozy security of a dinner prepared at home for the two of you to share? Your lover's ample imagination is entertainment enough—why bother with the movies?

Stubborn when pressed, this mate insists on doing things his or her own way, but rarely expresses anger directly. Even if an emotional explosion is about to erupt, it's easier to handle any conflict by surreptitiously continuing with set plans. Anger is just so hard for your lover to deal with that even a direct confrontation often fails to resolve the issue. Your best bet might be to adopt the attitude of live and let live, for an open debate rarely takes place.

In bed, Pisces-Taurus is willing to take forever to discover what pleases you both. Bed is this mate's favorite place, anyway, so be prepared for long, lazy evenings of lovemaking during which you explore your body from head to toe, your desires from beginning to end, and your fantasies from A to Z. No wonder he or she likes to say at home so much.

Venus in Pisces with Mars in Gemini

Friendly, outgoing, and social, you like to keep on the move, meeting new people, seeing new places, and never getting bogged down. You're a terrific storyteller, and children as well as adults love to be around you to hear your marvelous flights of fancy. You probably know more people than any five of your friends put together, and even though you may spend only a little time with each of them, you really get to know your friends both emotionally and intellectually. Although people like to come to you with their problems, you don't particularly enjoy being an unpaid therapist, although you do try to be sympathetic and empathetic, but heavy psychological conversations can be a bit ponderous for your itchy-footed nature.

Stability in relationships is not your long suit, and it may not even be a priority for you. You need your freedom to come and go as you like, and although you're quite romantic, you may feel that a committed relationship would be restricting. To you, love is a kind of magic that happens, and you want a permanent relationship that never loses the initial spark of attraction. The fact is that successful relationships are more than fifty percent hard work and determination, but to your way of thinking, that attitude defeats the beauty of romance. Perfection in love ought to endure without herculean efforts. Because you feel this way, you'd often rather abandon a relationship when it loses some of its early sparkle; another one always comes along, anyway.

Your Pisces-Gemini lover can keep you interested and amused for hours on end—if he or she could sit still that long—with all manner of funny and romantic stories that are created endlessly in a marvelously imaginative brain. Feeling listless? Your lover's brand of humor and a sensitivity to what's bothering you will set you to giggling in a flash. Need an inspiration for a vacation? This mate has thirty-five ideas ready before you open the first travel brochure.

This individual is the most popular guest at a party, the first one into the lake for skinny-dipping, and the only one who actually agrees to come along with you on that cross country bicycle trip. Will your lover make it all the way? Sometimes not, for this is one of those combinations quick to start and quick to abandon new schemes. Being free to experience life is what's important—not getting to the finish line.

In bed, Pisces-Gemini may spend more time talking about

romance than actually engaging in sex. It's up to you to reach out for the first hug, start the tickling contest, or to make a bet about who can turn the other on the most quickly. Once you focus that creativity on sex, who knows what can happen?

Venus in Pisces with Mars in Cancer

You're sensitive, emotional, and shy, but when you aren't feeling your best, you often need to retreat to a quiet place to restore your good humor and your energy. Because you're so moody, it's important for you to try to avoid negative or bombastic people; the negative vibrations that you pick up from perfectly normal, usually cheerful people are hard enough to filter out of your system.

You're caring, loving, and kind, and you help so many people with all sorts of problems that sometimes it's hard to keep track of them all. You're naturally the go-to person for other people who need advice and comfort. That's not so bad where friendship is concerned, but if you find yourself romancing a collection of stray dogs, it's not too hard to understand why most of these romances fail to become permanent. Your important life lesson is that love at its best is a two-way street. Partners should give as much as they get, although admittedly people have to take turns looking out for each other, but ultimately the balance sheet should be even. Once you make that your love life goal, it's much easier to find the sort of partner who will become your true love for a lifetime.

And that is just what you seek, true love for a lifetime. You want a mate you'll love and adore for the rest of your life, someone with whom you can build a home, rear a family, and share a joyful old age.

Your Pisces-Cancer mate is so giving and devoted that he or she can make you feel like the most special person on earth. Or your lover can make you feel smothered, depending on your own needs. If you delight in being the center of attention, having all your needs attended to (before you even realize them), being served your favorite meals, and having your frayed edges soothed with the tenderest devotion, then you're really in luck. Pisces-Cancer loves to stay at home and concentrate on you.

In bed, this mate wants to spin a web of gossamer magic in which the two of you can loll, hypnotically entranced by each other's bodies and each other's souls. There is all the time in the world for two lovers to gaze into each other's eyes, revealing what twenty volumes of sonnets couldn't cover. And to Pisces-Cancer, love is forever after, for this mate seeks a love that will endure and will provide a safe harbor where the two of you can retreat from all the cares of the world beyond.

Venus in Pisces with Mars in Leo

You're warm and friendly, kind and loving, and your generosity to both friends and lovers is probably legendary. Doing nice things for others without even a thought of repayment makes you feel wonderful, so you willingly give of your money, time, or talents whenever they are needed. Although you're quite sensitive to the feelings of others, often you prefer to keep yours to yourself. It's not that you're shy, but rather that you like to maintain your privacy. Emotions are nothing to be ashamed of, but they're to be shared with the few really intimate friends we each have, not the whole world.

You envision the perfect life, with the perfect mate by your side. Not only do you want to be madly in love, but you want to build the sort of life that everyone else finds mesmerizing. You want to be the ones to host the most fabulous bashes, produce the most wonderful children, and live in a bubble of happiness and joy for the rest of your life.

Early on, you're quite content to play the field, for there are so many exciting, attractive, and interesting people to date. You don't find dating as unappealing as many people do; you love it. As much fun as you have being single, there's always a nagging little voice in the back of your mind whispering, "When I find my true love...." And that's the eventuality you yearn for, finding that perfect soulmate who completes your destiny, and with whom you can build the magical life you envision.

Your Pisces-Leo lover likes to dream big dreams and then to carry them out. Even if you're just beginning to date, this individual acts as though you're involved in the love affair of the century, and spares no effort to make it such. Nothing is too extravagant for a beloved, and if the cash is available, you're treated to diamonds and weekends in Paris. If not, you receive whatever your mate can afford. In return, all you must grant is adequate personal freedom and a little respect. Of course, a healthy dose of loving attention from you won't be refused.

In bed, Pisces-Leo really wants to make you happy and never tires before you're satisfied. This mate does tend to take the lead quite often, but he or she is so huggable in the display of this grand passion that it's impossible not to enjoy being overwhelmed by such generosity of spirit. And when you realize that this adoration of you not only endures but also is amplified in time, you first begin to see how really lucky you are.

Venus in Pisces with Mars in Virgo

You're really out there to help the other guy, although you do sometimes alternate between behavior that is uncritically loving and unlovingly critical. Ultimately, it's your lesson to learn that we each must be encouraged to develop our individuality, whatever that is, and that compromise is essential, for it allows individuality to be expressed without relationships being destroyed.

To you, loving means being helpful, and as long as you're not trying to "improve" the one you love, your effort should be appreciated. You have the ability to hone in on another's preferences, feelings, and needs, which makes you a terrific gift buyer. When it's time to buy a present, you really put a great deal of effort into choosing just the right thing, and you usually succeed. Likewise, the little details of life come under your scrutiny quite effectively, and you find yourself able to do the sweet little things that make people happy. This in turn makes you happy, for you like giving pleasure to other people.

Your goal is to understand that compromise is a good thing, even if you don't feel that the right choices are being made. You recognize that other people have a right to have their voices heard, even if that voice is saying what to you is the wrong thing. Understanding this helps you create a happy relationship.

Your Pisces-Virgo lover is industrious and puts as much concerted effort into making your relationship work as is needed. Even though this individual has a terrific imagination and can be quite romantic, he or she is always responsible, reliable, and careful about everything. Whether or not your lover is an artist or craftsperson, he or she has the admirable ability of being able to bring to practical realization the creations of a fertile imagination. Thus where love is concerned, this mate can keep the machinery oiled without losing track of the magic. Pisces-Virgo is willing to settle down as long as there are not too many restrictions.

In bed, your mate knows all the special things you need to feel loved and desired, and never neglects a one. Making a lover feel really catered to is a special talent, and too few people possess such sensitivity in today's world of the quick, meaningless grapple. To this emotionally pristine individual, sex is only for true lovers—people who can merge both body and soul in the union of holy mingling, perfect communication, and total acceptance.

Venus in Pisces with Mars in Libra

Kind and gentle, sensitive and thoughtful, you'd rather cut off your arm than thoughtlessly hurt someone's feelings. Your nature is mannerly, and even courtly, and you feel that attention to etiquette—at least informally—is the way to show that you care about other people's feelings and needs.

You need to socialize and be around people, for it's easy for you to get quite lonely when isolated for too long. After you've had a good dose of human interaction, you're content to retire to the solitude of your room for refueling. Having a balance of companionship and solitude is important to you, although even when you do accomplish it, you often feel that you're alone when you want company, and with people when you prefer to be by yourself.

Love is very important to you, for it is through the loving act of give and take that you most strongly express yourself and learn about who you are. Just as great art speaks to the soul, so does the love that lives in eternity define and create us all. You feel that partnership is the best way to live, and you go out of your way to make a relationship work. You just want to know that the person you love also loves you and will stay with you throughout thick and thin.

Your Pisces-Libra lover doesn't like to make waves. Everything should be pretty, calm, and congenial. Having a pleasant time is more important than participating in an intense encounter, and in fact, intensity of any sort makes this individual nervous. A nice romance—or marriage—where two people have good times sharing mutual pleasures such as poetry, movies, concerts, and quiet dinners, is the ideal. It's good fun to relax together at home with the stereo on and the candles lit.

To this placid romantic, relationships are for fun and warm feelings, and the kind of work that must be put into any marriage seems a bit heavy. That doesn't mean that your mate is unwilling to do the work of a marriage, but he or she would rather think about love as a beautiful pink bubble, encasing the two of you forever.

In bed, Pisces-Libra is delighted to let you take the lead. Kisses and soft caresses are this mate's style, rather than impassioned embraces. So snuggle under your down quilt, feed each other strawberries, drink champagne, and do all the beautiful things that lovers have done together through the centuries.

Venus in Pisces with Mars in Scorpio

You're one of the most emotional people around, and just about everything you do is determined largely because of your feelings. Like some sort of psychic-energy sponge, you can pick up both the negative and positive emotions of your friends, or even residual emotional vibrations from the atmosphere. You can use your emotional sensitivity to help others deal with their feelings and their problems, for all sorts of people are drawn to you, sensing a deep compassion on your part. And you can be very healing, just in your ability to listen and understand, as long as you're not doing healing by absorbing the negative vibrations yourself.

You reveal very little of your own inner feelings and deep emotional nature. Private and shy, you're very elusive, even to the people who know you best. When in company, you have a good time socializing, but even though you're a pleasant and friendly guest, often you'd rather be at home, either alone or with your mate. You recognize that the social side of your nature is very appealing, but what matters more to you is being with a mate who knows and understands you, and who shares your tastes and pleasures. You want to be with someone you can trust and adore for the rest of your life. You go out of your way to make a mate happy and you'd like to feel that your partner does the same for you. This level of intimacy is what means the most to you, not group activities and not being around many casual friends. You know that fun is important in a casual way, but nothing takes the place of deep and passionate love, or that knowing gaze that you see in the eyes of someone with whom you're truly intimate.

Your Pisces-Scorpio lover wants to find one true love. Nothing less than the soulmate with whom he or she has shared thousands of lifetimes of loving union will satisfy. Even a nice affair with a well-loved partner isn't enough. This individual seeks that cosmic relationship that makes of your two souls a single entity, eternally mingled in the perfect harmony of true completion. At first glance this mate can determine if you're a potential soulmate, and if first glance disappoints, there's no way on earth to interest him or her. And if, after a time, it becomes obvious that you're not true soulmates, your lover has no choice but to depart, despite the very deep love that still endures and the pain you both suffer.

In bed, Pisces-Scorpio surrenders totally to the passion

that envelops and consumes you both in an intensely overwhelming, transformational fury that brings your bodies together in wordless ecstasy. Sexual satisfaction is not the primary focus; this type of loving communication takes place totally beyond thought.

It's the physical excitement and release that leads to the emotional, ethereal blending of essences with each other and with the source of all creation that is the ultimate goal of a loving sexual union sought by Pisces-Scorpio. It's through a loving relationship that we here on earth come closest to God, and that is why this mate seeks a partner as one on a holy crusade.

Venus in Pisces with Mars in Sagittarius

You're friendly and outgoing, the life of the party, and your healthy imagination can spin enough fantasies of magical, faraway lands to keep a room full of three-year-olds enraptured for hours. You're full of life and excitement, and you enjoy being on the move, meeting various people and having many opportunities for fun. It's easy for you to become involved quickly in romances, for you have the ability to like others in a genuine, very uncritical way. Often you find yourself in the middle of relationships that you never intended to have because of the initial enthusiasm that you bring to any encounter.

Being in a single, committed relationship can sometimes be a problem for you, for although your feelings are genuine, and you're capable of very unselfish devotion, it feels more natural to you to love and let go rather than to hold on. Mostly you feel that there are too many experiences and too many people to meet for you to want a single relationship. Also, you must be totally free to come and go as you like, or you begin to feel fenced in.

When the romantic side of your nature takes over, all you can think about is true love, and that perfect soulmate who would make you want to stay forever. It's just a question of finding the person without whom you'd be more miserable than you would be by staying together. Then you can be happy, as long as there's excitement that's ongoing and you're both free to grow and change as people.

Your Pisces-Sagittarius lover is as warm and loving as a puppy dog, and genuinely has your best interest at heart. The problem is that this individual feels the same way about a few hundred other people, so how can you feel that you're special? And when you express this insecurity and your mate replies, "Maybe you should try to meet someone else who can make you happier," you naturally feel like choking him or her. Remember, it's not that your mate doesn't love you; it's just that he or she is jumpy and can't concentrate on any one person for very long. And as much as you're adored, making a commitment is a difficult step for your lover to take.

In bed, Pisces-Sagittarius combines an emotional tenderness with an infectious physical vitality. Doing anything physical is good for the disposition, and sex is his or her absolute favorite physical activity. Using an active imagination to set all sorts of scenes and acting out playful fantasies can be a lot of fun. Why worry about propriety, timing, or tomorrow? And if this philosophy is acceptable, you're in for a fun filled romance with lots of hugs and surprises.

Venus in Pisces with Mars in Capricorn

You understand the importance of combining dreams with practical achievements, and more than most people, you have the ability to turn your fantasies into reality. You're friendly and helpful, but you don't like to waste too much time on people who bend your ear with their problems and then do nothing to solve them.

Achievement is important to you, as are successes and status, but you never lose sight of the human issues or of your own feelings. People respond to this trait in you, for it's rare to find someone so sensitive, responsible, and dependable as well. Your lively personality appeals to many people, and you're never lonely for company or without social invitations.

You enjoy interacting on a casual level, but it's your goal to be with one perfect soulmate for the rest of your life. You can envision quite early on the sort of happy marriage and joyful family that you want to build, and you may be congeniality paired from college onward. You can see good qualities in many people, and that's a very nice skill, but you know exactly what you want in a mate, and choose only the sort of person who meets your standards and your needs for the rest of your life. A mere infatuation isn't enough; it has to be true love that lasts.

Your Pisces-Capricorn lover wants a mate who shares in dreams and the efforts to realize them. A loving, working partnership of equals who inspire and encourage each other is the ideal relationship. Ultimately this individual may want to build something that the world can share and to which the two of you can point with pride as the fruition of your partnership.

When this sweetie finds the right mate, Pisces-Capricorn puts much effort into the relationship and into making you happy. Your lover is willing to listen sensitively to your feelings and to try to compromise so that both of you feel your needs are being met. And although always hard at work at one project or another, he or she never forgets that you and your relationship are priorities as well.

In bed, Pisces-Capricorn is emotional, sensual, and most of all enjoys having a good time. Sharing fantasies, special secrets, trading back rubs, and doing anything that makes you both feel as if you've had a vacation from your daily responsibilities is a delightful way to spend an evening. It's sort of like creating your own private amusement park for just the two of you to share.

Venus in Pisces with Mars in Aquarius

You have so many legions of friends that you may ignore the need for a single close relationship. A one-to-one involvement may just not be among your priorities, for love is more of a universal principle to you than a personal feeling. If you do choose to settle down, it's with someone who shares your commitment to help the world.

You like to feel the same sense of camaraderie with a lover

that you do with your closest friends. Although you can become infatuated, it's usually not your motivating force. You need to feel that you're genuinely seeing the person that you're with, and that that person sees you as well. Being seen and understood is to you the most important type of familiarity, and it goes far beyond the usual physical intimacy for which most people settle.

You're not always focused on marriage, or a long-term commitment. If you can find a relationship where you feel comfortable and happy, that may be enough. You do have your priorities, and often you're quite busy, and you don't always feel that more is necessary where relationships are concerned.

Your Pisces-Aquarius lover is always in the throes of some beautiful idealistic dream. Unconventional and uninterested in propriety, he or she meanders along, never noticing if anyone is watching. The problem is that you may feel your romance gets lost in the shuffle of your lover's dream world. Unselfish and unconcerned with personal gratification, this individual is loving and friendly toward everybody, so what does that mean about the two of you? Good question. Often it just means that that is the way he or she is, and you have nothing to do with it. It's hard for your mate to concentrate on a personal love affair, for the motivation and know-how to get a permanent relationship off the ground is difficult to muster.

In bed, Pisces-Aquarius has no trouble expressing genuine friendship and honestly loving feelings. Feel free to take the lead, and communicate openly that sex is important to you, and what your specific needs are, and your lover will be delighted to take any suggestions you offer. And because he or she is totally uninhibited and a fast learner as well, you both may be in for quite a surprise.

Venus in Pisces with Mars in Pisces

Emotional, sensitive, and dreamy, you need to spend some time quietly alone, meditating and gathering your energies. You enjoy being creative and you expend a great deal of your time and efforts expressing your imagination.

Even when you know that being selfish is appropriate, it's hard for you to do. You tend to focus on the other person, putting your own needs aside, and that can make a relationship difficult, unless you find a saintly partner who has the same sort of ethos that you do. If you and a friend both like the same romantic partner, you often step aside and let your pal take the mate. This is sweet, but it doesn't always get you true love.

True love is what you actually want to find. You can be happy in a casual relationship, and sometimes you succumb to infatuation—because your imagination is so strong you can envision any sort of romantic eventuality happening between you and another person. But ultimately what you want is the one person on earth into whose eyes you can look and know this is the person for you. Then you're willing to put that person first in every aspect of your life. The key is to find that one person who also puts you first. Then you share true love, for that is what true love is.

Your Pisces-Pisces lover is sensitive, artistic, receptive, and willing always to put aside his or her needs in favor of your own, so you must try to be fair-minded and rather unselfish as well. In fact, for you to be aggressively nice to your lover couldn't hurt, because he or she is always so giving that having the favor returned is only right.

Some people with his placement are more inclined toward a spiritual, reflective life than one that involves love, marriage, and ordinary reality. So if you find yourself enamored of this person, it's your job to be enticing enough so that Pisces-Pisces sees you as the soulmate who completes his or her destiny. If there's an aura of fate, you've done your job. That meant-to-be sensation has to be at work here for this relationship to come about, and for it to last.

In bed, Pisces-Pisces wants you to be happy, and it's not always about sex, lust, or heaving bodies. Sometimes it's just about snuggling, cuddling, stroking, or even just kissing. It's that emotional sensation of being nurtured, loved, and adored that this mate values. If you desire more passion, speak up. Say what you need, be precise, and expect your wish to be your mate's command.

A Few Caveats—
How Your Sun and Moon
Can Modify This Information

Early in this book, you were warned not to trust assertions about your love style which relied on information based only on your Sun sign. That is correct advice. The essence of who you are in terms of your romantic and sexual desires and preferences is described by your Venus and Mars. However, in a horoscope everything is connected and interacts. Everything impinges on everything else. You're not a collection of disconnected parts functioning independently, but rather a person with many interconnected qualities and expectations. Every little detail in your horoscope taken together adds up to the sum and total of you.

Although you can have this information synthesized by having a reading with a good astrologer, when reading about the part of your horoscope, this task is left to you to do. So I wanted to include a few words about how some things I've said in the many passages above could be modified.

In doing the delineations for every Venus-Mars combination, I tried to hit on the essence of each combination, the heart and soul of each particular love style, the archetype. Hopefully when you read about yourself—or a special loved one—you recognized the essence that lives inside you in what I wrote. But you might think, hmm I'm more emotional that that...hmm I crave commitment more than that...hmm I'm sexier than that. And so on. If so, there's a reason for that, and the reason is your Sun or Moon sign.

The Sun describes your basic nature and the way you approach life. An Aries is a certain kind of person, different from a Taurus, and so on. The Moon describes your inner landscape, your emotions, your need for nurturing and emotional security.

So, for example, if you have Venus in a communicative and relatively less emotional Air sign, such as Gemini or Aquarius, you're less romantic than someone with Venus in a more sensitive Water sign, such as Cancer or Pisces. Gemini and Aquarius Venus people want to play the field, enjoy dating, and need friendships almost more than romance. But if you're a sensitive Cancer Sun or Moon, then you're emotional in every aspect of your life, and you crave attachments that feed your need for nurturing and an emotional connection. It doesn't change the chatty way you like to express affection and your need to talk, but it does make you need a relationship more than a Gemini Venus who has Sun or Moon in Gemini, for example. The information about your Venus is still correct, but it's just shaded by your Sun and Moon, because everything in your horoscope is shaded by everything else.

Just as a little guide, keep the following in mind:

If your Sun or Moon is in Fire (Aries, Leo, or Sagittarius), you're more outgoing romantically, less shy, and a bit less sensitive. You put yourself first more often, no matter where your Venus or Mars are.

If your Sun or Moon is in Earth (Taurus, Virgo, or Capricorn), you're more practical and you seek physical security, so that can always create a dimension in the way you choose romantic partners. You may be more likely to stay in a relationship for practical or financial reasons.

If your Sun or Moon is in Air (Gemini, Libra, or Aquarius), you need conversation and social activities, but you're not always that emotional or sensitive to other people's feelings. You don't want to get bogged down in the sentimental stuff. If your Sun or Moon is sentimental, then you want closeness but not with someone you'd consider a whiner.

If your Sun or Moon is in Water (Cancer, Scorpio, or Pisces), you're sensitive and emotional, and you need a strong sense of emotional security. So even if your Venus is in one of the Air sigs that resist commitment, you want to find a way to make commitment happen. You just won't want to be there for other people in an emotional way as often as someone else might.

Likewise, commitment and longevity are an issue when considering romantic outlooks. The Mode of your Sun and Moon sign plays a part here, because it describes the basic level of stability at which you function.

If your Sun or Moon are in Cardinal signs (Aries, Cancer,

Libra, or Capricorn), you're more assertive, even if your Venus or Mars are shy and hesitant. You find a way to express your desires and seek what you want. And if you want to let go, you move on without too much hesitation. You don't want for love to come to you; you go get it.

If your Sun or Moon are in Fixed signs (Taurus, Leo, Scorpio, or Aquarius), you're a stable person who desires continuity and longevity. You don't let go or make changes easily. So even if your Venus is in a sign that likes to date and move on, you try to stay put. Or you may attract partners who leave because that way you don't have to let go of your own volition.

If your Sun or Moon are in Mutable signs (Gemini, Virgo, Sagittarius, or Pisces), you're more flexible. You enjoy variety and consider new things as good possibilities. You can let go and move on because you have faith that something new will come. Or if you're Mutable and your Venus or Mars are very fixed, you might attract the wrong partner so it's easy to ditch that person when the time comes.

Keep in mind that all these examples are designed to show you that everything places shades of meaning upon the archetypes we've already discussed. They don't negate the basic truths of who you are romantically, they just add slightly different flavors, such as when you're cooking and add a bit of a different spice or essence. You still have beef stew, but it tastes slightly different with cumin, or jalapeno, or basil.

Or suppose you come from a strongly traditional background, one in which marriage is considered the norm. Even if you have rebellious energies in your Venus and Mars, still in your mind resides the idea that everyone should marry, and stay married. Notions like that can create your life, even if your heart is a little wild inside.

Likewise there are other planets in your horoscope making connections to Venus and Mars and they too add shades of meaning that can somewhat change your basic archetype.

Despite all that, I hope you find the essence of yourself in the paragraphs about you, for that is why I wrote this book.

Tables to Locate Venus and Mars

Look below for the date of your birth. Then you can see where Venus (and of course Mars) were on that day. For most of you, your birthday will fall somewhere in the middle of any particular planetary stay in a sign. Only if you were born just as Venus or Mars was moving into a new sign, you may have to use your birth time to determine precisely where Venus and Mars were at the moment of your birth. The tables below were calculated for the global zero hour, in Greenwich, England. So you would need to determine what time it was in Greenwich at the moment of your birth.

Convert your birth time to Greenwich, England time by following the chart below. If you're in the United States, add the number of hours to your birth time and you'll have the time it was in Greenwich. This chart is configured for standard time. Daylight Savings Time has changed over the years, so it's difficult to adjust reliably for it without using a computer. If you know you were born during Daylight Savings Time, then subtract an hour from your birth time before doing the other calculations. There are sites online where you can calculate your planets for free. Keep in mind if you're adding, that might mean you're pushed into the next day. That is the whole point of doing this, so you know which day to use. Don't worry, though, you can still celebrate your birthday on your actual birthday!

UNITED STATES
Eastern Time add 5 hours
Central Time add 6 hours
Mountain Time add 7 hours
Pacific Time add 8 hours

For other parts of the world or to see this information visually, go to the following site and locate your birthplace on the map. http://www.worldtimezone.com/ Then you'll see how many hours to add to (or subtract from) your birth time so it matches Greenwich.

Please note once again that **this is necessary only if**

you were born close to the time at which Venus or Mars were moving into the next sign. Otherwise, all you need is the day of your birth. If you look below, you can see that Venus was in Aquarius on January 24th, 1930 at 12:22 AM in Greenwich. If you were born in California that day at 6 PM, then you'd need to add 8 hours, making your Greenwich birth time 2 AM on January 25th, which is after Venus had already entered. (12:22 AM is just after midnight.) If you were born at 5 PM on January 23rd in California, you'd add 8 hours, making your Greenwich time 1 AM on January 24th, and that was after Venus entered Aquarius. But if you were born on January 30th, you can see you're in the middle of the Aquarius period, so no calculations are needed. This will be true for most of you.

I know this can be confusing. Thank goodness for computers. But if you spend some time on Twitter or other social networking sites, it seems easier to understand, because you may befriend someone in another country. Then you get used to the idea that they're just getting up in England as you're heading into the wee hours. It's always later there. So if you're in California, your 11 PM Monday is their 7 AM Tuesday.

If this still stresses you, just read the passages that border the sign listed. You should be able to recognize the one that matches you!

Locate Your Venus

Jan 24, 1930	12:22 AM	Aquarius
Feb 16, 1930	10:11 PM	Pisces
Mar 12, 1930	10:34 PM	Aries
Apr 6, 1930	2:57 AM	Taurus
Apr 30, 1930	12:37 PM	Gemini
May 25, 1930	4:36 AM	Cancer
Jun 19, 1930	4:39 AM	Leo
Jul 14, 1930	4:34 PM	Virgo
Aug 10, 1930	12:54 AM	Libra
Sep 7, 1930	4:05 AM	Scorpio
Oct 12, 1930	2:45 AM	Sagittarius
Nov 22, 1930	7:44 AM	Scorpio
Jan 3, 1931	8:03 PM	Sagittarius
Feb 6, 1931	12:25 PM	Capricorn
Mar 5, 1931	9:46 PM	Aquarius
Mar 31, 1931	7:04 PM	Pisces
Apr 26, 1931	2:10 AM	Aries
May 21, 1931	2:38 AM	Taurus
Jun 14, 1931	11:04 PM	Gemini
Jul 9, 1931	3:35 PM	Cancer
Aug 3, 1931	3:29 AM	Leo
Aug 27, 1931	10:42 AM	Virgo
Sep 20, 1931	2:15 PM	Libra
Oct 14, 1931	3:45 PM	Scorpio
Nov 7, 1931	4:32 PM	Sagittarius
Dec 1, 1931	5:29 PM	Capricorn
Dec 25, 1931	7:44 PM	Aquarius
Jan 19, 1932	1:52 AM	Pisces
Feb 12, 1932	4:58 PM	Aries
Mar 9, 1932	2:07 AM	Taurus
Apr 5, 1932	12:19 AM	Gemini
May 6, 1932	9:04 AM	Cancer
Jul 13, 1932	10:33 AM	Gemini
Jul 28, 1932	12:36 PM	Cancer
Sep 8, 1932	7:45 PM	Leo
Oct 7, 1932	5:46 AM	Virgo
Nov 2, 1932	4:01 AM	Libra
Nov 27, 1932	12:06 AM	Scorpio
Dec 21, 1932	7:43 AM	Sagittarius

Jan 14, 1933	9:56 AM	Capricorn
Feb 7, 1933	10:30 AM	Aquarius
Mar 3, 1933	11:24 AM	Pisces
Mar 27, 1933	1:58 PM	Aries
Apr 20, 1933	7:00 PM	Taurus
May 15, 1933	2:47 AM	Gemini
Jun 8, 1933	1:01 PM	Cancer
Jul 3, 1933	1:29 AM	Leo
Jul 27, 1933	4:45 PM	Virgo
Aug 21, 1933	12:23 PM	Libra
Sep 15, 1933	2:54 PM	Scorpio
Oct 11, 1933	4:32 AM	Sagittarius
Nov 6, 1933	4:02 PM	Capricorn
Dec 5, 1933	6:00 PM	Aquarius
Apr 6, 1934	9:23 AM	Pisces
May 6, 1934	8:54 AM	Aries
Jun 2, 1934	10:11 AM	Taurus
Jun 28, 1934	9:38 AM	Gemini
Jul 23, 1934	6:22 PM	Cancer
Aug 17, 1934	3:45 PM	Leo
Sep 11, 1934	3:32 AM	Virgo
Oct 5, 1934	7:56 AM	Libra
Oct 29, 1934	7:37 AM	Scorpio
Nov 22, 1934	4:59 AM	Sagittarius
Dec 16, 1934	1:39 AM	Capricorn
Jan 8, 1935	10:44 PM	Aquarius
Feb 1, 1935	9:36 PM	Pisces
Feb 26, 1935	12:30 AM	Aries
Mar 22, 1935	10:29 AM	Taurus
Apr 16, 1935	7:37 AM	Gemini
May 11, 1935	10:01 PM	Cancer
Jun 7, 1935	7:11 PM	Leo
Jul 7, 1935	8:33 PM	Virgo
Nov 9, 1935	4:34 PM	Libra
Dec 8, 1935	2:36 PM	Scorpio
Jan 3, 1936	2:16 PM	Sagittarius
Jan 28, 1936	2:00 PM	Capricorn
Feb 22, 1936	4:14 AM	Aquarius
Mar 17, 1936	2:53 PM	Pisces
Apr 11, 1936	12:41 AM	Aries
May 5, 1936	10:53 AM	Taurus
May 29, 1936	9:39 PM	Gemini
Jun 23, 1936	8:16 AM	Cancer
Jul 17, 1936	5:51 PM	Leo

Aug 11, 1936	2:11 AM	Virgo
Sep 4, 1936	10:02 AM	Libra
Sep 28, 1936	6:36 PM	Scorpio
Oct 23, 1936	5:00 AM	Sagittarius
Nov 16, 1936	6:36 PM	Capricorn
Dec 11, 1936	2:51 PM	Aquarius
Jan 6, 1937	3:18 AM	Pisces
Feb 2, 1937	10:39 AM	Aries
Mar 9, 1937	1:19 PM	Taurus
Apr 14, 1937	4:19 AM	Aries
Jun 4, 1937	6:41 AM	Taurus
Jul 7, 1937	9:13 PM	Gemini
Aug 4, 1937	8:14 PM	Cancer
Aug 31, 1937	12:08 AM	Leo
Sep 25, 1937	4:03 AM	Virgo
Oct 19, 1937	4:33 PM	Libra
Nov 12, 1937	7:43 PM	Scorpio
Dec 6, 1937	6:06 PM	Sagittarius
Dec 30, 1937	2:42 PM	Capricorn
Jan 23, 1938	11:16 AM	Aquarius
Feb 16, 1938	9:00 AM	Pisces
Mar 12, 1938	9:20 AM	Aries
Apr 5, 1938	1:46 PM	Taurus
Apr 29, 1938	11:35 PM	Gemini
May 24, 1938	3:56 PM	Cancer
Jun 18, 1938	4:37 PM	Leo
Jul 14, 1938	5:44 AM	Virgo
Aug 9, 1938	4:26 PM	Libra
Sep 7, 1938	1:36 AM	Scorpio
Oct 13, 1938	6:49 PM	Sagittarius
Nov 15, 1938	4:07 PM	Scorpio
Jan 4, 1939	9:48 PM	Sagittarius
Feb 6, 1939	9:20 AM	Capricorn
Mar 5, 1939	1:29 PM	Aquarius
Mar 31, 1939	8:34 AM	Pisces
Apr 25, 1939	2:28 PM	Aries
May 20, 1939	2:13 PM	Taurus
Jun 14, 1939	10:11 AM	Gemini
Jul 9, 1939	2:25 AM	Cancer
Aug 2, 1939	2:11 PM	Leo
Aug 26, 1939	9:24 PM	Virgo
Sep 20, 1939	1:02 AM	Libra
Oct 14, 1939	2:41 AM	Scorpio
Nov 7, 1939	3:41 AM	Sagittarius

Dec 1, 1939	4:52 AM	Capricorn
Dec 25, 1939	7:25 AM	Aquarius
Jan 18, 1940	2:00 PM	Pisces
Feb 12, 1940	5:51 AM	Aries
Mar 8, 1940	4:25 PM	Taurus
Apr 4, 1940	6:10 PM	Gemini
May 6, 1940	6:47 PM	Cancer
Jul 5, 1940	4:17 PM	Gemini
Aug 1, 1940	2:20 AM	Cancer
Sep 8, 1940	4:59 PM	Leo
Oct 6, 1940	9:10 PM	Virgo
Nov 1, 1940	5:24 PM	Libra
Nov 26, 1940	12:32 PM	Scorpio
Dec 20, 1940	7:36 PM	Sagittarius
Jan 13, 1941	9:29 PM	Capricorn
Feb 6, 1941	9:49 PM	Aquarius
Mar 2, 1941	10:33 PM	Pisces
Mar 27, 1941	12:58 AM	Aries
Apr 20, 1941	5:53 AM	Taurus
May 14, 1941	1:36 PM	Gemini
Jun 7, 1941	11:53 PM	Cancer
Jul 2, 1941	12:33 PM	Leo
Jul 27, 1941	4:12 AM	Virgo
Aug 21, 1941	12:29 AM	Libra
Sep 15, 1941	4:01 AM	Scorpio
Oct 10, 1941	7:21 PM	Sagittarius
Nov 6, 1941	10:17 AM	Capricorn
Dec 5, 1941	11:04 PM	Aquarius
Apr 6, 1942	1:14 PM	Pisces
May 6, 1942	2:26 AM	Aries
Jun 2, 1942	12:26 AM	Taurus
Jun 27, 1942	10:18 PM	Gemini
Jul 23, 1942	6:10 AM	Cancer
Aug 17, 1942	3:04 AM	Leo
Sep 10, 1942	2:38 PM	Virgo
Oct 4, 1942	6:58 PM	Libra
Oct 28, 1942	6:40 PM	Scorpio
Nov 21, 1942	4:07 PM	Sagittarius
Dec 15, 1942	12:53 PM	Capricorn
Jan 8, 1943	10:03 AM	Aquarius
Feb 1, 1943	9:02 AM	Pisces
Feb 25, 1943	12:04 PM	Aries
Mar 21, 1943	10:24 PM	Taurus

Apr 15, 1943	8:12 PM	Gemini
May 11, 1943	11:56 AM	Cancer
Jun 7, 1943	12:09 PM	Leo
Jul 7, 1943	11:56 PM	Virgo
Nov 9, 1943	6:25 PM	Libra
Dec 8, 1943	7:45 AM	Scorpio
Jan 3, 1944	4:43 AM	Sagittarius
Jan 28, 1944	3:11 AM	Capricorn
Feb 21, 1944	4:40 PM	Aquarius
Mar 17, 1944	2:46 AM	Pisces
Apr 10, 1944	12:09 PM	Aries
May 4, 1944	10:04 PM	Taurus
May 29, 1944	8:39 AM	Gemini
Jun 22, 1944	7:12 PM	Cancer
Jul 17, 1944	4:47 AM	Leo
Aug 10, 1944	1:13 PM	Virgo
Sep 3, 1944	9:16 PM	Libra
Sep 28, 1944	6:12 AM	Scorpio
Oct 22, 1944	5:07 PM	Sagittarius
Nov 16, 1944	7:26 AM	Capricorn
Dec 11, 1944	4:47 AM	Aquarius
Jan 5, 1945	7:18 PM	Pisces
Feb 2, 1945	8:07 AM	Aries
Mar 11, 1945	11:17 AM	Taurus
Apr 7, 1945	7:15 PM	Aries
Jun 4, 1945	10:58 PM	Taurus
Jul 7, 1945	4:20 PM	Gemini
Aug 4, 1945	10:59 AM	Cancer
Aug 30, 1945	1:05 PM	Leo
Sep 24, 1945	4:06 PM	Virgo
Oct 19, 1945	4:09 AM	Libra
Nov 12, 1945	7:05 AM	Scorpio
Dec 6, 1945	5:22 AM	Sagittarius
Dec 30, 1945	1:56 AM	Capricorn
Jan 22, 1946	10:28 PM	Aquarius
Feb 15, 1946	8:11 PM	Pisces
Mar 11, 1946	8:32 PM	Aries
Apr 5, 1946	1:01 AM	Taurus
Apr 29, 1946	10:59 AM	Gemini
May 24, 1946	3:39 AM	Cancer
Jun 18, 1946	5:00 AM	Leo
Jul 13, 1946	7:22 PM	Virgo
Aug 9, 1946	8:34 AM	Libra
Sep 7, 1946	12:16 AM	Scorpio

Oct 16, 1946	10:45 AM	Sagittarius
Nov 8, 1946	8:56 AM	Scorpio
Jan 5, 1947	4:45 PM	Sagittarius
Feb 6, 1947	5:41 AM	Capricorn
Mar 5, 1947	5:09 AM	Aquarius
Mar 30, 1947	10:14 PM	Pisces
Apr 25, 1947	3:03 AM	Aries
May 20, 1947	2:06 AM	Taurus
Jun 13, 1947	9:35 PM	Gemini
Jul 8, 1947	1:30 PM	Cancer
Aug 2, 1947	1:06 AM	Leo
Aug 26, 1947	8:17 AM	Virgo
Sep 19, 1947	12:01 PM	Libra
Oct 13, 1947	1:49 PM	Scorpio
Nov 6, 1947	2:59 PM	Sagittarius
Nov 30, 1947	4:23 PM	Capricorn
Dec 24, 1947	7:13 PM	Aquarius
Jan 18, 1948	2:14 AM	Pisces
Feb 11, 1948	6:51 PM	Aries
Mar 8, 1948	6:59 AM	Taurus
Apr 4, 1948	12:40 PM	Gemini
May 7, 1948	8:27 AM	Cancer
Jun 29, 1948	7:58 AM	Gemini
Aug 3, 1948	2:15 AM	Cancer
Sep 8, 1948	1:40 PM	Leo
Oct 6, 1948	12:25 PM	Virgo
Nov 1, 1948	6:42 AM	Libra
Nov 26, 1948	12:55 AM	Scorpio
Dec 20, 1948	7:28 AM	Sagittarius
Jan 13, 1949	9:01 AM	Capricorn
Feb 6, 1949	9:05 AM	Aquarius
Mar 2, 1949	9:38 AM	Pisces
Mar 26, 1949	11:54 AM	Aries
Apr 19, 1949	4:44 PM	Taurus
May 14, 1949	12:25 AM	Gemini
Jun 7, 1949	10:47 AM	Cancer
Jul 1, 1949	11:40 PM	Leo
Jul 26, 1949	3:43 PM	Virgo
Aug 20, 1949	12:39 PM	Libra
Sep 14, 1949	5:12 PM	Scorpio
Oct 10, 1949	10:18 AM	Sagittarius
Nov 6, 1949	4:53 AM	Capricorn
Dec 6, 1949	6:06 AM	Aquarius

Apr 6, 1950	3:13 PM	Pisces
May 5, 1950	7:19 PM	Aries
Jun 1, 1950	2:19 PM	Taurus
Jun 27, 1950	10:45 AM	Gemini
Jul 22, 1950	5:50 PM	Cancer
Aug 16, 1950	2:18 PM	Leo
Sep 10, 1950	1:37 AM	Virgo
Oct 4, 1950	5:51 AM	Libra
Oct 28, 1950	5:33 AM	Scorpio
Nov 21, 1950	3:03 AM	Sagittarius
Dec 14, 1950	11:54 PM	Capricorn
Jan 7, 1951	9:10 PM	Aquarius
Jan 31, 1951	8:14 PM	Pisces
Feb 24, 1951	11:26 PM	Aries
Mar 21, 1951	10:05 AM	Taurus
Apr 15, 1951	8:33 AM	Gemini
May 11, 1951	1:41 AM	Cancer
Jun 7, 1951	5:10 AM	Leo
Jul 8, 1951	4:54 AM	Virgo
Nov 9, 1951	6:48 PM	Libra
Dec 8, 1951	12:19 AM	Scorpio
Jan 2, 1952	6:44 PM	Sagittarius
Jan 27, 1952	3:58 PM	Capricorn
Feb 21, 1952	4:42 AM	Aquarius
Mar 16, 1952	2:18 PM	Pisces
Apr 9, 1952	11:17 PM	Aries
May 4, 1952	8:55 AM	Taurus
May 28, 1952	7:19 PM	Gemini
Jun 22, 1952	5:46 AM	Cancer
Jul 16, 1952	3:23 PM	Leo
Aug 9, 1952	11:58 PM	Virgo
Sep 3, 1952	8:17 AM	Libra
Sep 27, 1952	5:36 PM	Scorpio
Oct 22, 1952	5:02 AM	Sagittarius
Nov 15, 1952	8:03 PM	Capricorn
Dec 10, 1952	6:30 PM	Aquarius
Jan 5, 1953	11:10 AM	Pisces
Feb 2, 1953	5:54 AM	Aries
Mar 14, 1953	6:58 PM	Taurus
Mar 31, 1953	5:17 AM	Aries
Jun 5, 1953	10:34 AM	Taurus
Jul 7, 1953	10:30 AM	Gemini
Aug 4, 1953	1:08 AM	Cancer
Aug 30, 1953	1:35 AM	Leo

Sep 24, 1953	3:48 AM	Virgo
Oct 18, 1953	3:27 PM	Libra
Nov 11, 1953	6:12 PM	Scorpio
Dec 5, 1953	4:24 PM	Sagittarius
Dec 29, 1953	12:53 PM	Capricorn
Jan 22, 1954	9:20 AM	Aquarius
Feb 15, 1954	7:01 AM	Pisces
Mar 11, 1954	7:22 AM	Aries
Apr 4, 1954	11:55 AM	Taurus
Apr 28, 1954	10:03 PM	Gemini
May 23, 1954	3:04 PM	Cancer
Jun 17, 1954	5:04 PM	Leo
Jul 13, 1954	8:43 AM	Virgo
Aug 9, 1954	12:34 AM	Libra
Sep 6, 1954	11:29 PM	Scorpio
Oct 23, 1954	10:08 PM	Sagittarius
Oct 27, 1954	10:41 AM	Scorpio
Jan 6, 1955	6:48 AM	Sagittarius
Feb 6, 1955	1:15 AM	Capricorn
Mar 4, 1955	8:22 PM	Aquarius
Mar 30, 1955	11:30 AM	Pisces
Apr 24, 1955	3:13 PM	Aries
May 19, 1955	1:35 PM	Taurus
Jun 13, 1955	8:38 AM	Gemini
Jul 8, 1955	12:15 AM	Cancer
Aug 1, 1955	11:43 AM	Leo
Aug 25, 1955	6:52 PM	Virgo
Sep 18, 1955	10:41 PM	Libra
Oct 13, 1955	12:39 AM	Scorpio
Nov 6, 1955	2:02 AM	Sagittarius
Nov 30, 1955	3:42 AM	Capricorn
Dec 24, 1955	6:52 AM	Aquarius
Jan 17, 1956	2:22 PM	Pisces
Feb 11, 1956	7:46 AM	Aries
Mar 7, 1956	9:31 PM	Taurus
Apr 4, 1956	7:23 AM	Gemini
May 8, 1956	2:17 AM	Cancer
Jun 23, 1956	12:10 PM	Gemini
Aug 4, 1956	9:49 AM	Cancer
Sep 8, 1956	9:23 AM	Leo
Oct 6, 1956	3:12 AM	Virgo
Oct 31, 1956	7:40 PM	Libra
Nov 25, 1956	1:01 PM	Scorpio
Dec 19, 1956	7:07 PM	Sagittarius

Jan 12, 1957	8:23 PM	Capricorn
Feb 5, 1957	8:16 PM	Aquarius
Mar 1, 1957	8:39 PM	Pisces
Mar 25, 1957	10:46 PM	Aries
Apr 19, 1957	3:28 AM	Taurus
May 13, 1957	11:08 AM	Gemini
Jun 6, 1957	9:35 PM	Cancer
Jul 1, 1957	10:42 AM	Leo
Jul 26, 1957	3:10 AM	Virgo
Aug 20, 1957	12:44 AM	Libra
Sep 14, 1957	6:20 AM	Scorpio
Oct 10, 1957	1:16 AM	Sagittarius
Nov 5, 1957	11:46 PM	Capricorn
Dec 6, 1957	3:26 PM	Aquarius
Apr 6, 1958	4:00 PM	Pisces
May 5, 1958	11:59 AM	Aries
Jun 1, 1958	4:07 AM	Taurus
Jun 26, 1958	11:08 PM	Gemini
Jul 22, 1958	5:26 AM	Cancer
Aug 16, 1958	1:28 AM	Leo
Sep 9, 1958	12:35 PM	Virgo
Oct 3, 1958	4:44 PM	Libra
Oct 27, 1958	4:26 PM	Scorpio
Nov 20, 1958	1:59 PM	Sagittarius
Dec 14, 1958	10:55 AM	Capricorn
Jan 7, 1959	8:16 AM	Aquarius
Jan 31, 1959	7:28 AM	Pisces
Feb 24, 1959	10:53 AM	Aries
Mar 20, 1959	9:55 PM	Taurus
Apr 14, 1959	9:08 PM	Gemini
May 10, 1959	3:45 PM	Cancer
Jun 6, 1959	10:43 PM	Leo
Jul 8, 1959	12:08 PM	Virgo
Sep 20, 1959	3:01 AM	Leo
Sep 25, 1959	8:15 AM	Virgo
Nov 9, 1959	6:11 PM	Libra
Dec 7, 1959	4:41 PM	Scorpio
Jan 2, 1960	8:43 AM	Sagittarius
Jan 27, 1960	4:46 AM	Capricorn
Feb 20, 1960	4:47 PM	Aquarius
Mar 16, 1960	1:53 AM	Pisces
Apr 9, 1960	10:32 AM	Aries
May 3, 1960	7:56 PM	Taurus

May 28, 1960	6:11 AM	Gemini
Jun 21, 1960	4:34 PM	Cancer
Jul 16, 1960	2:11 AM	Leo
Aug 9, 1960	10:54 AM	Virgo
Sep 2, 1960	7:29 PM	Libra
Sep 27, 1960	5:13 AM	Scorpio
Oct 21, 1960	5:12 PM	Sagittarius
Nov 15, 1960	8:57 AM	Capricorn
Dec 10, 1960	8:34 AM	Aquarius
Jan 5, 1961	3:31 AM	Pisces
Feb 2, 1961	4:46 AM	Aries
Jun 5, 1961	7:25 PM	Taurus
Jul 7, 1961	4:32 AM	Gemini
Aug 3, 1961	3:28 PM	Cancer
Aug 29, 1961	2:18 PM	Leo
Sep 23, 1961	3:43 PM	Virgo
Oct 18, 1961	2:58 AM	Libra
Nov 11, 1961	5:33 AM	Scorpio
Dec 5, 1961	3:40 AM	Sagittarius
Dec 29, 1961	12:07 AM	Capricorn
Jan 21, 1962	8:31 PM	Aquarius
Feb 14, 1962	6:09 PM	Pisces
Mar 10, 1962	6:28 PM	Aries
Apr 3, 1962	11:05 PM	Taurus
Apr 28, 1962	9:23 AM	Gemini
May 23, 1962	2:46 AM	Cancer
Jun 17, 1962	5:31 AM	Leo
Jul 12, 1962	10:32 PM	Virgo
Aug 8, 1962	5:13 PM	Libra
Sep 7, 1962	12:11 AM	Scorpio
Jan 6, 1963	5:35 PM	Sagittarius
Feb 5, 1963	8:36 PM	Capricorn
Mar 4, 1963	11:41 AM	Aquarius
Mar 30, 1963	1:00 AM	Pisces
Apr 24, 1963	3:39 AM	Aries
May 19, 1963	1:21 AM	Taurus
Jun 12, 1963	7:57 PM	Gemini
Jul 7, 1963	11:18 AM	Cancer
Jul 31, 1963	10:38 PM	Leo
Aug 25, 1963	5:49 AM	Virgo
Sep 18, 1963	9:43 AM	Libra
Oct 12, 1963	11:50 AM	Scorpio
Nov 5, 1963	1:25 PM	Sagittarius
Nov 29, 1963	3:21 PM	Capricorn

Dec 23, 1963	6:53 PM	Aquarius
Jan 17, 1964	2:54 AM	Pisces
Feb 10, 1964	9:09 PM	Aries
Mar 7, 1964	12:38 PM	Taurus
Apr 4, 1964	3:03 AM	Gemini
May 9, 1964	3:16 AM	Cancer
Jun 17, 1964	6:17 PM	Gemini
Aug 5, 1964	8:53 AM	Cancer
Sep 8, 1964	4:53 AM	Leo
Oct 5, 1964	6:10 PM	Virgo
Oct 31, 1964	8:54 AM	Libra
Nov 25, 1964	1:25 AM	Scorpio
Dec 19, 1964	7:02 AM	Sagittarius
Jan 12, 1965	8:00 AM	Capricorn
Feb 5, 1965	7:41 AM	Aquarius
Mar 1, 1965	7:55 AM	Pisces
Mar 25, 1965	9:54 AM	Aries
Apr 18, 1965	2:31 PM	Taurus
May 12, 1965	10:08 PM	Gemini
Jun 6, 1965	8:39 AM	Cancer
Jun 30, 1965	9:59 PM	Leo
Jul 25, 1965	2:51 PM	Virgo
Aug 19, 1965	1:06 PM	Libra
Sep 13, 1965	7:50 PM	Scorpio
Oct 9, 1965	4:46 PM	Sagittarius
Nov 5, 1965	7:36 PM	Capricorn
Dec 7, 1965	4:37 AM	Aquarius
Feb 6, 1966	12:46 PM	Capricorn
Feb 25, 1966	10:55 AM	Aquarius
Apr 6, 1966	3:53 PM	Pisces
May 5, 1966	4:33 AM	Aries
May 31, 1966	6:00 PM	Taurus
Jun 26, 1966	11:40 AM	Gemini
Jul 21, 1966	5:11 PM	Cancer
Aug 15, 1966	12:47 PM	Leo
Sep 8, 1966	11:40 PM	Virgo
Oct 3, 1966	3:44 AM	Libra
Oct 27, 1966	3:28 AM	Scorpio
Nov 20, 1966	1:06 AM	Sagittarius
Dec 13, 1966	10:09 PM	Capricorn
Jan 6, 1967	7:36 PM	Aquarius
Jan 30, 1967	6:53 PM	Pisces
Feb 23, 1967	10:30 PM	Aries

Mar 20, 1967	9:56 AM	Taurus
Apr 14, 1967	9:54 AM	Gemini
May 10, 1967	6:05 AM	Cancer
Jun 6, 1967	4:48 PM	Leo
Jul 8, 1967	10:11 PM	Virgo
Sep 9, 1967	11:58 AM	Leo
Oct 1, 1967	6:07 PM	Virgo
Nov 9, 1967	4:32 PM	Libra
Dec 7, 1967	8:48 AM	Scorpio
Jan 1, 1968	10:37 PM	Sagittarius
Jan 26, 1968	5:35 PM	Capricorn
Feb 20, 1968	4:55 AM	Aquarius
Mar 15, 1968	1:32 PM	Pisces
Apr 8, 1968	9:48 PM	Aries
May 3, 1968	6:56 AM	Taurus
May 27, 1968	5:02 PM	Gemini
Jun 21, 1968	3:20 AM	Cancer
Jul 15, 1968	12:59 PM	Leo
Aug 8, 1968	9:49 PM	Virgo
Sep 2, 1968	6:39 AM	Libra
Sep 26, 1968	4:45 PM	Scorpio
Oct 21, 1968	5:16 AM	Sagittarius
Nov 14, 1968	9:48 PM	Capricorn
Dec 9, 1968	10:40 PM	Aquarius
Jan 4, 1969	8:07 PM	Pisces
Feb 2, 1969	4:45 AM	Aries
Jun 6, 1969	1:48 AM	Taurus
Jul 6, 1969	10:04 PM	Gemini
Aug 3, 1969	5:30 AM	Cancer
Aug 29, 1969	2:48 AM	Leo
Sep 23, 1969	3:26 AM	Virgo
Oct 17, 1969	2:17 PM	Libra
Nov 10, 1969	4:40 PM	Scorpio
Dec 4, 1969	2:41 PM	Sagittarius
Dec 28, 1969	11:04 AM	Capricorn
Jan 21, 1970	7:26 AM	Aquarius
Feb 14, 1970	5:04 AM	Pisces
Mar 10, 1970	5:25 AM	Aries
Apr 3, 1970	10:05 AM	Taurus
Apr 27, 1970	8:33 PM	Gemini
May 22, 1970	2:19 PM	Cancer
Jun 16, 1970	5:49 PM	Leo
Jul 12, 1970	12:16 PM	Virgo
Aug 8, 1970	9:59 AM	Libra

Sep 7, 1970	1:54 AM	Scorpio
Jan 7, 1971	1:00 AM	Sagittarius
Feb 5, 1971	2:57 PM	Capricorn
Mar 4, 1971	2:24 AM	Aquarius
Mar 29, 1971	2:02 PM	Pisces
Apr 23, 1971	3:44 PM	Aries
May 18, 1971	12:48 PM	Taurus
Jun 12, 1971	6:58 AM	Gemini
Jul 6, 1971	10:02 PM	Cancer
Jul 31, 1971	9:15 AM	Leo
Aug 24, 1971	4:25 PM	Virgo
Sep 17, 1971	8:25 PM	Libra
Oct 11, 1971	10:43 PM	Scorpio
Nov 5, 1971	12:30 AM	Sagittarius
Nov 29, 1971	2:41 AM	Capricorn
Dec 23, 1971	6:32 AM	Aquarius
Jan 16, 1972	3:01 PM	Pisces
Feb 10, 1972	10:08 AM	Aries
Mar 7, 1972	3:25 AM	Taurus
Apr 3, 1972	10:48 PM	Gemini
May 10, 1972	1:51 PM	Cancer
Jun 11, 1972	8:08 PM	Gemini
Aug 6, 1972	1:26 AM	Cancer
Sep 7, 1972	11:27 PM	Leo
Oct 5, 1972	8:33 AM	Virgo
Oct 30, 1972	9:40 PM	Libra
Nov 24, 1972	1:23 PM	Scorpio
Dec 18, 1972	6:34 PM	Sagittarius
Jan 11, 1973	7:15 PM	Capricorn
Feb 4, 1973	6:43 PM	Aquarius
Feb 28, 1973	6:45 PM	Pisces
Mar 24, 1973	8:34 PM	Aries
Apr 18, 1973	1:05 AM	Taurus
May 12, 1973	8:42 AM	Gemini
Jun 5, 1973	7:20 PM	Cancer
Jun 30, 1973	8:55 AM	Leo
Jul 25, 1973	2:13 AM	Virgo
Aug 19, 1973	1:10 AM	Libra
Sep 13, 1973	9:05 AM	Scorpio
Oct 9, 1973	8:08 AM	Sagittarius
Nov 5, 1973	3:39 PM	Capricorn
Dec 7, 1973	9:37 PM	Aquarius
Jan 29, 1974	7:51 PM	Capricorn

Feb 28, 1974	2:25 PM	Aquarius
Apr 6, 1974	2:17 PM	Pisces
May 4, 1974	8:21 PM	Aries
May 31, 1974	7:19 AM	Taurus
Jun 25, 1974	11:44 PM	Gemini
Jul 21, 1974	4:34 AM	Cancer
Aug 14, 1974	11:47 PM	Leo
Sep 8, 1974	10:28 AM	Virgo
Oct 2, 1974	2:27 PM	Libra
Oct 26, 1974	2:12 PM	Scorpio
Nov 19, 1974	11:56 AM	Sagittarius
Dec 13, 1974	9:06 AM	Capricorn
Jan 6, 1975	6:39 AM	Aquarius
Jan 30, 1975	6:05 AM	Pisces
Feb 23, 1975	9:53 AM	Aries
Mar 19, 1975	9:42 PM	Taurus
Apr 13, 1975	10:26 PM	Gemini
May 9, 1975	8:11 PM	Cancer
Jun 6, 1975	10:54 AM	Leo
Jul 9, 1975	11:06 AM	Virgo
Sep 2, 1975	3:34 PM	Leo
Oct 4, 1975	5:19 AM	Virgo
Nov 9, 1975	1:52 PM	Libra
Dec 7, 1975	12:29 AM	Scorpio
Jan 1, 1976	12:14 PM	Sagittarius
Jan 26, 1976	6:09 AM	Capricorn
Feb 19, 1976	4:50 PM	Aquarius
Mar 15, 1976	12:59 AM	Pisces
Apr 8, 1976	8:56 AM	Aries
May 2, 1976	5:49 PM	Taurus
May 27, 1976	3:43 AM	Gemini
Jun 20, 1976	1:56 PM	Cancer
Jul 14, 1976	11:36 PM	Leo
Aug 8, 1976	8:36 AM	Virgo
Sep 1, 1976	5:44 PM	Libra
Sep 26, 1976	4:17 AM	Scorpio
Oct 20, 1976	5:22 PM	Sagittarius
Nov 14, 1976	10:42 AM	Capricorn
Dec 9, 1976	12:53 PM	Aquarius
Jan 4, 1977	1:01 PM	Pisces
Feb 2, 1977	5:54 AM	Aries
Jun 6, 1977	6:10 AM	Taurus
Jul 6, 1977	3:09 PM	Gemini
Aug 2, 1977	7:19 PM	Cancer

Aug 28, 1977	3:09 PM	Leo
Sep 22, 1977	3:05 PM	Virgo
Oct 17, 1977	1:37 AM	Libra
Nov 10, 1977	3:52 AM	Scorpio
Dec 4, 1977	1:49 AM	Sagittarius
Dec 27, 1977	10:09 PM	Capricorn
Jan 20, 1978	6:29 PM	Aquarius
Feb 13, 1978	4:07 PM	Pisces
Mar 9, 1978	4:29 PM	Aries
Apr 2, 1978	9:14 PM	Taurus
Apr 27, 1978	7:53 AM	Gemini
May 22, 1978	2:03 AM	Cancer
Jun 16, 1978	6:19 AM	Leo
Jul 12, 1978	2:14 AM	Virgo
Aug 8, 1978	3:08 AM	Libra
Sep 7, 1978	5:07 AM	Scorpio
Jan 7, 1979	6:38 AM	Sagittarius
Feb 5, 1979	9:16 AM	Capricorn
Mar 3, 1979	5:18 PM	Aquarius
Mar 29, 1979	3:18 AM	Pisces
Apr 23, 1979	4:02 AM	Aries
May 18, 1979	12:29 AM	Taurus
Jun 11, 1979	6:13 PM	Gemini
Jul 6, 1979	9:02 AM	Cancer
Jul 30, 1979	8:07 PM	Leo
Aug 24, 1979	3:16 AM	Virgo
Sep 17, 1979	7:21 AM	Libra
Oct 11, 1979	9:48 AM	Scorpio
Nov 4, 1979	11:50 AM	Sagittarius
Nov 28, 1979	2:20 PM	Capricorn
Dec 22, 1979	6:35 PM	Aquarius
Jan 16, 1980	3:37 AM	Pisces
Feb 9, 1980	11:39 PM	Aries
Mar 6, 1980	6:54 PM	Taurus
Apr 3, 1980	7:46 PM	Gemini
May 12, 1980	8:53 PM	Cancer
Jun 5, 1980	5:44 AM	Gemini
Aug 6, 1980	2:25 PM	Cancer
Sep 7, 1980	5:57 PM	Leo
Oct 4, 1980	11:07 PM	Virgo
Oct 30, 1980	10:38 AM	Libra
Nov 24, 1980	1:35 AM	Scorpio
Dec 18, 1980	6:21 AM	Sagittarius

Jan 11, 1981	6:48 AM	Capricorn
Feb 4, 1981	6:07 AM	Aquarius
Feb 28, 1981	6:01 AM	Pisces
Mar 24, 1981	7:43 AM	Aries
Apr 17, 1981	12:08 PM	Taurus
May 11, 1981	7:45 PM	Gemini
Jun 5, 1981	6:29 AM	Cancer
Jun 29, 1981	8:20 PM	Leo
Jul 24, 1981	2:04 PM	Virgo
Aug 18, 1981	1:44 PM	Libra
Sep 12, 1981	10:51 PM	Scorpio
Oct 9, 1981	12:04 AM	Sagittarius
Nov 5, 1981	12:39 PM	Capricorn
Dec 8, 1981	8:52 PM	Aquarius
Jan 23, 1982	2:56 AM	Capricorn
Mar 2, 1982	11:25 AM	Aquarius
Apr 6, 1982	12:20 PM	Pisces
May 4, 1982	12:27 PM	Aries
May 30, 1982	9:02 PM	Taurus
Jun 25, 1982	12:13 PM	Gemini
Jul 20, 1982	4:21 PM	Cancer
Aug 14, 1982	11:09 AM	Leo
Sep 7, 1982	9:38 PM	Virgo
Oct 2, 1982	1:32 AM	Libra
Oct 26, 1982	1:19 AM	Scorpio
Nov 18, 1982	11:07 PM	Sagittarius
Dec 12, 1982	8:20 PM	Capricorn
Jan 5, 1983	5:58 PM	Aquarius
Jan 29, 1983	5:31 PM	Pisces
Feb 22, 1983	9:35 PM	Aries
Mar 19, 1983	9:51 AM	Taurus
Apr 13, 1983	11:26 AM	Gemini
May 9, 1983	10:56 AM	Cancer
Jun 6, 1983	6:04 AM	Leo
Jul 10, 1983	5:25 AM	Virgo
Aug 27, 1983	11:43 AM	Leo
Oct 5, 1983	7:35 PM	Virgo
Nov 9, 1983	10:52 AM	Libra
Dec 6, 1983	4:15 PM	Scorpio
Jan 1, 1984	2:00 AM	Sagittarius
Jan 25, 1984	6:51 PM	Capricorn
Feb 19, 1984	4:53 AM	Aquarius
Mar 14, 1984	12:35 PM	Pisces
Apr 7, 1984	8:13 PM	Aries

May 2, 1984	4:53 AM	Taurus
May 26, 1984	2:40 PM	Gemini
Jun 20, 1984	12:48 AM	Cancer
Jul 14, 1984	10:30 AM	Leo
Aug 7, 1984	7:40 PM	Virgo
Sep 1, 1984	5:07 AM	Libra
Sep 25, 1984	4:05 PM	Scorpio
Oct 20, 1984	5:45 AM	Sagittarius
Nov 13, 1984	11:54 PM	Capricorn
Dec 9, 1984	3:26 AM	Aquarius
Jan 4, 1985	6:23 AM	Pisces
Feb 2, 1985	8:29 AM	Aries
Jun 6, 1985	8:53 AM	Taurus
Jul 6, 1985	8:01 AM	Gemini
Aug 2, 1985	9:10 AM	Cancer
Aug 28, 1985	3:39 AM	Leo
Sep 22, 1985	2:53 AM	Virgo
Oct 16, 1985	1:04 PM	Libra
Nov 9, 1985	3:08 PM	Scorpio
Dec 3, 1985	1:00 PM	Sagittarius
Dec 27, 1985	9:17 AM	Capricorn
Jan 20, 1986	5:36 AM	Aquarius
Feb 13, 1986	3:11 AM	Pisces
Mar 9, 1986	3:32 AM	Aries
Apr 2, 1986	8:19 AM	Taurus
Apr 26, 1986	7:10 PM	Gemini
May 21, 1986	1:46 PM	Cancer
Jun 15, 1986	6:52 PM	Leo
Jul 11, 1986	4:23 PM	Virgo
Aug 7, 1986	8:46 PM	Libra
Sep 7, 1986	10:15 AM	Scorpio
Jan 7, 1987	10:20 AM	Sagittarius
Feb 5, 1987	3:03 AM	Capricorn
Mar 3, 1987	7:55 AM	Aquarius
Mar 28, 1987	4:20 PM	Pisces
Apr 22, 1987	4:07 PM	Aries
May 17, 1987	11:56 AM	Taurus
Jun 11, 1987	5:15 AM	Gemini
Jul 5, 1987	7:50 PM	Cancer
Jul 30, 1987	6:49 AM	Leo
Aug 23, 1987	2:00 PM	Virgo
Sep 16, 1987	6:12 PM	Libra
Oct 10, 1987	8:49 PM	Scorpio
Nov 3, 1987	11:04 PM	Sagittarius

Nov 28, 1987	1:51 AM	Capricorn
Dec 22, 1987	6:29 AM	Aquarius
Jan 15, 1988	4:04 PM	Pisces
Feb 9, 1988	1:04 PM	Aries
Mar 6, 1988	10:21 AM	Taurus
Apr 3, 1988	5:07 PM	Gemini
May 17, 1988	4:26 PM	Cancer
May 27, 1988	7:36 AM	Gemini
Aug 6, 1988	11:24 PM	Cancer
Sep 7, 1988	11:37 AM	Leo
Oct 4, 1988	1:15 PM	Virgo
Oct 29, 1988	11:20 PM	Libra
Nov 23, 1988	1:34 PM	Scorpio
Dec 17, 1988	5:56 PM	Sagittarius
Jan 10, 1989	6:08 PM	Capricorn
Feb 3, 1989	5:15 PM	Aquarius
Feb 27, 1989	4:59 PM	Pisces
Mar 23, 1989	6:32 PM	Aries
Apr 16, 1989	10:52 PM	Taurus
May 11, 1989	6:28 AM	Gemini
Jun 4, 1989	5:17 PM	Cancer
Jun 29, 1989	7:21 AM	Leo
Jul 24, 1989	1:31 AM	Virgo
Aug 18, 1989	1:58 AM	Libra
Sep 12, 1989	12:22 PM	Scorpio
Oct 8, 1989	4:00 PM	Sagittarius
Nov 5, 1989	10:13 AM	Capricorn
Dec 10, 1989	4:54 AM	Aquarius
Jan 16, 1990	3:23 PM	Capricorn
Mar 3, 1990	5:52 PM	Aquarius
Apr 6, 1990	9:13 AM	Pisces
May 4, 1990	3:52 AM	Aries
May 30, 1990	10:13 AM	Taurus
Jun 25, 1990	12:14 AM	Gemini
Jul 20, 1990	3:41 AM	Cancer
Aug 13, 1990	10:05 PM	Leo
Sep 7, 1990	8:21 AM	Virgo
Oct 1, 1990	12:13 PM	Libra
Oct 25, 1990	12:03 PM	Scorpio
Nov 18, 1990	9:58 AM	Sagittarius
Dec 12, 1990	7:18 AM	Capricorn
Jan 5, 1991	5:03 AM	Aquarius
Jan 29, 1991	4:44 AM	Pisces

Feb 22, 1991	9:02 AM	Aries
Mar 18, 1991	9:45 PM	Taurus
Apr 13, 1991	12:10 AM	Gemini
May 9, 1991	1:28 AM	Cancer
Jun 6, 1991	1:16 AM	Leo
Jul 11, 1991	5:06 AM	Virgo
Aug 21, 1991	3:06 PM	Leo
Oct 6, 1991	9:15 PM	Virgo
Nov 9, 1991	6:37 AM	Libra
Dec 6, 1991	7:21 AM	Scorpio
Dec 31, 1991	3:19 PM	Sagittarius
Jan 25, 1992	7:14 AM	Capricorn
Feb 18, 1992	4:40 PM	Aquarius
Mar 13, 1992	11:57 PM	Pisces
Apr 7, 1992	7:16 AM	Aries
May 1, 1992	3:41 PM	Taurus
May 26, 1992	1:18 AM	Gemini
Jun 19, 1992	11:22 AM	Cancer
Jul 13, 1992	9:07 PM	Leo
Aug 7, 1992	6:26 AM	Virgo
Aug 31, 1992	4:09 PM	Libra
Sep 25, 1992	3:31 AM	Scorpio
Oct 19, 1992	5:47 PM	Sagittarius
Nov 13, 1992	12:48 PM	Capricorn
Dec 8, 1992	5:49 PM	Aquarius
Jan 3, 1993	11:54 PM	Pisces
Feb 2, 1993	12:37 PM	Aries
Jun 6, 1993	10:03 AM	Taurus
Jul 6, 1993	12:21 AM	Gemini
Aug 1, 1993	10:38 PM	Cancer
Aug 27, 1993	3:48 PM	Leo
Sep 21, 1993	2:22 PM	Virgo
Oct 16, 1993	12:13 AM	Libra
Nov 9, 1993	2:07 AM	Scorpio
Dec 2, 1993	11:54 PM	Sagittarius
Dec 26, 1993	8:09 PM	Capricorn
Jan 19, 1994	4:28 PM	Aquarius
Feb 12, 1994	2:04 PM	Pisces
Mar 8, 1994	2:28 PM	Aries
Apr 1, 1994	7:20 PM	Taurus
Apr 26, 1994	6:24 AM	Gemini
May 21, 1994	1:26 AM	Cancer
Jun 15, 1994	7:23 AM	Leo
Jul 11, 1994	6:33 AM	Virgo

Aug 7, 1994	2:36 PM	Libra
Sep 7, 1994	5:12 PM	Scorpio
Jan 7, 1995	12:07 PM	Sagittarius
Feb 4, 1995	8:12 PM	Capricorn
Mar 2, 1995	10:10 PM	Aquarius
Mar 28, 1995	5:10 AM	Pisces
Apr 22, 1995	4:07 AM	Aries
May 16, 1995	11:22 PM	Taurus
Jun 10, 1995	4:18 PM	Gemini
Jul 5, 1995	6:39 AM	Cancer
Jul 29, 1995	5:32 PM	Leo
Aug 23, 1995	12:43 AM	Virgo
Sep 16, 1995	5:01 AM	Libra
Oct 10, 1995	7:48 AM	Scorpio
Nov 3, 1995	10:18 AM	Sagittarius
Nov 27, 1995	1:23 PM	Capricorn
Dec 21, 1995	6:23 PM	Aquarius
Jan 15, 1996	4:30 AM	Pisces
Feb 9, 1996	2:30 AM	Aries
Mar 6, 1996	2:01 AM	Taurus
Apr 3, 1996	3:26 PM	Gemini
Aug 7, 1996	6:15 AM	Cancer
Sep 7, 1996	5:07 AM	Leo
Oct 4, 1996	3:22 AM	Virgo
Oct 29, 1996	12:02 PM	Libra
Nov 23, 1996	1:34 AM	Scorpio
Dec 17, 1996	5:34 AM	Sagittarius
Jan 10, 1997	5:32 AM	Capricorn
Feb 3, 1997	4:28 AM	Aquarius
Feb 27, 1997	4:01 AM	Pisces
Mar 23, 1997	5:26 AM	Aries
Apr 16, 1997	9:43 AM	Taurus
May 10, 1997	5:20 PM	Gemini
Jun 4, 1997	4:18 AM	Cancer
Jun 28, 1997	6:38 PM	Leo
Jul 23, 1997	1:16 PM	Virgo
Aug 17, 1997	2:31 PM	Libra
Sep 12, 1997	2:17 AM	Scorpio
Oct 8, 1997	8:25 AM	Sagittarius
Nov 5, 1997	8:50 AM	Capricorn
Dec 12, 1997	4:39 AM	Aquarius
Jan 9, 1998	9:03 PM	Capricorn
Mar 4, 1998	4:14 PM	Aquarius

Apr 6, 1998	5:38 AM	Pisces
May 3, 1998	7:16 PM	Aries
May 29, 1998	11:32 PM	Taurus
Jun 24, 1998	12:27 PM	Gemini
Jul 19, 1998	3:17 PM	Cancer
Aug 13, 1998	9:19 AM	Leo
Sep 6, 1998	7:24 PM	Virgo
Sep 30, 1998	11:13 PM	Libra
Oct 24, 1998	11:06 PM	Scorpio
Nov 17, 1998	9:06 PM	Sagittarius
Dec 11, 1998	6:33 PM	Capricorn
Jan 4, 1999	4:25 PM	Aquarius
Jan 28, 1999	4:17 PM	Pisces
Feb 21, 1999	8:49 PM	Aries
Mar 18, 1999	9:59 AM	Taurus
Apr 12, 1999	1:17 PM	Gemini
May 8, 1999	4:29 PM	Cancer
Jun 5, 1999	9:25 PM	Leo
Jul 12, 1999	3:18 PM	Virgo
Aug 15, 1999	2:12 PM	Leo
Oct 7, 1999	4:51 PM	Virgo
Nov 9, 1999	2:19 AM	Libra
Dec 5, 1999	10:41 PM	Scorpio
Dec 31, 1999	4:54 AM	Sagittarius
Jan 24, 2000	7:52 PM	Capricorn
Feb 18, 2000	4:43 AM	Aquarius
Mar 13, 2000	11:36 AM	Pisces
Apr 6, 2000	6:37 PM	Aries
May 1, 2000	2:49 AM	Taurus
May 25, 2000	12:15 PM	Gemini
Jun 18, 2000	10:15 PM	Cancer
Jul 13, 2000	8:02 AM	Leo
Aug 6, 2000	5:32 PM	Virgo
Aug 31, 2000	3:35 AM	Libra
Sep 24, 2000	3:26 PM	Scorpio
Oct 19, 2000	6:18 AM	Sagittarius
Nov 13, 2000	2:14 AM	Capricorn
Dec 8, 2000	8:48 AM	Aquarius
Jan 3, 2001	6:14 PM	Pisces
Feb 2, 2001	7:14 PM	Aries
Jun 6, 2001	10:25 AM	Taurus
Jul 5, 2001	4:44 PM	Gemini
Aug 1, 2001	12:18 PM	Cancer

Aug 27, 2001	4:12 AM	Leo
Sep 21, 2001	2:09 AM	Virgo
Oct 15, 2001	11:42 AM	Libra
Nov 8, 2001	1:28 PM	Scorpio
Dec 2, 2001	11:11 AM	Sagittarius
Dec 26, 2001	7:25 AM	Capricorn
Jan 19, 2002	3:42 AM	Aquarius
Feb 12, 2002	1:18 AM	Pisces
Mar 8, 2002	1:42 AM	Aries
Apr 1, 2002	6:39 AM	Taurus
Apr 25, 2002	5:57 PM	Gemini
May 20, 2002	1:27 PM	Cancer
Jun 14, 2002	8:16 PM	Leo
Jul 10, 2002	9:09 PM	Virgo
Aug 7, 2002	9:09 AM	Libra
Sep 8, 2002	3:05 AM	Scorpio
Jan 7, 2003	1:07 PM	Sagittarius
Feb 4, 2003	1:27 PM	Capricorn
Mar 2, 2003	12:40 PM	Aquarius
Mar 27, 2003	6:14 PM	Pisces
Apr 21, 2003	4:18 PM	Aries
May 16, 2003	10:58 AM	Taurus
Jun 10, 2003	3:32 AM	Gemini
Jul 4, 2003	5:39 PM	Cancer
Jul 29, 2003	4:25 AM	Leo
Aug 22, 2003	11:36 AM	Virgo
Sep 15, 2003	3:58 PM	Libra
Oct 9, 2003	6:56 PM	Scorpio
Nov 2, 2003	9:42 PM	Sagittarius
Nov 27, 2003	1:07 AM	Capricorn
Dec 21, 2003	6:32 AM	Aquarius
Jan 14, 2004	5:16 PM	Pisces
Feb 8, 2004	4:20 PM	Aries
Mar 5, 2004	6:12 PM	Taurus
Apr 3, 2004	2:57 PM	Gemini
Aug 7, 2004	11:02 AM	Cancer
Sep 6, 2004	10:16 PM	Leo
Oct 3, 2004	5:20 PM	Virgo
Oct 29, 2004	12:39 AM	Libra
Nov 22, 2004	1:31 PM	Scorpio
Dec 16, 2004	5:10 PM	Sagittarius
Jan 9, 2005	4:56 PM	Capricorn
Feb 2, 2005	3:42 PM	Aquarius

Feb 26, 2005	3:07 PM	Pisces
Mar 22, 2005	4:25 PM	Aries
Apr 15, 2005	8:37 PM	Taurus
May 10, 2005	4:14 AM	Gemini
Jun 3, 2005	3:18 PM	Cancer
Jun 28, 2005	5:53 AM	Leo
Jul 23, 2005	1:01 AM	Virgo
Aug 17, 2005	3:05 AM	Libra
Sep 11, 2005	4:14 PM	Scorpio
Oct 8, 2005	1:00 AM	Sagittarius
Nov 5, 2005	8:10 AM	Capricorn
Dec 15, 2005	3:57 PM	Aquarius
Jan 1, 2006	8:18 PM	Capricorn
Mar 5, 2006	8:39 AM	Aquarius
Apr 6, 2006	1:21 AM	Pisces
May 3, 2006	10:25 AM	Aries
May 29, 2006	12:41 PM	Taurus
Jun 24, 2006	12:31 AM	Gemini
Jul 19, 2006	2:41 AM	Cancer
Aug 12, 2006	8:21 PM	Leo
Sep 6, 2006	6:15 AM	Virgo
Sep 30, 2006	10:02 AM	Libra
Oct 24, 2006	9:58 AM	Scorpio
Nov 17, 2006	8:02 AM	Sagittarius
Dec 11, 2006	5:33 AM	Capricorn
Jan 4, 2007	3:31 AM	Aquarius
Jan 28, 2007	3:32 AM	Pisces
Feb 21, 2007	8:21 AM	Aries
Mar 17, 2007	10:00 PM	Taurus
Apr 12, 2007	2:15 AM	Gemini
May 8, 2007	7:28 AM	Cancer
Jun 5, 2007	5:59 PM	Leo
Jul 14, 2007	6:23 PM	Virgo
Aug 9, 2007	1:10 AM	Leo
Oct 8, 2007	6:53 AM	Virgo
Nov 8, 2007	9:05 PM	Libra
Dec 5, 2007	1:29 PM	Scorpio
Dec 30, 2007	6:02 PM	Sagittarius
Jan 24, 2008	8:06 AM	Capricorn
Feb 17, 2008	4:22 PM	Aquarius
Mar 12, 2008	10:51 PM	Pisces
Apr 6, 2008	5:35 AM	Aries
Apr 30, 2008	1:34 PM	Taurus
May 24, 2008	10:52 PM	Gemini

Jun 18, 2008	8:48 AM	Cancer
Jul 12, 2008	6:39 PM	Leo
Aug 6, 2008	4:20 AM	Virgo
Aug 30, 2008	2:41 PM	Libra
Sep 24, 2008	2:59 AM	Scorpio
Oct 18, 2008	6:31 PM	Sagittarius
Nov 12, 2008	3:25 PM	Capricorn
Dec 7, 2008	11:37 PM	Aquarius
Jan 3, 2009	12:35 PM	Pisces
Feb 3, 2009	3:41 AM	Aries
Apr 11, 2009	12:47 PM	Pisces
Apr 24, 2009	7:18 AM	Aries
Jun 6, 2009	9:07 AM	Taurus
Jul 5, 2009	8:23 AM	Gemini
Aug 1, 2009	1:28 AM	Cancer
Aug 26, 2009	4:12 PM	Leo
Sep 20, 2009	1:32 PM	Virgo
Oct 14, 2009	10:46 PM	Libra
Nov 8, 2009	12:23 AM	Scorpio
Dec 1, 2009	10:04 PM	Sagittarius
Dec 25, 2009	6:17 PM	Capricorn
Jan 18, 2010	2:35 PM	Aquarius
Feb 11, 2010	12:10 PM	Pisces
Mar 7, 2010	12:33 PM	Aries
Mar 31, 2010	5:35 PM	Taurus
Apr 25, 2010	5:05 AM	Gemini
May 20, 2010	1:05 AM	Cancer
Jun 14, 2010	8:50 AM	Leo
Jul 10, 2010	11:32 AM	Virgo
Aug 7, 2010	3:47 AM	Libra
Sep 8, 2010	3:44 PM	Scorpio
Nov 8, 2010	3:06 AM	Libra
Nov 30, 2010	12:33 AM	Scorpio
Jan 7, 2011	12:30 PM	Sagittarius
Feb 4, 2011	5:58 AM	Capricorn
Mar 2, 2011	2:39 AM	Aquarius
Mar 27, 2011	6:53 AM	Pisces
Apr 21, 2011	4:06 AM	Aries
May 15, 2011	10:12 PM	Taurus
Jun 9, 2011	2:23 PM	Gemini
Jul 4, 2011	4:17 AM	Cancer
Jul 28, 2011	2:59 PM	Leo
Aug 21, 2011	10:11 PM	Virgo
Sep 15, 2011	2:40 AM	Libra

Oct 9, 2011	5:50 AM	Scorpio
Nov 2, 2011	8:51 AM	Sagittarius
Nov 26, 2011	12:36 PM	Capricorn
Dec 20, 2011	6:26 PM	Aquarius
Jan 14, 2012	5:47 AM	Pisces
Feb 8, 2012	6:01 AM	Aries
Mar 5, 2012	10:25 AM	Taurus
Apr 3, 2012	3:18 PM	Gemini
Aug 7, 2012	1:43 PM	Cancer
Sep 6, 2012	2:48 PM	Leo
Oct 3, 2012	6:59 AM	Virgo
Oct 28, 2012	1:04 PM	Libra
Nov 22, 2012	1:20 AM	Scorpio
Dec 16, 2012	4:38 AM	Sagittarius
Jan 9, 2013	4:11 AM	Capricorn
Feb 2, 2013	2:47 AM	Aquarius
Feb 26, 2013	2:03 AM	Pisces
Mar 22, 2013	3:15 AM	Aries
Apr 15, 2013	7:25 AM	Taurus
May 9, 2013	3:03 PM	Gemini
Jun 3, 2013	2:13 AM	Cancer
Jun 27, 2013	5:03 PM	Leo
Jul 22, 2013	12:41 PM	Virgo
Aug 16, 2013	3:37 PM	Libra
Sep 11, 2013	6:16 AM	Scorpio
Oct 7, 2013	5:54 PM	Sagittarius
Nov 5, 2013	8:43 AM	Capricorn
Mar 5, 2014	9:03 PM	Aquarius
Apr 5, 2014	8:31 PM	Pisces
May 3, 2014	1:21 AM	Aries
May 29, 2014	1:45 AM	Taurus
Jun 23, 2014	12:33 PM	Gemini
Jul 18, 2014	2:06 PM	Cancer
Aug 12, 2014	7:24 AM	Leo
Sep 5, 2014	5:07 PM	Virgo
Sep 29, 2014	8:52 PM	Libra
Oct 23, 2014	8:52 PM	Scorpio
Nov 16, 2014	7:03 PM	Sagittarius
Dec 10, 2014	4:42 PM	Capricorn
Jan 3, 2015	2:48 PM	Aquarius
Jan 27, 2015	3:00 PM	Pisces
Feb 20, 2015	8:05 PM	Aries
Mar 17, 2015	10:15 AM	Taurus

Apr 11, 2015	3:28 PM	Gemini
May 7, 2015	10:52 PM	Cancer
Jun 5, 2015	3:33 PM	Leo
Jul 18, 2015	10:38 PM	Virgo
Jul 31, 2015	3:27 PM	Leo
Oct 8, 2015	5:29 PM	Virgo
Nov 8, 2015	3:31 PM	Libra
Dec 5, 2015	4:15 AM	Scorpio
Dec 30, 2015	7:16 AM	Sagittarius
Jan 23, 2016	8:31 PM	Capricorn
Feb 17, 2016	4:17 AM	Aquarius
Mar 12, 2016	10:24 AM	Pisces
Apr 5, 2016	4:50 PM	Aries
Apr 30, 2016	12:36 AM	Taurus
May 24, 2016	9:44 AM	Gemini
Jun 17, 2016	7:39 PM	Cancer
Jul 12, 2016	5:34 AM	Leo
Aug 5, 2016	3:27 PM	Virgo
Aug 30, 2016	2:06 AM	Libra
Sep 23, 2016	2:51 PM	Scorpio
Oct 18, 2016	7:01 AM	Sagittarius
Nov 12, 2016	4:54 AM	Capricorn
Dec 7, 2016	2:51 PM	Aquarius
Jan 3, 2017	7:46 AM	Pisces
Feb 3, 2017	3:51 PM	Aries
Apr 3, 2017	12:25 AM	Pisces
Apr 28, 2017	1:13 PM	Aries
Jun 6, 2017	7:26 AM	Taurus
Jul 5, 2017	12:11 AM	Gemini
Jul 31, 2017	2:54 PM	Cancer
Aug 26, 2017	4:30 AM	Leo
Sep 20, 2017	1:15 AM	Virgo
Oct 14, 2017	10:11 AM	Libra
Nov 7, 2017	11:38 AM	Scorpio
Dec 1, 2017	9:14 AM	Sagittarius
Dec 25, 2017	5:26 AM	Capricorn
Jan 18, 2018	1:43 AM	Aquarius
Feb 10, 2018	11:19 PM	Pisces
Mar 6, 2018	11:45 PM	Aries
Mar 31, 2018	4:54 AM	Taurus
Apr 24, 2018	4:40 PM	Gemini
May 19, 2018	1:10 PM	Cancer
Jun 13, 2018	9:54 PM	Leo
Jul 10, 2018	2:32 AM	Virgo

Aug 6, 2018	11:27 PM	Libra
Sep 9, 2018	9:25 AM	Scorpio
Oct 31, 2018	7:42 PM	Libra
Dec 2, 2018	5:02 PM	Scorpio
Jan 7, 2019	11:18 AM	Sagittarius
Feb 3, 2019	10:29 PM	Capricorn
Mar 1, 2019	4:45 PM	Aquarius
Mar 26, 2019	7:43 PM	Pisces
Apr 20, 2019	4:10 PM	Aries
May 15, 2019	9:46 AM	Taurus
Jun 9, 2019	1:37 AM	Gemini
Jul 3, 2019	3:18 PM	Cancer
Jul 28, 2019	1:54 AM	Leo
Aug 21, 2019	9:06 AM	Virgo
Sep 14, 2019	1:43 PM	Libra
Oct 8, 2019	5:06 PM	Scorpio
Nov 1, 2019	8:25 PM	Sagittarius
Nov 26, 2019	12:28 AM	Capricorn
Dec 20, 2019	6:41 AM	Aquarius
Jan 13, 2020	6:39 PM	Pisces
Feb 7, 2020	8:02 PM	Aries
Mar 5, 2020	3:07 AM	Taurus
Apr 3, 2020	5:10 PM	Gemini
Aug 7, 2020	3:21 PM	Cancer
Sep 6, 2020	7:21 AM	Leo
Oct 2, 2020	8:48 PM	Virgo
Oct 28, 2020	1:41 AM	Libra
Nov 21, 2020	1:22 PM	Scorpio
Dec 15, 2020	4:21 PM	Sagittarius
Jan 8, 2021	3:41 PM	Capricorn
Feb 1, 2021	2:05 PM	Aquarius
Feb 25, 2021	1:11 PM	Pisces
Mar 21, 2021	2:16 PM	Aries
Apr 14, 2021	6:22 PM	Taurus
May 9, 2021	2:01 AM	Gemini
Jun 2, 2021	1:18 PM	Cancer
Jun 27, 2021	4:27 AM	Leo
Jul 22, 2021	12:37 AM	Virgo
Aug 16, 2021	4:26 AM	Libra
Sep 10, 2021	8:39 PM	Scorpio
Oct 7, 2021	11:21 AM	Sagittarius
Nov 5, 2021	10:44 AM	Capricorn
Mar 6, 2022	6:30 AM	Aquarius

Apr 5, 2022	3:17 PM	Pisces
May 2, 2022	4:10 PM	Aries
May 28, 2022	2:46 PM	Taurus
Jun 23, 2022	12:34 AM	Gemini
Jul 18, 2022	1:32 AM	Cancer
Aug 11, 2022	6:30 PM	Leo
Sep 5, 2022	4:05 AM	Virgo
Sep 29, 2022	7:49 AM	Libra
Oct 23, 2022	7:52 AM	Scorpio
Nov 16, 2022	6:08 AM	Sagittarius
Dec 10, 2022	3:54 AM	Capricorn
Jan 3, 2023	2:09 AM	Aquarius
Jan 27, 2023	2:33 AM	Pisces
Feb 20, 2023	7:55 AM	Aries
Mar 16, 2023	10:34 PM	Taurus
Apr 11, 2023	4:47 AM	Gemini
May 7, 2023	2:24 PM	Cancer
Jun 5, 2023	1:46 PM	Leo
Oct 9, 2023	1:10 AM	Virgo
Nov 8, 2023	9:30 AM	Libra
Dec 4, 2023	6:51 PM	Scorpio
Dec 29, 2023	8:23 PM	Sagittarius
Jan 23, 2024	8:50 AM	Capricorn
Feb 16, 2024	4:05 PM	Aquarius
Mar 11, 2024	9:50 PM	Pisces
Apr 5, 2024	4:00 AM	Aries
Apr 29, 2024	11:31 AM	Taurus
May 23, 2024	8:30 PM	Gemini
Jun 17, 2024	6:20 AM	Cancer
Jul 11, 2024	4:19 PM	Leo
Aug 5, 2024	2:23 AM	Virgo
Aug 29, 2024	1:22 PM	Libra
Sep 23, 2024	2:36 AM	Scorpio
Oct 17, 2024	7:28 PM	Sagittarius
Nov 11, 2024	6:25 PM	Capricorn
Dec 7, 2024	6:13 AM	Aquarius
Jan 3, 2025	3:24 AM	Pisces
Feb 4, 2025	7:57 AM	Aries
Mar 27, 2025	8:40 AM	Pisces
Apr 30, 2025	5:16 PM	Aries
Jun 6, 2025	4:42 AM	Taurus
Jul 4, 2025	3:31 PM	Gemini
Jul 31, 2025	3:57 AM	Cancer
Aug 25, 2025	4:27 PM	Leo

Sep 19, 2025	12:39 PM	Virgo
Oct 13, 2025	9:18 PM	Libra
Nov 6, 2025	10:39 PM	Scorpio
Nov 30, 2025	8:13 PM	Sagittarius
Dec 24, 2025	4:26 PM	Capricorn

Locating Your Mars

Feb 6, 1930	6:21 PM	Aquarius
Mar 17, 1930	5:55 AM	Pisces
Apr 24, 1930	5:27 PM	Aries
Jun 3, 1930	3:15 AM	Taurus
Jul 14, 1930	12:54 PM	Gemini
Aug 28, 1930	11:27 AM	Cancer
Oct 20, 1930	2:43 PM	Leo
Feb 16, 1931	2:27 PM	Cancer
Mar 30, 1931	3:48 AM	Leo
Jun 10, 1931	2:58 PM	Virgo
Aug 1, 1931	4:38 PM	Libra
Sep 17, 1931	8:43 AM	Scorpio
Oct 30, 1931	12:46 PM	Sagittarius
Dec 10, 1931	3:11 AM	Capricorn
Jan 18, 1932	12:35 AM	Aquarius
Feb 25, 1932	2:36 AM	Pisces
Apr 3, 1932	7:02 AM	Aries
May 12, 1932	10:53 AM	Taurus
Jun 22, 1932	9:19 AM	Gemini
Aug 4, 1932	7:52 PM	Cancer
Sep 20, 1932	7:43 PM	Leo
Nov 13, 1932	9:25 PM	Virgo
Jul 6, 1933	10:03 PM	Libra
Aug 26, 1933	6:34 AM	Scorpio
Oct 9, 1933	11:35 AM	Sagittarius
Nov 19, 1933	7:18 AM	Capricorn
Dec 28, 1933	3:43 AM	Aquarius
Feb 4, 1934	4:13 AM	Pisces
Mar 14, 1934	9:09 AM	Aries
Apr 22, 1934	3:40 PM	Taurus
Jun 2, 1934	4:21 PM	Gemini
Jul 15, 1934	9:33 PM	Cancer
Aug 30, 1934	1:43 PM	Leo
Oct 18, 1934	4:59 AM	Virgo
Dec 11, 1934	9:32 AM	Libra

Jul 29, 1935	5:32 PM	Scorpio
Sep 16, 1935	12:59 PM	Sagittarius
Oct 28, 1935	6:22 PM	Capricorn
Dec 7, 1935	4:34 AM	Aquarius
Jan 14, 1936	1:59 PM	Pisces
Feb 22, 1936	4:09 AM	Aries
Apr 1, 1936	9:30 PM	Taurus
May 13, 1936	9:17 AM	Gemini
Jun 25, 1936	9:53 PM	Cancer
Aug 10, 1936	9:43 AM	Leo
Sep 26, 1936	2:51 PM	Virgo
Nov 14, 1936	2:52 PM	Libra
Jan 5, 1937	8:39 PM	Scorpio
Mar 13, 1937	3:16 AM	Sagittarius
May 14, 1937	10:52 PM	Scorpio
Aug 8, 1937	10:14 PM	Sagittarius
Sep 30, 1937	9:08 AM	Capricorn
Nov 11, 1937	6:31 PM	Aquarius
Dec 21, 1937	5:46 PM	Pisces
Jan 30, 1938	12:44 PM	Aries
Mar 12, 1938	7:48 AM	Taurus
Apr 23, 1938	6:39 PM	Gemini
Jun 7, 1938	1:28 AM	Cancer
Jul 22, 1938	10:26 PM	Leo
Sep 7, 1938	8:22 PM	Virgo
Oct 25, 1938	6:20 AM	Libra
Dec 11, 1938	11:25 PM	Scorpio
Jan 29, 1939	9:49 AM	Sagittarius
Mar 21, 1939	7:25 AM	Capricorn
May 25, 1939	12:19 AM	Aquarius
Jul 21, 1939	7:31 PM	Capricorn
Sep 24, 1939	1:13 AM	Aquarius
Nov 19, 1939	3:56 PM	Pisces
Jan 4, 1940	12:05 AM	Aries
Feb 17, 1940	1:54 AM	Taurus
Apr 1, 1940	6:41 PM	Gemini
May 17, 1940	2:45 PM	Cancer
Jul 3, 1940	10:32 AM	Leo
Aug 19, 1940	3:58 PM	Virgo
Oct 5, 1940	2:21 PM	Libra
Nov 20, 1940	5:16 PM	Scorpio

Jan 4, 1941	7:42 PM	Sagittarius
Feb 17, 1941	11:32 PM	Capricorn
Apr 2, 1941	11:46 AM	Aquarius
May 16, 1941	5:05 AM	Pisces
Jul 2, 1941	5:17 AM	Aries
Jan 11, 1942	10:21 PM	Taurus
Mar 7, 1942	8:04 AM	Gemini
Apr 26, 1942	6:18 AM	Cancer
Jun 14, 1942	3:56 AM	Leo
Aug 1, 1942	8:27 AM	Virgo
Sep 17, 1942	10:11 AM	Libra
Nov 1, 1942	10:36 PM	Scorpio
Dec 15, 1942	4:51 PM	Sagittarius
Jan 26, 1943	7:10 PM	Capricorn
Mar 8, 1943	12:42 PM	Aquarius
Apr 17, 1943	10:25 AM	Pisces
May 27, 1943	9:25 AM	Aries
Jul 7, 1943	11:05 PM	Taurus
Aug 23, 1943	11:58 PM	Gemini
Mar 28, 1944	9:54 AM	Cancer
May 22, 1944	2:16 PM	Leo
Jul 12, 1944	2:54 AM	Virgo
Aug 29, 1944	12:23 AM	Libra
Oct 13, 1944	12:09 PM	Scorpio
Nov 25, 1944	4:11 PM	Sagittarius
Jan 5, 1945	7:31 PM	Capricorn
Feb 14, 1945	9:58 AM	Aquarius
Mar 25, 1945	3:43 AM	Pisces
May 2, 1945	8:29 PM	Aries
Jun 11, 1945	11:52 AM	Taurus
Jul 23, 1945	8:59 AM	Gemini
Sep 7, 1945	8:56 PM	Cancer
Nov 11, 1945	9:05 PM	Leo
Dec 26, 1945	3:04 PM	Cancer
Apr 22, 1946	7:31 PM	Leo
Jun 20, 1946	8:31 AM	Virgo
Aug 9, 1946	1:17 PM	Libra
Sep 24, 1946	4:35 PM	Scorpio
Nov 6, 1946	6:22 PM	Sagittarius
Dec 17, 1946	10:56 AM	Capricorn
Jan 25, 1947	11:44 AM	Aquarius

Mar 4, 1947	4:46 PM	Pisces
Apr 11, 1947	11:03 PM	Aries
May 21, 1947	3:40 AM	Taurus
Jul 1, 1947	3:34 AM	Gemini
Aug 13, 1947	9:26 PM	Cancer
Oct 1, 1947	2:31 AM	Leo
Dec 1, 1947	11:44 AM	Virgo
Feb 12, 1948	10:28 AM	Leo
May 18, 1948	8:54 PM	Virgo
Jul 17, 1948	5:25 AM	Libra
Sep 3, 1948	1:58 PM	Scorpio
Oct 17, 1948	5:43 AM	Sagittarius
Nov 26, 1948	9:59 PM	Capricorn
Jan 4, 1949	5:50 PM	Aquarius
Feb 11, 1949	6:05 PM	Pisces
Mar 21, 1949	10:02 PM	Aries
Apr 30, 1949	2:33 AM	Taurus
Jun 10, 1949	12:57 AM	Gemini
Jul 23, 1949	5:54 AM	Cancer
Sep 7, 1949	4:51 AM	Leo
Oct 27, 1949	12:58 AM	Virgo
Dec 26, 1949	5:23 AM	Libra
Mar 28, 1950	11:05 AM	Virgo
Jun 11, 1950	8:27 PM	Libra
Aug 10, 1950	4:48 PM	Scorpio
Sep 25, 1950	7:48 PM	Sagittarius
Nov 6, 1950	6:40 AM	Capricorn
Dec 15, 1950	8:59 AM	Aquarius
Jan 22, 1951	1:05 PM	Pisces
Mar 1, 1951	10:03 PM	Aries
Apr 10, 1951	9:37 AM	Taurus
May 21, 1951	3:32 PM	Gemini
Jul 3, 1951	11:42 PM	Cancer
Aug 18, 1951	10:55 AM	Leo
Oct 5, 1951	12:20 AM	Virgo
Nov 24, 1951	6:11 AM	Libra
Jan 20, 1952	1:33 AM	Scorpio
Aug 27, 1952	6:53 PM	Sagittarius
Oct 12, 1952	4:45 AM	Capricorn
Nov 21, 1952	7:40 PM	Aquarius
Dec 30, 1952	9:35 PM	Pisces

Feb 8, 1953	1:07 AM	Aries
Mar 20, 1953	6:54 AM	Taurus
May 1, 1953	6:08 AM	Gemini
Jun 14, 1953	3:49 AM	Cancer
Jul 29, 1953	7:25 PM	Leo
Sep 14, 1953	5:59 PM	Virgo
Nov 1, 1953	2:19 PM	Libra
Dec 20, 1953	11:22 AM	Scorpio
Feb 9, 1954	7:18 PM	Sagittarius
Apr 12, 1954	4:28 PM	Capricorn
Jul 3, 1954	7:23 AM	Sagittarius
Aug 24, 1954	1:22 PM	Capricorn
Oct 21, 1954	12:03 PM	Aquarius
Dec 4, 1954	7:41 AM	Pisces
Jan 15, 1955	4:33 AM	Aries
Feb 26, 1955	10:22 AM	Taurus
Apr 10, 1955	11:09 PM	Gemini
May 26, 1955	12:50 AM	Cancer
Jul 11, 1955	9:22 AM	Leo
Aug 27, 1955	10:13 AM	Virgo
Oct 13, 1955	11:20 AM	Libra
Nov 29, 1955	1:33 AM	Scorpio
Jan 14, 1956	2:28 AM	Sagittarius
Feb 28, 1956	8:05 PM	Capricorn
Apr 14, 1956	11:40 PM	Aquarius
Jun 3, 1956	7:51 AM	Pisces
Dec 6, 1956	11:24 AM	Aries
Jan 28, 1957	2:19 PM	Taurus
Mar 17, 1957	9:34 PM	Gemini
May 4, 1957	3:22 PM	Cancer
Jun 21, 1957	12:18 PM	Leo
Aug 8, 1957	5:27 AM	Virgo
Sep 24, 1957	4:31 AM	Libra
Nov 8, 1957	9:04 PM	Scorpio
Dec 23, 1957	1:29 AM	Sagittarius
Feb 3, 1958	6:57 PM	Capricorn
Mar 17, 1958	7:11 AM	Aquarius
Apr 27, 1958	2:31 AM	Pisces
Jun 7, 1958	6:21 AM	Aries
Jul 21, 1958	7:03 AM	Taurus
Sep 21, 1958	5:26 AM	Gemini
Oct 29, 1958	12:01 AM	Taurus

Feb 10, 1959	1:57 PM	Gemini
Apr 10, 1959	9:46 AM	Cancer
Jun 1, 1959	2:26 AM	Leo
Jul 20, 1959	11:03 AM	Virgo
Sep 5, 1959	10:46 PM	Libra
Oct 21, 1959	9:40 AM	Scorpio
Dec 3, 1959	6:09 PM	Sagittarius
Jan 14, 1960	4:59 AM	Capricorn
Feb 23, 1960	4:11 AM	Aquarius
Apr 2, 1960	6:24 AM	Pisces
May 11, 1960	7:19 AM	Aries
Jun 20, 1960	9:05 AM	Taurus
Aug 2, 1960	4:32 AM	Gemini
Sep 21, 1960	4:06 AM	Cancer
Feb 5, 1961	12:23 AM	Gemini
Feb 7, 1961	5:25 AM	Cancer
May 6, 1961	1:13 AM	Leo
Jun 28, 1961	11:47 PM	Virgo
Aug 17, 1961	12:41 AM	Libra
Oct 1, 1961	8:02 PM	Scorpio
Nov 13, 1961	9:50 PM	Sagittarius
Dec 24, 1961	5:50 PM	Capricorn
Feb 1, 1962	11:06 PM	Aquarius
Mar 12, 1962	7:58 AM	Pisces
Apr 19, 1962	4:58 PM	Aries
May 28, 1962	11:47 PM	Taurus
Jul 9, 1962	3:50 AM	Gemini
Aug 22, 1962	11:37 AM	Cancer
Oct 11, 1962	11:54 PM	Leo
Jun 3, 1963	6:30 AM	Virgo
Jul 27, 1963	4:14 AM	Libra
Sep 12, 1963	9:11 AM	Scorpio
Oct 25, 1963	5:31 PM	Sagittarius
Dec 5, 1963	9:03 AM	Capricorn
Jan 13, 1964	6:13 AM	Aquarius
Feb 20, 1964	7:33 AM	Pisces
Mar 29, 1964	11:24 AM	Aries
May 7, 1964	2:41 PM	Taurus
Jun 17, 1964	11:43 AM	Gemini
Jul 30, 1964	6:23 PM	Cancer
Sep 15, 1964	5:22 AM	Leo

Nov 6, 1964	3:20 AM	Virgo
Jun 29, 1965	1:12 AM	Libra
Aug 20, 1965	12:16 PM	Scorpio
Oct 4, 1965	6:46 AM	Sagittarius
Nov 14, 1965	7:19 AM	Capricorn
Dec 23, 1965	5:36 AM	Aquarius
Jan 30, 1966	7:01 AM	Pisces
Mar 9, 1966	12:55 PM	Aries
Apr 17, 1966	8:35 PM	Taurus
May 28, 1966	10:07 PM	Gemini
Jul 11, 1966	3:15 AM	Cancer
Aug 25, 1966	3:52 PM	Leo
Oct 12, 1966	6:37 PM	Virgo
Dec 4, 1966	12:55 AM	Libra
Feb 12, 1967	12:20 PM	Scorpio
Mar 31, 1967	6:10 AM	Libra
Jul 19, 1967	10:56 PM	Scorpio
Sep 10, 1967	1:44 AM	Sagittarius
Oct 23, 1967	2:14 AM	Capricorn
Dec 1, 1967	8:12 PM	Aquarius
Jan 9, 1968	9:49 AM	Pisces
Feb 17, 1968	3:18 AM	Aries
Mar 27, 1968	11:43 PM	Taurus
May 8, 1968	2:14 PM	Gemini
Jun 21, 1968	5:03 AM	Cancer
Aug 5, 1968	5:07 PM	Leo
Sep 21, 1968	6:39 PM	Virgo
Nov 9, 1968	6:10 AM	Libra
Dec 29, 1968	10:07 PM	Scorpio
Feb 25, 1969	6:21 AM	Sagittarius
Sep 21, 1969	6:35 AM	Capricorn
Nov 4, 1969	6:51 PM	Aquarius
Dec 15, 1969	2:22 PM	Pisces
Jan 24, 1970	9:29 PM	Aries
Mar 7, 1970	1:28 AM	Taurus
Apr 18, 1970	6:59 PM	Gemini
Jun 2, 1970	6:51 AM	Cancer
Jul 18, 1970	6:43 AM	Leo
Sep 3, 1970	4:57 AM	Virgo
Oct 20, 1970	10:57 AM	Libra
Dec 6, 1970	4:34 PM	Scorpio

Jan 23, 1971	1:34 AM	Sagittarius
Mar 12, 1971	10:11 AM	Capricorn
May 3, 1971	8:57 PM	Aquarius
Nov 6, 1971	12:31 PM	Pisces
Dec 26, 1971	6:04 PM	Aries
Feb 10, 1972	2:04 PM	Taurus
Mar 27, 1972	4:30 AM	Gemini
May 12, 1972	1:14 PM	Cancer
Jun 28, 1972	4:09 PM	Leo
Aug 15, 1972	12:59 AM	Virgo
Sep 30, 1972	11:23 PM	Libra
Nov 15, 1972	10:17 PM	Scorpio
Dec 30, 1972	4:12 PM	Sagittarius
Feb 12, 1973	5:51 AM	Capricorn
Mar 26, 1973	8:59 PM	Aquarius
May 8, 1973	4:09 AM	Pisces
Jun 20, 1973	8:54 PM	Aries
Aug 12, 1973	2:56 PM	Taurus
Oct 29, 1973	10:56 PM	Aries
Dec 24, 1973	8:09 AM	Taurus
Feb 27, 1974	10:11 AM	Gemini
Apr 20, 1974	8:18 AM	Cancer
Jun 9, 1974	12:54 AM	Leo
Jul 27, 1974	2:04 PM	Virgo
Sep 12, 1974	7:08 PM	Libra
Oct 28, 1974	7:05 AM	Scorpio
Dec 10, 1974	10:05 PM	Sagittarius
Jan 21, 1975	6:49 PM	Capricorn
Mar 3, 1975	5:32 AM	Aquarius
Apr 11, 1975	7:15 PM	Pisces
May 21, 1975	8:14 AM	Aries
Jul 1, 1975	3:53 AM	Taurus
Aug 14, 1975	8:47 PM	Gemini
Oct 17, 1975	8:44 AM	Cancer
Nov 25, 1975	6:30 PM	Gemini
Mar 18, 1976	1:15 PM	Cancer
May 16, 1976	11:10 AM	Leo
Jul 6, 1976	11:27 PM	Virgo
Aug 24, 1976	5:55 AM	Libra
Oct 8, 1976	8:23 PM	Scorpio
Nov 20, 1976	11:53 PM	Sagittarius

Jan 1, 1977	12:42 AM	Capricorn
Feb 9, 1977	11:57 AM	Aquarius
Mar 20, 1977	2:19 AM	Pisces
Apr 27, 1977	3:46 PM	Aries
Jun 6, 1977	3:00 AM	Taurus
Jul 17, 1977	3:13 PM	Gemini
Sep 1, 1977	12:20 AM	Cancer
Oct 26, 1977	6:56 PM	Leo
Jan 26, 1978	1:59 AM	Cancer
Apr 10, 1978	6:50 PM	Leo
Jun 14, 1978	2:38 AM	Virgo
Aug 4, 1978	9:07 AM	Libra
Sep 19, 1978	8:57 PM	Scorpio
Nov 2, 1978	1:20 AM	Sagittarius
Dec 12, 1978	5:39 PM	Capricorn
Jan 20, 1979	5:07 PM	Aquarius
Feb 27, 1979	8:25 PM	Pisces
Apr 7, 1979	1:08 AM	Aries
May 16, 1979	4:25 AM	Taurus
Jun 26, 1979	1:55 AM	Gemini
Aug 8, 1979	1:28 PM	Cancer
Sep 24, 1979	9:21 PM	Leo
Nov 19, 1979	9:36 PM	Virgo
Mar 11, 1980	8:46 PM	Leo
May 4, 1980	2:27 AM	Virgo
Jul 10, 1980	5:59 PM	Libra
Aug 29, 1980	5:50 AM	Scorpio
Oct 12, 1980	6:27 AM	Sagittarius
Nov 22, 1980	1:42 AM	Capricorn
Dec 30, 1980	10:30 PM	Aquarius
Feb 6, 1981	10:48 PM	Pisces
Mar 17, 1981	2:40 AM	Aries
Apr 25, 1981	7:17 AM	Taurus
Jun 5, 1981	5:26 AM	Gemini
Jul 18, 1981	8:54 AM	Cancer
Sep 2, 1981	1:52 AM	Leo
Oct 21, 1981	1:56 AM	Virgo
Dec 16, 1981	12:14 AM	Libra
Aug 3, 1982	11:45 AM	Scorpio
Sep 20, 1982	1:20 AM	Sagittarius
Oct 31, 1982	11:05 PM	Capricorn

Dec 10, 1982	6:17 AM	Aquarius
Jan 17, 1983	1:10 PM	Pisces
Feb 25, 1983	12:19 AM	Aries
Apr 5, 1983	2:03 PM	Taurus
May 16, 1983	9:43 PM	Gemini
Jun 29, 1983	6:54 AM	Cancer
Aug 13, 1983	4:54 PM	Leo
Sep 30, 1983	12:12 AM	Virgo
Nov 18, 1983	10:26 AM	Libra
Jan 11, 1984	3:20 AM	Scorpio
Aug 17, 1984	7:50 PM	Sagittarius
Oct 5, 1984	6:02 AM	Capricorn
Nov 15, 1984	6:09 PM	Aquarius
Dec 25, 1984	6:38 AM	Pisces
Feb 2, 1985	5:19 PM	Aries
Mar 15, 1985	5:06 AM	Taurus
Apr 26, 1985	9:13 AM	Gemini
Jun 9, 1985	10:40 AM	Cancer
Jul 25, 1985	4:04 AM	Leo
Sep 10, 1985	1:31 AM	Virgo
Oct 27, 1985	3:16 PM	Libra
Dec 14, 1985	6:59 PM	Scorpio
Feb 2, 1986	6:27 AM	Sagittarius
Mar 28, 1986	3:47 AM	Capricorn
Oct 9, 1986	1:01 AM	Aquarius
Nov 26, 1986	2:35 AM	Pisces
Jan 8, 1987	12:20 PM	Aries
Feb 20, 1987	2:44 PM	Taurus
Apr 5, 1987	4:37 PM	Gemini
May 21, 1987	3:01 AM	Cancer
Jul 6, 1987	4:46 PM	Leo
Aug 22, 1987	7:51 PM	Virgo
Oct 8, 1987	7:27 PM	Libra
Nov 24, 1987	3:19 AM	Scorpio
Jan 8, 1988	3:24 PM	Sagittarius
Feb 22, 1988	10:15 AM	Capricorn
Apr 6, 1988	9:44 PM	Aquarius
May 22, 1988	7:42 AM	Pisces
Jul 13, 1988	8:00 PM	Aries
Oct 23, 1988	10:01 PM	Pisces
Nov 1, 1988	12:57 PM	Aries

Jan 19, 1989	8:11 AM	Taurus
Mar 11, 1989	8:51 AM	Gemini
Apr 29, 1989	4:37 AM	Cancer
Jun 16, 1989	2:10 PM	Leo
Aug 3, 1989	1:35 PM	Virgo
Sep 19, 1989	2:38 PM	Libra
Nov 4, 1989	5:29 AM	Scorpio
Dec 18, 1989	4:57 AM	Sagittarius
Jan 29, 1990	2:10 PM	Capricorn
Mar 11, 1990	3:54 PM	Aquarius
Apr 20, 1990	10:09 PM	Pisces
May 31, 1990	7:11 AM	Aries
Jul 12, 1990	2:44 PM	Taurus
Aug 31, 1990	11:40 AM	Gemini
Dec 14, 1990	7:46 AM	Taurus
Jan 21, 1991	1:15 AM	Gemini
Apr 3, 1991	12:49 AM	Cancer
May 26, 1991	12:19 PM	Leo
Jul 15, 1991	12:36 PM	Virgo
Sep 1, 1991	6:38 AM	Libra
Oct 16, 1991	7:05 PM	Scorpio
Nov 29, 1991	2:19 AM	Sagittarius
Jan 9, 1992	9:47 AM	Capricorn
Feb 18, 1992	4:38 AM	Aquarius
Mar 28, 1992	2:04 AM	Pisces
May 5, 1992	9:36 PM	Aries
Jun 14, 1992	3:56 PM	Taurus
Jul 26, 1992	6:59 PM	Gemini
Sep 12, 1992	6:05 AM	Cancer
Apr 27, 1993	11:40 PM	Leo
Jun 23, 1993	7:42 AM	Virgo
Aug 12, 1993	1:10 AM	Libra
Sep 27, 1993	2:15 AM	Scorpio
Nov 9, 1993	5:29 AM	Sagittarius
Dec 20, 1993	12:34 AM	Capricorn
Jan 28, 1994	4:05 AM	Aquarius
Mar 7, 1994	11:01 AM	Pisces
Apr 14, 1994	6:02 PM	Aries
May 23, 1994	10:37 PM	Taurus
Jul 3, 1994	10:30 PM	Gemini
Aug 16, 1994	7:15 PM	Cancer

Oct 4, 1994	3:48 PM	Leo
Dec 12, 1994	11:32 AM	Virgo
Jan 22, 1995	11:48 PM	Leo
May 25, 1995	4:09 PM	Virgo
Jul 21, 1995	9:21 AM	Libra
Sep 7, 1995	7:00 AM	Scorpio
Oct 20, 1995	9:02 PM	Sagittarius
Nov 30, 1995	1:57 PM	Capricorn
Jan 8, 1996	11:02 AM	Aquarius
Feb 15, 1996	11:50 AM	Pisces
Mar 24, 1996	3:12 PM	Aries
May 2, 1996	6:16 PM	Taurus
Jun 12, 1996	2:42 PM	Gemini
Jul 25, 1996	6:32 PM	Cancer
Sep 9, 1996	8:02 PM	Leo
Oct 30, 1996	7:13 AM	Virgo
Jan 3, 1997	8:10 AM	Libra
Mar 8, 1997	7:49 PM	Virgo
Jun 19, 1997	8:30 AM	Libra
Aug 14, 1997	8:42 AM	Scorpio
Sep 28, 1997	10:22 PM	Sagittarius
Nov 9, 1997	5:33 AM	Capricorn
Dec 18, 1997	6:37 AM	Aquarius
Jan 25, 1998	9:26 AM	Pisces
Mar 4, 1998	4:18 PM	Aries
Apr 13, 1998	1:05 AM	Taurus
May 24, 1998	3:42 AM	Gemini
Jul 6, 1998	9:00 AM	Cancer
Aug 20, 1998	7:16 PM	Leo
Oct 7, 1998	12:28 PM	Virgo
Nov 27, 1998	10:10 AM	Libra
Jan 26, 1999	11:59 AM	Scorpio
May 5, 1999	9:32 PM	Libra
Jul 5, 1999	3:59 AM	Scorpio
Sep 2, 1999	7:29 PM	Sagittarius
Oct 17, 1999	1:35 AM	Capricorn
Nov 26, 1999	6:56 AM	Aquarius
Jan 4, 2000	3:01 AM	Pisces
Feb 12, 2000	1:04 AM	Aries
Mar 23, 2000	1:25 AM	Taurus
May 3, 2000	7:18 PM	Gemini

Jun 16, 2000	12:30 PM	Cancer
Aug 1, 2000	1:21 AM	Leo
Sep 17, 2000	12:19 AM	Virgo
Nov 4, 2000	2:00 AM	Libra
Dec 23, 2000	2:37 PM	Scorpio
Feb 14, 2001	8:06 PM	Sagittarius
Sep 8, 2001	5:51 PM	Capricorn
Oct 27, 2001	5:19 PM	Aquarius
Dec 8, 2001	9:52 PM	Pisces
Jan 18, 2002	10:53 PM	Aries
Mar 1, 2002	3:05 PM	Taurus
Apr 13, 2002	5:36 PM	Gemini
May 28, 2002	11:43 AM	Cancer
Jul 13, 2002	3:23 PM	Leo
Aug 29, 2002	2:38 PM	Virgo
Oct 15, 2002	5:38 PM	Libra
Dec 1, 2002	2:26 PM	Scorpio
Jan 17, 2003	4:22 AM	Sagittarius
Mar 4, 2003	9:17 PM	Capricorn
Apr 21, 2003	11:48 PM	Aquarius
Jun 17, 2003	2:25 AM	Pisces
Dec 16, 2003	1:24 PM	Aries
Feb 3, 2004	10:04 AM	Taurus
Mar 21, 2004	7:39 AM	Gemini
May 7, 2004	8:46 AM	Cancer
Jun 23, 2004	8:50 PM	Leo
Aug 10, 2004	10:14 AM	Virgo
Sep 26, 2004	9:15 AM	Libra
Nov 11, 2004	5:11 AM	Scorpio
Dec 25, 2004	4:04 PM	Sagittarius
Feb 6, 2005	6:32 PM	Capricorn
Mar 20, 2005	6:02 PM	Aquarius
May 1, 2005	2:58 AM	Pisces
Jun 12, 2005	2:30 AM	Aries
Jul 28, 2005	5:12 AM	Taurus
Feb 17, 2006	10:44 PM	Gemini
Apr 14, 2006	12:59 AM	Cancer
Jun 3, 2006	6:43 PM	Leo
Jul 22, 2006	6:53 PM	Virgo
Sep 8, 2006	4:18 AM	Libra
Oct 23, 2006	4:38 PM	Scorpio

Dec 6, 2006	4:58 AM	Sagittarius
Jan 16, 2007	8:54 PM	Capricorn
Feb 26, 2007	1:32 AM	Aquarius
Apr 6, 2007	8:49 AM	Pisces
May 15, 2007	2:06 PM	Aries
Jun 24, 2007	9:27 PM	Taurus
Aug 7, 2007	6:01 AM	Gemini
Sep 28, 2007	11:55 PM	Cancer
Dec 31, 2007	4:00 PM	Gemini
Mar 4, 2008	10:01 AM	Cancer
May 9, 2008	8:20 PM	Leo
Jul 1, 2008	4:21 PM	Virgo
Aug 19, 2008	10:03 AM	Libra
Oct 4, 2008	4:34 AM	Scorpio
Nov 16, 2008	8:27 AM	Sagittarius
Dec 27, 2008	7:30 AM	Capricorn
Feb 4, 2009	3:55 PM	Aquarius
Mar 15, 2009	3:20 AM	Pisces
Apr 22, 2009	1:44 PM	Aries
May 31, 2009	9:18 PM	Taurus
Jul 12, 2009	2:56 AM	Gemini
Aug 25, 2009	5:15 PM	Cancer
Oct 16, 2009	3:32 PM	Leo
Jun 7, 2010	6:11 AM	Virgo
Jul 29, 2010	11:46 PM	Libra
Sep 14, 2010	10:38 PM	Scorpio
Oct 28, 2010	6:48 AM	Sagittarius
Dec 7, 2010	11:49 PM	Capricorn
Jan 15, 2011	10:41 PM	Aquarius
Feb 23, 2011	1:06 AM	Pisces
Apr 2, 2011	4:51 AM	Aries
May 11, 2011	7:03 AM	Taurus
Jun 21, 2011	2:50 AM	Gemini
Aug 3, 2011	9:22 AM	Cancer
Sep 19, 2011	1:51 AM	Leo
Nov 11, 2011	4:15 AM	Virgo
Jul 3, 2012	12:32 PM	Libra
Aug 23, 2012	3:24 PM	Scorpio
Oct 7, 2012	3:21 AM	Sagittarius
Nov 17, 2012	2:36 AM	Capricorn
Dec 26, 2012	12:49 AM	Aquarius

Feb 2, 2013	1:54 AM	Pisces
Mar 12, 2013	6:26 AM	Aries
Apr 20, 2013	11:48 AM	Taurus
May 31, 2013	10:39 AM	Gemini
Jul 13, 2013	1:22 PM	Cancer
Aug 28, 2013	2:05 AM	Leo
Oct 15, 2013	11:05 AM	Virgo
Dec 7, 2013	8:41 PM	Libra
Jul 26, 2014	2:25 AM	Scorpio
Sep 13, 2014	9:57 PM	Sagittarius
Oct 26, 2014	10:43 AM	Capricorn
Dec 4, 2014	11:57 PM	Aquarius
Jan 12, 2015	10:20 AM	Pisces
Feb 20, 2015	12:11 AM	Aries
Mar 31, 2015	4:26 PM	Taurus
May 12, 2015	2:40 AM	Gemini
Jun 24, 2015	1:33 PM	Cancer
Aug 8, 2015	11:32 PM	Leo
Sep 25, 2015	2:18 AM	Virgo
Nov 12, 2015	9:41 PM	Libra
Jan 3, 2016	2:32 PM	Scorpio
Mar 6, 2016	2:29 AM	Sagittarius
May 27, 2016	1:51 PM	Scorpio
Aug 2, 2016	5:49 PM	Sagittarius
Sep 27, 2016	8:07 AM	Capricorn
Nov 9, 2016	5:51 AM	Aquarius
Dec 19, 2016	9:23 AM	Pisces
Jan 28, 2017	5:39 AM	Aries
Mar 10, 2017	12:34 AM	Taurus
Apr 21, 2017	10:32 AM	Gemini
Jun 4, 2017	4:16 PM	Cancer
Jul 20, 2017	12:19 PM	Leo
Sep 5, 2017	9:35 AM	Virgo
Oct 22, 2017	6:29 PM	Libra
Dec 9, 2017	8:59 AM	Scorpio
Jan 26, 2018	12:56 PM	Sagittarius
Mar 17, 2018	4:40 PM	Capricorn
May 16, 2018	4:55 AM	Aquarius
Aug 13, 2018	2:14 AM	Capricorn
Sep 11, 2018	12:56 AM	Aquarius
Nov 15, 2018	10:21 PM	Pisces

Jan 1, 2019	2:20 AM	Aries
Feb 14, 2019	10:51 AM	Taurus
Mar 31, 2019	6:12 AM	Gemini
May 16, 2019	3:09 AM	Cancer
Jul 1, 2019	11:19 PM	Leo
Aug 18, 2019	5:18 AM	Virgo
Oct 4, 2019	4:22 AM	Libra
Nov 19, 2019	7:40 AM	Scorpio
Jan 3, 2020	9:37 AM	Sagittarius
Feb 16, 2020	11:33 AM	Capricorn
Mar 30, 2020	7:43 PM	Aquarius
May 13, 2020	4:17 AM	Pisces
Jun 28, 2020	1:45 AM	Aries
Jan 6, 2021	10:27 PM	Taurus
Mar 4, 2021	3:29 AM	Gemini
Apr 23, 2021	11:49 AM	Cancer
Jun 11, 2021	1:34 PM	Leo
Jul 29, 2021	8:32 PM	Virgo
Sep 15, 2021	12:14 AM	Libra
Oct 30, 2021	2:21 PM	Scorpio
Dec 13, 2021	9:53 AM	Sagittarius
Jan 24, 2022	12:53 PM	Capricorn
Mar 6, 2022	6:23 AM	Aquarius
Apr 15, 2022	3:05 AM	Pisces
May 24, 2022	11:17 PM	Aries
Jul 5, 2022	6:04 AM	Taurus
Aug 20, 2022	7:56 AM	Gemini
Mar 25, 2023	11:45 AM	Cancer
May 20, 2023	3:31 PM	Leo
Jul 10, 2023	11:40 AM	Virgo
Aug 27, 2023	1:20 PM	Libra
Oct 12, 2023	4:04 AM	Scorpio
Nov 24, 2023	10:15 AM	Sagittarius
Jan 4, 2024	2:58 PM	Capricorn
Feb 13, 2024	6:05 AM	Aquarius
Mar 22, 2024	11:47 PM	Pisces
Apr 30, 2024	3:33 PM	Aries
Jun 9, 2024	4:35 AM	Taurus
Jul 20, 2024	8:43 PM	Gemini
Sep 4, 2024	7:46 PM	Cancer
Nov 4, 2024	4:09 AM	Leo

Jan 6, 2025	10:44 AM	Cancer
Apr 18, 2025	4:20 AM	Leo
Jun 17, 2025	8:35 AM	Virgo
Aug 6, 2025	11:23 PM	Libra
Sep 22, 2025	7:54 AM	Scorpio
Nov 4, 2025	1:01 PM	Sagittarius

Friends And Family

Name	Birthdate	Venus	Mars

About the Author

Nancy Frederick is an internationally acclaimed astrologer who has been consistently in print for over twenty-five years. If you read astrology magazines, you've read Nancy! She has published thousands of articles in all the national astrology magazines. Nancy contributes frequently to *Dell Horoscope*, with a bi-monthly column, many articles, features like the *Yearbook, Purse Books* and *Love Sign Guides*. As the founding editor of *ASTRO SIGNS*, she conceptualized the popular mini-magazine, designed its format, and wrote much of its contents for many years. She also wrote most of the contents of *Astrology Your Daily Horoscope* for fifteen years.

She is the author of five books combining various aspects of metaphysics with romance. They are: *Love and Sex Under the Stars*, Dell, 1989; *Tarot: Love is in the Cards; The Lover's Dream; Palmistry: All Lines Lead to Love; Love Games: Psychic Paths to Love,* Lynx Books, 1988. Her latest book, THE ASTRO TUTOR, AFA, 2008, is a collection of her most popular articles teaching astrology to appear in DELL HOROSCOPE Magazine. It has been newly expanded and updated for its electronic version.

Nancy is certified by many astrology organizations: American Federation of Astrologers, NCGR in New York and Aquarius Workshops in Los Angeles. She has taught astrology privately in New York and Los Angeles, has lectured in New York and taught through the Learning Annex in Los Angeles as well as at conferences sponsored by the AFA.

In addition to being an astrologer, she is a master of the Tarot and uses the cards as well as astrology in her counselling work. Nancy has done much research over many years into other aspects of metaphysics. A spiritualist, she worked for some years with a trance medium, talking directly to spirit and getting information about Karma, reincarnation, and technical astrological details.

Ms. Frederick spends much of her time counselling a large international clientele. She's also the author of six popular novels. Visit www.nancyfrederick.com to contact her.